CROSSROADS

JEANNE GODFREY
MARIA CARTY
MIKE OUELLETTE

Gage Editorial Team
Joe Banel
Maggie Goh
Sue Kanhai
Diane Robitaille
Susan Skivington

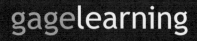

© 2000 Gage Learning Corporation
Nelson
1120 Birchmount Road
Toronto, Ontario M1K 5G4
1-800-668-0671
www.nelson.com

Managing Editor: Darleen Rotozinski
Contributing Writer: Chelsea Donaldson
Copy Editor: Sue Kanhai
Permissions Editor: Elizabeth Long
Photo Researcher: Mary Rose MacLachlan
Researchers: Monika Croyden, Carol Milne Smith, Catherine Rondina, Jennifer Sweeney
Proofreader: Sandy Manley
Bias Reviewer: Margaret Hoogeveen
Cover Illustration: Cathy Chatterton
**Design, Art Direction
& Electronic Assembly:** Wycliffe Smith Design

**National Library of Canada
Cataloguing in Publication Data**

Main entry under title:

Gage crossroads 8

ISBN 0-7715-1322-4

1. Readers (Elementary). I. Godfrey, Jeanne.
II. Title: Crossroads eight. III. Title: Crossroads 8.

PE1121.G255 2000   428.6   C99-932482-9

ISBN-13: 978-0-7715-1322-0
ISBN-10: 0-7715-1322-4
  5 TCP 07
Printed and bound in Canada

Lines
for a
Bookmark
by Gael Turnbull

You who read...
May you seek
As you look;
May you keep
What you need;
May you care
What you choose;
And know here
In this book
Something strange,
Something sure,
That will change
You and be yours.

TABLE OF CONTENTS

ALTERNATE TABLE OF CONTENTS

PERSONAL FOCUS

"Only with
the heart
can a person
see rightly;
what is
essential
is invisible
to the eye."

Antoine de Saint-Exupéry
from The Little Prince

What if, with the wave of a wand, your life could be changed?

The Transformations of Cindy R.

Short Story by Anne Mazer

"Cin, Cin, Cindy!" the three girls call out.

"Cindy! Will you help me put up the decorations for the dance?" Agnes says.

"Could you find my scissors, Cindy?" Marybeth chimes in.

"We need more cups!" Dara cries. "Cindy, where are the cups?"

Cindy hurries over. "Here I come, Agnes," she says in a low voice. "Okay, Marybeth. I'll find them, Dara."

Agnes is small and exquisite. Marybeth is strong and graceful. Dara is tall, dark, and statuesque. All three girls are beautiful. And popular. And busy.

Cindy is only busy. She sweeps the floor, brushes off the costumes, puts up the posters, runs the errands, counts the money, twists the crepe paper into bright spirals and hangs it from the gymnasium ceiling.

"You're serving the punch tonight, aren't you, Cindy?" Agnes says. It isn't really a question.

Cindy nods. Of course she is. She always serves the punch. She never dances.

If you look at her eyes—you don't, nobody does—but if you did, you'd wonder why blue eyes are considered attractive. Cindy's eyes do not remind anyone of the sky or the sea. Faded blue jeans have more colour. Worn flannel sheets possess more sparkle. Old dishwater is more lively.

As for her hair, it hangs there, lank and mousy and dull, without even the energy to snarl. Her nose is nondescript, her mouth twists nervously whenever anyone asks her a question. Her eyes blink. She bites her lips, she whispers, she winds her hair around her fingers and then chews on it.

"Where'd you get the shirt, Cin?" Agnes takes the sleeve between her thumb and forefinger. It's a flannel shirt, big and baggy, like Cindy's other clothes.

"My brother," Cindy says.

"Give it back to your brother," Agnes says. "The colour's all wrong. You look washed out."

"Oh," says Cindy. She imagines her face like a piece of cloth, loose and empty. Her shoulders slump even more.

Agnes turns away. A tall boy has just walked into the gymnasium. He has broad shoulders and shaggy blond hair. His eyes are blue and sparkling.

"Jeff!" Dara cries, holding open her arms.

Marybeth runs to him, but it is Agnes who gets there first. She puts her hand on his arm and smiles triumphantly at the other two.

"Let's go for ice cream," Jeff says. "Are we done working?"

"Cindy will finish," says Dara. "Won't you, Cindy?"

Cindy glances at the posters on the floor, the unfurled wheels of crepe paper, the piles of dust in the corners of the gymnasium, and nods. "Of course," she says. She always does.

Jeff links arms with Agnes and Marybeth, while Dara follows somewhat sulkily behind.

No one asks Cindy to go for ice cream. She wouldn't dream of it, anyway. Broom in hand, she hurries around the gymnasium, making sure everything is ready for the dance.

Tonight Cindy will stand behind the refreshment table, pouring punch and serving cookies on paper plates. Dara, Agnes, and Marybeth will all dance with Jeff, who will gaze adoringly at each in turn. Dara will be splendid in a rose gown that sets off her dark hair and eyes. Agnes will be exquisite in white with a wreath of flowers

in her pale hair. Marybeth will wear a braided ribbon around her neck and a dress of many colours, and as she dances, she will look like a fountain shooting off sparks of coloured light.

Cindy will wear a dress that Marybeth gave her. It is dark blue and tight in the shoulders, too short, and the zipper cuts into her back. On Marybeth it looked graceful and lovely, but it's cut all wrong for Cindy. But it's better at least than her only other dress, a shapeless brown tent also handed down to her.

When Cindy pours the punch tonight, she will try not to spill it on her classmates. Otherwise Agnes might yell—she has a temper. When the dance is done, Cindy will sweep up, count the money, and put it in a safe. Then she will go home, eke out a few tears, and fall asleep.

But it doesn't happen like that.

◆ ◆ ◆

At seven o'clock, Cindy goes home to eat and change into her dress. Her mother has left her supper on the plate. The mashed potatoes are cold and lumpy, and a thin layer of grease has congealed over the roast beef.

"What do you expect when you come home at all hours?" her mother complains. "I'm not a servant, you know."

"Sorry," Cindy says.

"Sorry isn't enough. You ought to help out a little more. I'm tired. I've been working all day. Don't expect to get out of here tonight without doing the dishes and mopping the floor."

To drown out the sound of her mother's nagging, Cindy picks up a magazine. As she turns the pages, her eye is caught by a picture of one of those ceramic statues that you buy in six instalments of $24.99 a month.

"Yes, you, too, can own this enchanting one-of-a-kind figurine," says the ad. "Your very own fairy godmother will watch over and protect you with her realistic magic wand. Hand-painted silver stars decorate the edges of her robe. Tiny crystal slippers adorn her feet. Produced in a very limited edition by the acclaimed European porcelain artist, Tiddly Wink."

"And *blah, blah, blah*," Cindy says. But she takes another quick look at the fairy godmother. And then she grabs a pen and begins filling out the order form. It's silly, really; she doesn't know why she's doing it. For one thing, she doesn't have the money; for another, she doesn't like painted porcelain statues. But something is pushing her—almost like a hand on her back, a voice in her ear—that she can't resist.

Cindy fills in her name, address, phone number, and age, then carefully tears out the coupon. If anyone needs a fairy godmother, it's her, even if it's a phony porcelain one.

And she puts the coupon in her pocket, thinking that maybe she'll mail it later.

But it doesn't happen that way.

◆ ◆ ◆

Poof! A small figure has appeared on the table in front of her, right between the dinner plate and the water glass. She is about fifteen centimetres tall, with pretty porcelain cheeks, and bright blue eyes. She is wearing a long, flowing silk gown with hand-painted stars along the hem and sleeves.

"Oh!" Cindy cries out, then claps her hand over her mouth.

The figurine is beautifully made. She almost seems to breathe. Slowly Cindy reaches out and touches the masses of silver hair piled into a bun.

"Stop poking at me!" snaps the figurine.

Cindy hastily withdraws her hand.

"I'm your fairy godmother," she says with a haughty toss of her head. "In case you didn't notice."

Cindy feels in her pocket for the coupon, but it's gone. And she didn't even mail it.

The fairy godmother casts a shrewd, appraising glance at her and whistles low under her breath. "You're a mess," she says. "No wonder you called me."

"I actually never called you." Cindy twists a strand of lank hair around her finger and starts to chew on it. "I mean, I meant to..."

"Oh, stop blathering!" says the fairy godmother. "Take it from me. I can fix you up good. I know just what you need."

"You do?" Cindy asks.

"Cindy! Did you clear the dishes? Is the floor washed? Don't forget to take out the garbage!" her mother calls from the other room.

"You need me." The fairy godmother raises a tiny golden wand. "Put yourself under my tutelage. All you have to say is yes and you'll be completely transformed. Is that an offer you can refuse?"

Cindy opens her mouth, then shuts it. Does she really want a fairy godmother that much? Have things gotten to that point? Hasn't she been getting along fine? Well, maybe not *fine*, but she's coping.

"Do you hear me, Cindy?" her mother says. "Answer me! If that kitchen isn't completely clean when I come in, you can forget about the dance!"

"Okay," Cindy says to the fairy godmother.

"Okay, what?" the fairy godmother retorts. "Follow instructions! You have to say yes."

"Yes!" Cindy says.

The fairy godmother waves her wand. *Poof!* The dishes are washed, the floor is clean, the garbage is empty.

"Cindy!!" her mother calls.

"All done, Mom!" She picks up the fairy godmother and runs up the stairs to her room.

◆ ◆ ◆

"Stand over there." The fairy godmother points to the corner. "Take off those clothes," she orders.

"Do I have to?" Cindy shrinks back. But at the commanding look in the fairy godmother's eye, she takes off first the big faded flannel shirt her brother gave her, then the baggy jeans, the sneakers and heavy socks, and finally the old T-shirt she wears over her underwear.

Cindy wraps her arms around herself. Her skin is too pale, her arms and legs too long, and her hips are too narrow. It doesn't help that she needed to buy new underwear six months ago. Three safety pins hold her bra together; her underpants are ripped at the seams.

The fairy godmother gives her a sharp, appraising glance. "You don't have a bad figure, you know. You should show it off more."

"Uh..." Cindy doesn't know what to say. She wishes that she could melt into the floor. The fairy godmother mutters a few words to herself, then waves her wand again. The air rustles like silk and releases the scent of a hundred flowers. *Poof!* A large mirror appears across from Cindy. She stares at the stranger reflected there. Who is it? She doesn't recognize herself. She is completely transformed.

Her hair is piled on her head in shining, graceful curls. The blush on her cheeks and lips is not natural, but it has been so artfully applied that no one can tell.

And then there is the dress. It is pale apricot, with a long sweeping skirt, a tightly-cut bodice, and lace-covered sleeves. Her feet are shod in matching apricot-coloured slippers. There are rings on her fingers and a velvet choker around her neck.

"You're a vision," says the fairy godmother, clasping her hands.

Cindy twirls around. The dress is looped in the back, with a full sash. Indeed, the dress is so full of lace and ribbons and bows, hoops and sleeves and sashes, that she feels as if she could set sail in it.

She frowns at herself in the mirror, wondering if she has new underwear, too, perhaps something in French silk. To tell the truth, she's not that crazy about the dress.

"What's the matter?" the fairy godmother demands. "Don't you like it?"

"It's the colour," Cindy says hesitantly. If she asks for a simpler dress, she might offend the fairy godmother. "Don't you think blue or violet would look better on me?"

The fairy godmother shakes her head. "You young girls just don't know left from right, or up from down. The colour is perfect for you, trust me."

Cindy nods. "Okay." It's what she's been saying all her life to everyone.

"This dress will change your life," the fairy godmother says. "It will make you happy. And beautiful. And loved."

Cindy looks at herself again. She resembles an overdressed box of candy. She's never seen Agnes, or Dara, or Marybeth wearing anything like this. "Really? You're sure?"

The fairy godmother has a tinkling, chime-like laugh. "You'll be the belle of the ball. Do you know how to dance?"

"No." Her voice quavers a little. Even when she gets a break from serving punch, she always stands at the edge of the crowd and watches the others dance. No one has ever asked her to dance. Not even the other girls want to dance with her.

The fairy godmother raises the tiny golden wand again and points it at Cindy's feet. *Poof!* They begin to tingle. Heat rushes to her toes. She begins to move. One, two, three; one, two, three. Step, glide, step. Cindy swirls and swoops around her bedroom as if she's done it for a lifetime, while the fairy godmother claps in time.

"Bravo!" the fairy godmother cries. "Bravo! Babe, you're terrific!"

Cindy comes to a halt. Was that really her, Cindy, dancing? Automatically she reaches up for a strand of hair to chew on.

"Oh, no! None of that!" The fairy godmother waves her wand once more. *Poof!*

Cindy's hand freezes in midair. How could she ever have chewed on her hair? What a disgusting habit! The very thought of it makes her stomach churn.

As she lowers her hand, Cindy notices that her nails are all perfectly shaped and polished a pale apricot. She wants to bite them, but somehow she can't. She can only gaze admiringly at the sapphire-and-gold rings on her fingers.

She dances a few steps, then halts in front of the mirror. Is that really her, she wonders again. She's like a little girl dressed up in her mother's clothes. Everyone is going to see through this costume.

"Oh!! Oh!!!" Cindy cries out at the very thought of it. Tears streak down her face, but her make-up does not smear.

She knows what is going to happen. They are going to send her to the washroom to scrub off the make-up and change back into her old, dark hand-me-downs. Then she will return to serve punch all night to Jeff and Marybeth and Dara and Agnes, and everything will be the way it's always been.

But it doesn't happen like that.

◆ ◆ ◆

When Cindy walks into the room, everyone falls silent and stares at her. She panics, she wants to run, but in these shoes, she'd fall on her face.

But no, instead, a girl named Alicia, who has never spoken to Cindy before, cries, "You look so *fabulous*!"

The fairy godmother is right. The dress is a hit; it transforms the evening. Everyone loves it. Everyone loves her.

"That dress!" Dara moans.

"Who does your hair?" Marybeth cries.

"Those bows!" Agnes screams. "And the lace, too!"

"You're stunning! Beautiful! Fabulous!" The compliments rain down on her like flowers.

Do they recognize her? No one calls her by name. They all stare at her with big eyes. Can they be envious eyes?

As Cindy walks—or rather glides—across the gymnasium, Jeff takes her hand and says, "Will you dance?"

Cindy nods. This really is a fairy tale. The music begins. They dance together as if they've done it all their lives. She moves as if enchanted—and of course she is. She only hopes there are no side effects; after all, she never takes so much as an aspirin.

Jeff gazes adoringly into her eyes. "You're beautiful," he says. "That colour...what is it?"

"Apricot," Cindy says.

As they dance around and around, not missing a step, his eyes never leave her face. "I *know* I've seen you before."

"Yes," Cindy says. "You've seen me before."

"Where?"

Cindy almost smiles. "Maybe in another life."

"I knew it!" he cries out triumphantly.

He leans toward her and whispers in her ear, "We were meant to be together."

Cindy is beginning to have her doubts. Did he actually say those words? "Meant to be together?" How corny can you get? Dancing with Jeff isn't all it's cracked up to be. This conversation is actually dumber than dumb, and she's beginning to feel a little annoyed by all the other girls staring and smiling at her.

She glances over at the refreshment table. A thin girl in an ill-fitting dress is pouring drinks. Cindy doesn't wish she were back there again, but she doesn't one hundred percent like where she is, either. Maybe not even ninety percent. Or even eighty.

The music stops. She sighs with relief, but Jeff won't let her go.

"I want the next dance and the next dance and the next," he says.

But her feet hurt. She wonders if the fairy godmother goofed and made the slippers too tight. Could a fairy godmother make a mistake? "I want to sit down."

"You can't." Jeff holds her arm tightly. "I'll die of unhappiness if I can't have just one more dance. Please."

Now he's definitely getting on her nerves. Maybe it's that pleading but possessive look in his eyes, or maybe it's that he's not listening to anything she says.

Cindy tries to pull away, but he won't let her go.

"Dance with me now," he insists.

Tears well up in her eyes. "Please..." she mutters.

Then she stops and takes a breath. She is different tonight. She's not the old, shy, scared Cindy. The fairy godmother has transformed her, made her a new person. Very well, she will be that new person.

She smiles sweetly at Jeff, and then kicks him hard in the shins.

◆ ◆ ◆

In the bathroom, where she has escaped, dozens of girls mob her. They want to know about the dress, about her hair, her make-up, how she made Jeff fall in love with her so quickly, and why he looked so forlorn and stunned just now on the dance floor.

"What's your secret?" Agnes asks breathlessly.

"I have a fairy godmother," Cindy says, pretending to touch up her make-up. It still looks as flawless as when she left the house.

The other girls laugh.

"What's it like dancing with Jeff?" asks a shy, plump girl.

"Boring."

"Is anyone else going to get to dance with Jeff tonight?" This is Dara speaking.

"I hope so," Cindy says.

"How come we've never seen you before?" one of the girls demands.

Cindy shrugs. "But you have. I always served the punch at the refreshment table."

"No—not you! Cindy's the one who always does it. Have you ever run into her? She's nothing like you. You'd never allow yourself to even be seen with her!" Dara, Marybeth, Agnes, and the other girls laugh.

They don't know who she is. They think she's beautiful and poised and glamorous. They smooth her dress, tug at her bows, and pat the ribbons in her hair.

"We want to see how this lace is made. How did you get your hair to curl on top of your head like that? Are your shoes made of silk?"

Touching, prodding, and admiring, they crowd her into a corner. Cindy can barely breathe. "Give me some air, girls," she pleads.

They don't listen to her.

Once again, she is about to burst into tears. But again she stops. This is her night; she is the belle of the ball. She is not shy, scared, slouching, slumping Cindy anymore. She's a new person. She already had a trial run with Jeff. She just needs some more practice.

Cindy opens her mouth and yells at the top of her lungs, "BUG OFF!"

Dara, Marybeth, Agnes, and the others flee.

Cindy smiles at herself in the bathroom mirror. She rips away her sash, kicks off the uncomfortable slippers, ties them to a loop on her dress, and walks barefoot to the gymnasium.

Jeff is waiting for her. He is limping slightly, but his eyes still light up when he sees her. "The next dance?" he asks, eyeing her bare feet and the slippers dangling from her dress.

"No, thank you."

"We have to see each other again. You're so—different." He reaches for her hand, but she jerks it away and runs off.

She looks back once at Jeff. Good riddance! she thinks. That's the end of that.

It is ten minutes before midnight. Cindy is looking forward to getting off this horrid dress, scrubbing all the make-up from her face, and having a long, hot soak in the tub.

But it doesn't happen like that.

◆ ◆ ◆

Her parents are asleep when Cindy lets herself in with the key, but the fairy godmother is awake. Her blue porcelain eyes glitter with excitement as she paces back and forth on the shelf next to Cindy's bed.

"Well? How was it?"

"Different," Cindy says.

"The experience of a lifetime?"

"Yes."

"I knew it would be!" the fairy godmother crows triumphantly.

"I hated it."

The fairy godmother crosses her arms. "And just what was so bad about it, Miss Unreasonable? Weren't you the most beautiful girl at the dance? The belle of the ball? Didn't the most handsome boy fall in love with you?"

"Yes, yes, yes..." With clumsy fingers, Cindy unfastens the dress. "Can you help me get these hoops off?"

The fairy godmother points the wand at Cindy's costume. *Poof!* It's gone. All that's left is a sash and a pair of slippers. She's sitting in her underwear again. At least it's French silk.

"You had an evening any girl would die for," says the fairy godmother, stamping her tiny porcelain foot. "How can you complain?"

Cindy tosses the apricot slippers to the floor. "You made them too tight," she says. "I could hardly breathe in that dress. And Jeff is a bore."

"Picky, picky, picky. Don't let little details stand in the way of your happiness."

"You call this happiness?" Cindy tugs at the pins in her hair.

"It will be soon. We haven't even begun..." The fairy godmother has a determined look that Cindy doesn't like. "By next week, every boy in the school will be mad for you."

"No, thank you," says Cindy, imagining a long line of Jeffs approaching her with that stubborn, possessive gleam in their eyes.

"We'll wow 'em," says the fairy godmother. "We'll pow 'em. They'll love you. They won't leave you alone."

"*No*, thank you!"

"Tonight was just a warm-up." The fairy godmother's eyes sparkle. "Wait until you see what I can really do." She waves her wand again and again.

Poof! Poof! Poof! As if in a slide show, Cindy sees herself in one outfit after another. There are leggings in bright colours, cabled sweaters, gauzy blouses with lace and pearl buttons, silk skirts that cling, jungle print dresses, leather boots, and matching backpacks... And her hair is short, long, wavy, straight, piled on her head, cascading around her shoulders, curling over her ears.

It makes her dizzy to see herself in so many ways. She can hardly remember what she really looks like.

"Enough!" she cries. "Please! I don't want to see any more."

The fairy godmother's eyes burn more brightly than ever. She points her wand at Cindy again.

"We'll redo your face," she says. "Make your nose a little straighter and your eyes a little larger. We'll put highlights in your hair and sculpt your thighs. We'll change your name to Cinda. No, to Synda, Cyndina..."

"*Stop!*" Cindy cries.

The fairy godmother keeps waving her wand. Cindy, Cinda, Synda, Cyndina, or whoever she is now, seizes the fairy godmother, plucks the wand from her fingers, and breaks it in two.

Instantly, Cindy—no doubt who she is now—returns to her former self. The straight, lank brown hair. The ripped underwear held together by pins.

"You'll be sorry!" sobs the fairy godmother, her little porcelain features distorted by rage. "A fairy godmother's curse on you! You'll go back to serving sodas! You're nothing without me! Twerp! Brat! Ingrate!"

Knowing that in fairy tales it's always important to be polite, Cindy smiles and says, "Thank you," once more before she picks up the shrieking figurine and drops her onto the bare floor, where she shatters into a thousand pieces.

Cindy sweeps her up carefully. She wouldn't want to cut herself on pieces of her fairy godmother.

◆ ◆ ◆

At school the next day, between classes, she runs into Dara, Agnes, and Marybeth.

"Where were you last night?" Agnes complains. "We had to find someone else to serve the punch. And no one swept the floor."

"You've got to start making posters for the next dance," says Dara.

"And I have a dress for you to mend," Marybeth adds. "I need it by tomorrow."

"Tomorrow?" Cindy's eyes prickle with tears. "I can't possibly—" Suddenly she stops. Is she still shy, scared, slumping, slouching Cindy? Is she still going to sweep the floor, mend the dress, make the posters? Now that she isn't the new Cindy anymore, is she the old Cindy again?

It might happen that way...or maybe it won't.

Cindy faces the three girls.

"I'm out of the picture," she says. Her voice begins to quaver, but she takes a breath and goes on. "Mend your own dress, Marybeth."

"What?" The girls stare at her in shock.

Cindy stands up straighter. "Make your own posters," she says.

Her mouth is firm. Her eyes are clear. Her voice is strong. This isn't a fairy tale anymore, so when she smiles, she isn't being polite.

She walks away. And then turns and yells, "Sweep your own floors!"

And that's the end of that.

She made it happen that way. ◆

1. RESPONDING TO THE STORY

a. Describe the relationship between Cindy and her friends. What do you think of it?

b. What do the transformations do for Cindy?

c. In a short paragraph, describe the main message of this story. Exchange your writing with a partner and compare your views.

d. Which events in this story do you find unrealistic? Which are realistic?

S T R A T E G I E S

2. READING COMPARE STORIES

With a partner, discuss what happens in *Cinderella*. Read the definition of **parody** at right. Do you think that "The Transformations of Cindy R." is a parody of *Cinderella*? Explain. Copy the chart below into your notebook and complete it with your partner, comparing the stories. Do you think this was an effective way for Anne Mazer to tell her story? Give reasons for your answer.

> A **parody** is a humorous imitation of a serious writing format. It follows the form of the original, but changes its sense to nonsense.

	Cinderella	"The Transformations of Cindy R."
Main Character		
Her Problem		
What the Main Character Is Like		
What Happens to the Main Character		
Other Characters		
Where and When the Story Takes Place		
How the Story Ends		
Message		

3. WRITING A FAIRY TALE

Use the chart that you created in "Compare Stories" to help you write a short fairy tale, or a parody of one. It could be a contemporary fairy tale that has a message, such as "You can't buy happiness." Begin by jotting down notes about the characters and events. Remember to use strong adjectives and adverbs when describing your characters. Read your story to a younger student.

4. LANGUAGE CONVENTIONS ADJECTIVES AND ADVERBS

Adjectives are words that are used to describe nouns. *Adverbs* are used to describe verbs. For example:

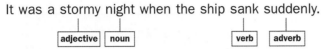

It was a stormy night when the ship sank suddenly.

In this story, the author uses both adjectives and adverbs to create vivid images of Cindy's physical appearance and personality, both before and after her "transformation." Copy the following chart into your notebook and list the adjectives and adverbs that the author has used to describe her. Pick one word from your chart that you think best describes Cindy "before" and "after."

	Cindy "Before"	Cindy "After"
Adjectives		
Adverbs		

SELF-ASSESSMENT: In one paragraph, describe Cindy, either before or after her transformation, using adjectives and adverbs that you have chosen. Show your writing to a partner and discuss your choice of descriptive words.

5. MEDIA TRUTH IN ADVERTISING

Reread the details of the advertisement, on page 13 of the story, in which Cindy finds her fairy godmother. How is this like a real ad? How does it parody one? What does it promise?

Record in your notebook the details of at least three TV or magazine ads that make similar promises. In your opinion, which is the most effective or persuasive? Why? Explain fully.

You Should Wear Khakis with That

GOALS AT A GLANCE

■ Analyse the message of a comic strip.
■ Develop a dialogue between two characters.

----

1. RESPONDING TO THE COMIC STRIP

Discuss the content and message of this comic strip with a small group. Why will Jeremy take his girlfriend's advice, but not his mother's? Do you agree that how you dress is "who you are"? Explain.

2. ORAL COMMUNICATION DEVELOP DIALOGUE

Think of a similar situation that you've experienced or witnessed. Develop eight lines of dialogue focussing on the experience. Role-play your dialogue with a classmate.

Does it matter to you what your friends look like?
Read this article to find out how Canadian teens
answered this survey question.

FEELING GOOD, LOOKING GREAT

Magazine Article by
Mary Walters Riskin

A recent survey from teen magazine *ZOOT* asked 66 teens between the ages of 13 and 18 whether they chose their friends on the basis of appearance. Two said "Yes." Two said "Sometimes." One said "Partly." But 61 (or 92%) of them said "No."

They said their friends' other qualities—personality, sense of humour, loyalty—were more important than appearance. And yet 25 of these same teens said they'd like to change something about the way *they* looked. Usually they wanted to change their shapes—be stronger, thinner, taller. Sometimes they wanted to get rid of freckles or change the colour of their eyes or the shapes of their noses. How come so many teens think other people are keeping an eye on their appearance when they don't worry about how other people look? Why do they tell themselves that other people's

---

GOALS AT A GLANCE

■ Draw conclusions about ideas in an article.
■ Generate ideas as a group.

looks don't matter, but theirs do? Actually, a lot of the teens in the survey knew the answer to that question. They said the reason they wanted to change was because "I'd feel better about myself," "I'd have more confidence," or "I'd feel more secure." In other words, it isn't the actual change in appearance they want so much as the feeling they think will go with it. What they really want is to feel good about themselves.

"I'D LIKE TO HAVE A FLAWLESS COMPLEXION, AND BE A BIT SKINNIER AND TALLER."
Jan, 15

A lot of adults have difficulty with the whole body-image issue, but it's particularly tough for teens. During the teen years, you get a first real look at what you're going to look like as an adult. Sometime during your teens, you reach your maximum height and your body shape begins to stabilize. Naturally, your body doesn't look like anyone else's body, and it probably doesn't look like any of those "ideal" bodies you see on television or in magazines.

To make things even tougher, some teens begin to have trouble with their weight and a lot have trouble with acne. Some find out they need glasses, or braces, or both.

It's tough to learn to accept yourself the way you are, and feel confident about it, when your body's going through so many changes.

"I WOULD RATHER BE SOMEONE ELSE."
Fran, 15

Some people are so determined to change the way they look that they actually damage their bodies by going on starvation diets, over-exercising, or using steroids or other drugs. They're often doing these things because of other problems in their lives that have nothing to do with the shape of their bodies, and they can end up with major, long-term illnesses.

Some people get onto a treadmill. They don't like the way they look so they don't look after themselves. They don't eat properly or get enough exercise.

Too much junk food and too little exercise make them feel depressed. Depressed people usually look as bad as they feel.

Others become like mismatched jigsaw puzzles, picking up bits and pieces of appearance from other people, but with no clear sense of what they really want to look like. As a result, they're never satisfied with their appearances.

"NOBODY REALLY LIKES EVERYTHING ABOUT THEMSELVES."
Sandy, 14

Teens who focus on the way they look and want to change their bodies are focussing on the wrong part of the equation. What needs changing is not their shapes or heights, but the way they see themselves. "If I looked better, I'd feel better about myself" is backward. When you are confident about yourself, you feel better. And when you feel better, you look better.

So, how do you build self-confidence?

Psychologists point out that people are always talking to themselves, and that the talk can get pretty negative. They think things like, "That was a dumb move," or "I shouldn't have said that." Sometimes the self-talk is more general—and more destructive. "I'm so ugly." "I'm so stupid." "I'm no good."

The good news is that you can train yourself to think self-confidently. The following exercises can help improve the way you think—and the way you feel:

1. Remember that few people are satisfied with everything about themselves. Everyone's good at some things, and not so good at others. Train yourself to focus on your strengths, your talents, and your interests, rather than your shortcomings.
2. Every time you notice you're dumping on yourself, substitute a more positive thought. Remind yourself of the things you're good at. Say, "So I messed up. I can't be perfect at everything."
3. Remember that feelings change. It's happened to you before: a situation looks terrible one day, not so bad the next. By the day after that, it's forgotten.

Remind yourself that you've overcome problems before, and know that you can do it again.

4. Imagine that your life is a movie, with you in the starring role. Are your problems really disasters, or are you just seeing them that way? When you stand back from your problems, sometimes it's easier to put them in perspective.

5. Spend time with people you trust and feel comfortable with. Talking to them about things that are bothering you can make problems seem less important. (If the problems are bigger than you can handle on your own, talk to a professional counsellor.)

6. Remember that you're in charge of your emotions. People can make you feel badly if you let them, and you can make yourself feel badly, too. Everyone has "down" times, but you can make yourself feel better if you work on the positive thoughts.

Building self-confidence is mostly a matter of teaching yourself to think differently.

Think of Danny de Vito, Roseanne, and Bart Simpson. Think of the people in your own life who are so self-confident that their appearances don't matter.

"IF I LOOKED BETTER, I'D FEEL BETTER ABOUT MYSELF."
  Fiona, 14

Statements about who you are come more from the way you speak and act rather than from the way you look. You can develop an image that you like without being taller, shorter, or thinner. Everybody is different from everybody else—not just in appearance, but in every way. You just have to find out what *you* like.

People with acne can get help from their doctors. People who really are overweight can diet safely. People who want to improve their physical condition can work on exercise and body building.

"I DON'T LIKE MY NOSE. IT'S A PIGGY NOSE—JUST LIKE MY MOTHER'S!"
  Jonathon, 13

It's human nature to want to change for the better. It's a great quality—and it can lead to outstanding achievement. The big thing is deciding what you can control and change, and what you can't. When you're working on the things you can—and want—to change, the other stuff doesn't seem so important.

"I'M HAPPY JUST THE WAY I AM. EVEN IF I'M A BIT WEIRD."
Mark, 14

The bottom line is that the self-confident look is what's good-looking. It has very little to do with the actual appearance of your body, and changing the way your body looks isn't what brings self-confidence.

Self-confidence comes from seeing your good qualities and accepting your imperfections, instead of focussing on your flaws. It comes from knowing that you have the power to change the way you think. It comes from knowing that the way you think affects the way you feel.

People who feel good about themselves look good, too.

At Face Value

Profile by Lorna Renooy

Ani Aubin is a singer and songwriter living in Toronto. She spoke with Lorna Renooy about art, beauty, and facial difference.

Lorna: Could you start by telling me a bit about yourself?
Ani: As a child, I felt different a lot of the time because of my birthmark. When you have a facial difference, you can either be introverted, or you can go out and face the world. That's what I chose to do, with the help of my family.

I began singing at an early age. That set me apart from other kids, too. On stage, you're so vulnerable. You're alone there under bright lights that shine right on your face, in front of all these people who are staring at you.

I started wearing make-up to cover my birth-mark when I was eight years old. By Grade Seven, I was wearing make-up every day. Two years ago, I stopped because I decided I still wasn't myself. The make-up was a mask, and I realized I was wearing it to protect myself from the meanness of people, but I also knew I was hiding who I was.

Lorna: What would you like to share with people who have facial differences?

Ani: You have to acknowledge that it is very, very hard to be different because of society and the way other people often see us. If we acknowledge this, it becomes less hard. Other people can be very cruel, or insensitive, but we shouldn't feel limited by that. We can accept ourselves the way we are.

---

1. RESPONDING TO THE ARTICLE

a. Were you surprised by the survey results in "Feeling Good, Looking Great"? Why or why not?

b. Do you think the opinions of singer Ani Aubin in "At Face Value" support the author's main idea in "Feeling Good, Looking Great"? Give reasons for your answer.

2. READING GENERATE IDEAS

In the article, Mary Walters Riskin lists many things young people can do to build self-confidence. In a small group, examine the steps that she suggests. Discuss why you think they will or will not work. Compile a list of your own ideas about how young people can learn to feel good about themselves. You could create a Web page and post these suggestions, or ask for comments on these ideas in a chat room.

HOW TO

CONDUCT A SURVEY

Goals at a Glance

- Follow instructions to conduct a survey. • Tally and present survey results.

ZOOT magazine conducted a survey. They thought their readers would want to know what kids their own age thought about an important topic—the self-image of teens. A survey is a research method used to find out the opinions, preferences, or habits of a group of people.

With a small group, discuss an issue that concerns all of you. Find out how your group members feel about this issue. Share your ideas.

Plan the Survey

There are several questions you will need to answer in planning your survey:

1. What is your *purpose* for conducting a survey? What do you want to find out?
2. What do you predict will be the *results* of your survey? What will you do with the results?
3. Who will be your *subjects*? How many will you need? How will you select them—at random, based on age or gender? What general information will you record about them? Generally, the greater the number of subjects, the greater the reliability of your results.
4. Will the *format* be oral or written responses? Will you ask for facts, opinions, or both? Remember that people are more likely to respond to surveys that can be completed in a minute or two.

Generate Questions

Make your questions clear, brief, specific, and *objective* (without any implied judgment). How you ask a question can influence the way it is answered. Be careful not to ask questions that lead to a particular response, or that use *loaded* (judgmental) words. Instead of:

How often do you cave in to peer pressure?

use

Are you influenced by peer pressure?

Use one, or a combination, of these types of questions:

- **MULTIPLE CHOICE**

  Follow a simple question with a list of possible answers.

PROCESS

Would your life be better without peer pressure?

    a) ❏ yes   b) ❏ no   c) ❏ not sure

Allow more than one answer to be chosen, or let subjects add their own.

Which of your decisions are most affected by peer pressure? Please check all that apply.

  ❏ buying clothes ❏ choosing friends
  ❏ obeying authorities
  ❏ choosing extra-curricular activities
  ❏ other (please specify)_____

• RANKING

Ask your subjects to number their choices in order of importance.

What influences what you buy? Rank your answers from 1-5, with #1 as the most important and #5 as the least important.

  ❏ cost ❏ brand name
  ❏ friend's recommendation
  ❏ TV advertisement
  ❏ popular kids have it

• OPEN-ENDED

An open-ended question has many possible answers. This makes it more difficult to group the answers and tally the results.

How do you feel about peer pressure?

_____

Produce the Survey Form

Use a computer to develop a rough draft of your survey. You may wish to include space for some general information from your subjects, such as age or gender. Design your survey so that it is neat and easy to read.

Edit and proofread your survey form before you distribute copies. If it's an oral survey, each group member must have at least one copy. If it's a written survey, include a sentence that explains why you are gathering the information. Set a deadline for the questionnaire to be completed and returned.

Conduct the Survey

Refer to the answers you provided to question three of "Plan the Survey." Have at least twenty people respond to your survey. Remember to thank your subjects for their help.

Share the Results

Tally the responses to each question and analyse your data. How do the results compare with your predictions?

You might wish to write a summary of your findings. You might also want to display your data visually using a graph.

Present your findings to the class and answer questions about the survey. Perhaps you could publish the survey results on your school's Web site or in a newsletter.

Group Assessment

❏ Did we state the purpose of our survey clearly?

❏ Did we follow our plan for the format and subjects?

❏ Did we develop our questions carefully?

❏ Did we tabulate and analyse our data correctly?

❏ Did we summarize or graph our results clearly?

PROCESS

*What does it take
to be a champion?*

Joy-riding

Short Story
by Jim Naughton

P eter glanced at the clock on the bookshelf. It was quarter
after four. "Fifteen minutes to freedom," he said to himself.
Fifteen minutes until he could turn off the metronome—*two,
three, four*—and stop moving his fingers across the keys.

For Peter the best part of the day began at the moment he
stopped practising the piano. Beginning at four-thirty each day
he had an entire hour to himself. He could read science fiction.
He could play video games in the den. He just couldn't leave
the house.

This had never really bothered him until the afternoon three
weeks earlier when he'd seen the runner gliding up Putnam Street
hill. Something about the way the older boy looked, something
about the way he moved, drew Peter away from his music and
out onto the porch to watch the runner race by in his maroon
and gold Darden High School sweat suit.

GOALS AT A GLANCE

- Analyse character using a Venn diagram.
- Analyse point of view.

That night at dinner his mother had said, "Mrs. Kennedy says she saw you on the porch this afternoon. I hope you weren't neglecting your music."

"I was just saying hello to a friend," Peter lied. He didn't even know the other boy's name.

Intimidated by his mother's intelligence network, Peter had not ventured back onto the porch for three weeks, content to watch from his bench as the older boy churned up the hill and off to the oval behind Peter's junior high school. But the previous afternoon, as he'd watched the second hand on the parlour clock ticking away the final seconds of his captivity, *two, three, four,* Peter had decided to go back out on the porch. He thought he might wave as the runner strode by, but instead he studied the older boy in silence.

The runner was tall, lean, and broad-shouldered. *I am none of that stuff*, Peter thought.

The runner had sharp features. Peter's nose looked like he had flattened it against a window and it had stayed that way. The runner had a clear, steady gaze. Peter was near-sighted and tended to squint. The runner had a shock of copper-coloured hair. Peter had a frizz so fine it was hard to say what colour it was.

In spite of these differences, Peter could have imagined himself in the other boy's place were it not for the runner's grace. The way the boy moved reminded him of music. His legs had the spring of a sprightly melody. His arms pumped a relentless rhythm. He ascended the hill almost effortlessly, as though gravity were no greater hindrance on this steep incline than it had been on the prairie-flat main street below.

He must never lose, Peter thought.

That was another way in which they were different. Peter had just come in third in the piano competition sponsored by the university, after coming in second in the contest sponsored by the orchestra, and third in the contest sponsored by the bank.

"Peter," his mother said, "you are a perpetual runner-up." Then she decided that rather than practise for one hour every day, he should practise for two. Two hours!

But two hours were now up. And as Peter stopped the metronome, he spotted a familiar figure in a maroon sweat suit at the bottom of the hill.

◆ ◆ ◆

Who is this kid? Kevin asked himself.

Kevin McGrail had not yet reached the crest of Putnam Street when he noticed the pudgy boy in the orange T-shirt on the porch of the white stucco house.

At least he's on the porch today, Kevin thought. For three weeks the kid had watched him from his piano bench. Every day as he pounded up the hill Kevin would hear this weird tinkly music coming from the stucco house across the street. Then there would be a pause as he passed by, and he would see the little frizzy-headed kid looking at him through the window. Then the weird tinkly music would begin again.

At first Kevin felt kind of spooked when the music stopped, like maybe Freddy Krueger was going to jump out of the bushes or something. But after a while he just wondered why the kid was so interested in him.

It wasn't like he was a big star or anything. Kevin was number three on the Darden cross-country team, a nice steady runner who could be counted on to come in ahead of number three on the opposing team. Coach Haggerty always told him he could be number two if he worked at it, but Kevin thought working at something was the surest way to turn it from a pleasure into a chore.

Just look at what happened with Mark Fairbanks. He and Kevin used to hang out together, but that was before Haggerty had convinced Mark that if he devoted his entire life to cross-country he could be a star. Well, Markie was a star all right. He was the fastest guy on the team and one of the top runners in the district. But he was also the biggest drone in the school. Every day at the beginning of practice he would shout, "Okay, it's time to go to *work!*"

Kevin felt the strain on his legs lighten as he reached the top of the hill. He saw the road flatten before him and felt the crisp autumn air tingling pleasantly in his lungs. *As soon as this becomes work*, he said to himself, *I quit.*

◆ ◆ ◆

"Mom," Peter said at dinner, "I want to go out for the football team."

His mother looked up from her Caesar salad with an expression of exaggerated horror. "Think of your hands!" she said.

Peter had known she would say that. "Well, maybe basketball then," he replied.

"That is every bit as dangerous."

Peter had kind of figured she would say that too. "Well, I want to do something," he said. "Something where there's people. Where there's guys."

His mother put down her fork, pressed her palms together in front of her face, hooked her thumbs under her chin, and regarded him from over her fingertips. *Now we are getting serious*, Peter thought.

"What about choir?" his mother proposed. "I haven't wanted you exposed to a lot of influences. Musically, I mean. But I am not insensitive to your need for companionship."

Peter shook his head. "How about cross-country?" he asked. "It's only running. How about that?"

"Sports are nothing but trouble," his mother said. "Trouble and disappointment. I think you will agree it is much more satisfying to devote yourself to something at which you can really excel."

"There is a boy on the high-school team who runs up at the oval every day," Peter said. "He told me I could practise with him."

His mother pursed her lips. If Peter could only have explained his plan to her, he was certain she would have said yes. But he wasn't ready to try that. He could barely make sense of it himself.

One thing he was sure of: That boy who ran past the house every day was a champion. He would know what separates winners from perpetual runners-up. And if Peter could learn that, well then, his mother would be happy, and if his mother was happy, well then, everything would be okay again. All she had to do was say yes.

"You still owe me two hours at that piano every day," she said.

◆ ◆ ◆

Kevin was surprised to see the little piano player up at the oval the next day. The kid was dressed in one of those shapeless sweat suits they wore in junior-high-school gym class.

Looks like he's already winded, Kevin thought as he watched the kid struggle through about a dozen jumping jacks. *I hope he doesn't hurt himself.*

Kevin was beginning his second lap when the kid fell in beside him.

"Hi," the boy said.

"Hey," said Kevin without slowing down.

"I'm getting in shape for next season," said the boy, who was already breathing heavily and losing ground.

"It's good to give yourself a lot of time," Kevin said, not meaning to sound quite so smart-alecky.

"See you around," the boy called as Kevin opened up the space between them.

Every day for the next three weeks the routine was the same: The kid was always waiting when Kevin arrived. He would puff along beside Kevin for a few strides, try to start a gasping conversation, and then fall hopelessly behind. The kid was obviously

never going to be a runner, Kevin thought, and he sure didn't look like he was enjoying himself. Yet there he was, grinding away, just like Fairbanks only without the talent.

You're a better person than I am, Kevin thought. *Or a sicker one.*

That Friday when Kevin got to the oval the chubby kid took one look at him and started to run. It was as though he were giving himself a head start in some kind of private race. The thought of some competition between the two of them made Kevin laugh, because he generally lapped the kid at least five or six times each session.

He put the little piano player out of his mind and tried to focus on the rhythm of his own footfalls. The following weekend he and the rest of the Darden team would be competing in the district championships, and Kevin had begun to think it might be a good time to answer a question that had been nagging at him for the last month. He wanted to know how good he was—not how good he could be if he devoted his entire life to cross-country, but how good he was at that moment. What would happen, he wondered, if he ran one race as hard as he could?

Part of him did not want to know. Suppose he beat out Billy Kovacs, number two on the Darden team? That would mean Coach Haggerty would be all over him. He'd expect Kevin to have a big season in his senior year, maybe even make it to the state championships. Just thinking about the way Haggerty put his gaunt face up next to yours and shouted "Go for the goal!" was enough to stop Kevin in his tracks.

On the other hand, he might not beat Billy Kovacs, and that would be depressing too. Kevin liked to think of himself as some-body who *could* run faster if he *wanted* to run faster. But if he went all out and still finished in the middle of the pack, it would mean he was just another mediocre high-school runner.

Maybe I should just run a nice easy race and forget about this, Kevin thought. *It would be less complicated.*

As he began the seventh of his eight laps, Kevin noticed that the chubby kid was still running—puffing and panting and lurching from one foot to another. "This is my bell lap," he gasped as Kevin trotted by.

Kevin chuckled at the idea of the little piano player in a race, but when he finished his workout he stopped to watch the other boy circle the track one last time. This was the kid's fourth lap. Kevin had never seen him run more than a kilometre before, and he felt a sneaky sense of pride in his training partner's accomplishment.

The kid came chugging down the track, gulping huge bites of air, and clutching his right side. But when he reached his imaginary finish line, he threw both hands into the air and held that pose for a moment before collapsing onto the grass. Kevin was about to jog over when he heard a voice in the stands announce: "And the winner in the Pudge Ball Olympics: Peter Whitney."

Kevin turned quickly and recognized three kids from the freshman class at school. "Hey, why don't you bozos take off," he said sharply, and looked at them long enough for the kids to understand that he meant it.

The piano player was still lying flat on his back when Kevin reached him and extended a hand to help him to his feet.

"Thanks," the boy said, in a barely audible voice.

◆ ◆ ◆

Hours after he had arrived home, Peter kept replaying the details in his head to see if there was something he had missed. First the fudge-brains from Grade Nine had made fun of him and the runner had taken his side. Next the older boy had waited around while Peter caught his breath. Then they'd walked down the hill together all the way to Peter's house. It was almost like they were friends.

But things had begun to go wrong as soon as Peter tried to ask him his secret. The trouble was he couldn't figure out how to put the question in his own words, and so he began talking like the books his mother read to help her get ahead at her office.

"Do you visualize your goals?" he blurted.

The boy looked at him quizzically.

"Some people do that," Peter continued, eager to fill the silence. "But other people, they say that you should concentrate on developing the habits of a highly effective person."

The runner didn't respond, so Peter felt compelled to keep talking. "Do you think your habits are effective? I mean, are they consistent with your aspirations? You know?"

The other boy shrugged. "You still play the piano?" he asked.

"Two hours a day," Peter said.

"You like it?"

"No," Peter said. "I mean, yes. I used to."

"But now you don't?"

Peter did not want to waste time talking about himself, but the older boy seemed genuinely interested. "Before we came here I had a different teacher," he said, and as he did every time he sat down at the piano, he began to think of Mickey Ray.

Mickey was his teacher back in Rochester. He taught part-time at the university and at night he played in clubs. Peter's mother didn't like him because he wore a ponytail. But everybody told her that he was the best teacher in town. She let Peter take lessons from him on one condition: that they play only "performance pieces"— compositions Peter might later play in a competition.

But Mickey did not always abide by this condition. Every once in a while he would pull a new piece of music from his satchel, wink conspiratorially at Peter, and ask him to give it a try. This was how Peter got to know jazz and ragtime and gospel music.

After Peter played through the piece once, Mickey would sit down on the bench beside him. "Next time," he would say, "a little more like this." And off he would go, playing the same notes in the same order, but making the piece sound more fluid, more powerful, more alive.

"It is not about hitting the right key at the right time," Mickey used to say. "It is about taking this baby for a ride." Peter began to tell the other boy about Mickey Ray.

"He sounds cool," the runner said.

"My teacher now is better," Peter said. Actually he wasn't sure if that was true. "Mr. Brettone is a superior musical pedagogue," his mother had said. But lately Peter had found himself imagining that Mr. Brettone had tiny pickaxes attached to his fingertips and that each time he struck a key it would crack and crumble.

They were standing in front of the house by the time Peter finished the story, and he was no closer to learning the other boy's secret than he had been before all those gruelling afternoons on the oval. Finally, just as the other boy was about to leave, he blurted: "How do you do it?"

"Do what?"

"Win."

"I don't know anything about winning," the runner said. "I just know about running."

Then came what Peter found the most puzzling exchange of all. "I hope you win at the districts," he said as the boy jogged away.

"Now what would I want to do that for?" the runner called back.

◆ ◆ ◆

Kevin stood among the throng of two hundred runners packed into a clearing just off the first fairway at the Glen Oaks Golf Club. At the crack of the starter's pistol they would all surge forward onto the manicured expanse of the fairway. The sight of all those bodies churning and all those bright uniforms bobbing up and down was so captivating that during his first two seasons Kevin had hung back at the beginning just to take in the spectacle.

Not this year, though. He had decided to run the race of his life, and moments after the gun was fired, he found himself in the first fourth of the great mob of runners struggling for position as they tore toward the first green, where the course cut sharply downhill and into the woods. As he hit what he thought of as a good cruising speed for the first stage of the race, Kevin couldn't help wondering if he would wear himself out too quickly or collapse on the grass at the finish line like that crazy little piano player.

It was strange to be thinking of him at a time like this. Or maybe it wasn't. Because what Kevin had been trying to figure out all along was whether excelling at his sport would somehow ruin it for him, the way excelling at the piano had ruined it for Peter. He half suspected that it would, but something the kid had told him that day Kevin had walked him home had given him a half-hearted kind of hope.

In the pack just ahead of him Kevin picked out Mark Fairbanks, Kovacs, and a couple of the top runners from other schools he had raced against during the year. No question—he was a lot closer to them than he usually was at the kilometre mark.

◆ ◆ ◆

As the runner streaked by, Peter cheered and pointed his friend out to his mother. It had taken heroic persuasion to get Mom to come out to a cross-country meet on a Saturday morning, but now he was sure that everything would go just the way he planned. His friend would win the race and then Peter would introduce him to Mom. He wasn't really certain what would happen after that. He couldn't really explain why he wanted them to meet. It wasn't so that Mom could see that he was making friends at school, because she thought friends only distracted him from his piano. And it wasn't because he thought she would be impressed by a cross-country champion, since Mom didn't really appreciate sports.

Peter wanted them to meet so that Mom could see that he had a little of the runner in him, a little bit of the champion, a little bit of something that would lift him beyond the status of a "perpetual runner-up." If he could only convince her of that, maybe it wouldn't be so hard to keep sitting down alone at the piano. Or to keep sitting down to dinner with her.

"He's not winning," Peter's mother said as they watched the runners cut off the fairway and into the woods.

"It's strategy, Mom," Peter told her, though he too was wondering why his friend was not at the head of the pack.

◆ ◆ ◆

They were tearing along an old railroad bed at the top of a ridge near the fourth tee. Kevin's legs still felt strong. His breath came easily. Fairbanks, who was fighting for the lead, was just a speck up along the train tracks, but Billy Kovacs was only eighteen metres or so ahead of Kevin.

I can take him, Kevin thought, *but then I'll have to hold him off the rest of the way*. He hesitated for a second, and then decided to pick up his pace.

◆ ◆ ◆

A single runner in the maroon Darden uniform came streaking out of the woods and onto the tenth fairway. There was less than a kilometre remaining in the race.

"That isn't your friend," Peter's mother said.

Another runner in red and white charged out of the woods a few metres behind. In a few moments there were six, seven, and then eight other runners pounding the last kilometre toward the finish line. Peter didn't recognize any of them.

"I'm sorry, dear," his mother said, rummaging in her purse for her car keys.

Peter felt as though he had bet a lifetime of allowances on the wrong horse.

◆ ◆ ◆

As he tore out of the woods and onto the tenth fairway, Kevin began counting the people ahead of him, a feat made more difficult by the sweat dripping into his eyes. There were fifteen of them, as nearly as he could tell. The top ten finishers went on to the state finals. Somewhere up along the railroad tracks the desire to be in that group had seized him and he had picked up his pace. Now the wind burned in his lungs and the acid burned in his calves. His Achilles tendons felt like guitar strings being tightened with each footfall. He had less than a kilometre to make up six places.

He glanced quickly across the fairway and saw Fairbanks duelling for the lead with Pat Connors of Tech. In the crowd behind them he saw the little piano player. He was gazing in Kevin's direction, disappointment etched on his face.

I'm running the race of my life and it isn't good enough for him, Kevin thought. He could feel the anger rising inside him. The race was ruined for him now, and he began to doubt his motives. Was he really running all out just to see what it felt like, or had the attention of this peculiar little kid made him hungry for more?

Kevin wanted his sense of purity back. He wanted to stop caring whether he finished in the top ten. Something inside him whispered "Slow down" but instead he emptied his mind and kept running.

Into that emptiness floated the memory of the conversation he and the little piano player had had just a few days before. The kid had been talking about his old teacher, the one who liked to take the piano "for a ride." *I can't play*, Kevin thought, *but I can run. This can be my ride.*

Imagining that he was Mickey Ray, Kevin focussed his eyes on the ground in front of him and sprinted the last couple hundred metres, unaware of the screaming fans or the other runners on the course.

◆ ◆ ◆

Peter couldn't understand what the big fuss was about. The kid had come in eleventh. That wasn't even good enough to qualify for the state finals, yet people were acting like that was a bigger deal than Mark Fairbanks, who had come in second. It was pretty cool to take a minute off your best time, he supposed, but still, eleventh place wasn't worth all the cheering the Darden fans did when the kid crossed the finish line.

Besides that, Kevin McGrail looked horrible. When he had glided up Putnam Street six weeks ago he had been so smooth, so poised. Now he was bent over, walking like he had a sunburn on the bottoms of his feet.

Peter saw the boy's coach, a gaunt man wearing a baseball cap, put an arm around Kevin's shoulder. "You dug down deep and you came up big," the coach barked.

Kevin drew a few rapid breaths. "I was joy-riding," he said.

"Joy-riding," Peter repeated to himself as he sat at his piano later that afternoon. "Joy-riding lands you in eleventh place." He stood up, opened the piano bench, and withdrew the exercises Mr. Brettone had assigned for that week. Beneath it he found *The Fats Waller Songbook*. Mickey had given it to him as a going-away present. Peter thumbed through the pages until he found "Your Feet's Too Big." Just the title made him laugh. And the way Mickey used to play it…

He looked up to see his mother standing in the doorway. "What are we featuring this afternoon?" she asked.

"Exercises for the left hand," Peter said, and he sat down to work.

----

1. RESPONDING TO THE STORY

a. What does the phrase "joy-riding" mean? Is "Joy-riding" a good title? Give reasons for your answer. Suggest another title for the story. Compare your title with those of your classmates.

b. Why do you think Kevin at first resists becoming the best that he can be? Why does he change his mind?

c. In your opinion, did Peter get to joy-ride? If so, how?

d. What advice would you like to give to Kevin? Peter? Peter's mom?

2. READING CHARACTER ANALYSIS

Read through the story carefully a second time. As you read, record on a Venn diagram the similarities and differences between the two boys. To create a Venn diagram, draw two circles that partially overlap. Label one circle "Kevin" and the other "Peter." Where the circles overlap, insert characteristics that the boys have in common. Where the circles are separate, record characteristics that are unique to each boy. Include both physical and personality traits.

Imagine that you are the editor of the school yearbook and are responsible for gathering information on your fellow classmates. Using the information from the Venn diagram write two paragraphs in which you describe the characteristics of Kevin and Peter. Include these paragraphs in your writing portfolio.

3. STORY CRAFT POINT OF VIEW

In small groups, discuss point of view in this story. *Point of view* refers to the position from which the events of a story are presented. In "Joy-riding," Jim Naughton tells the story from the points of view of both Kevin and Peter. Why might he have chosen to do this? Does using two points of view make the story easier or harder to follow? Explain.

4. WRITING CONTINUE THE STORY

Imagine that Kevin and Peter meet again as adults. In your notebook, write a conversation in which they exchange information on what they have accomplished in their lives. You should reveal whether or not they have reached their goals.

S T R A T E G I E S

5. EDITOR'S DESK PUNCTUATING DIALOGUE

This story contains a lot of *dialogue* (characters speaking with and to each other). What do you notice about the structure of dialogue in this story? What kind of punctuation is used? Here are some basic guidelines to follow when including dialogue in a story.

- Use proper punctuation.

    Begin and end direct speech with quotation marks.

    "May I please sit here?" asked the girl.

    Ending punctuation remains within the quotation marks.

    "The fire is on the first floor!" exclaimed the officer.

    Use commas in a broken quotation. Capitalize the first word in the quote, but not the first word that begins the second half of the quote.

    "If we can't find the answer," said John, "we'll move on to the next question."

- Vary the vocabulary used in dialogue. Instead of always using *said*, try words such as *stated* or *exclaimed*. Instead of *asked*, try *questioned* or *inquired*. You may find a thesaurus helpful.
- New speakers require new paragraphs.

Have you ever been
hurt by gossip?

FEATHERS
in the
WIND

FABLE RETOLD BY DIANE ROBITAILLE

Long, long ago in a small village there lived a man who was neither young nor old, neither evil nor good, neither ugly nor handsome, neither stupid nor smart. He was an average man. His name was Rumour.

One day, as Rumour was speaking to the baker, he heard, or thought he heard, someone say something vicious about one of his neighbours. His eyes lit up.

Rumour repeated this bit of news about his neighbour to others in the village. He told the butcher, who told her brother, who told his wife, who told her neighbour, and so on. Rumour also told his cousin the story, and he told his neighbour, who told her friends, and so on. And so on.

By sunset, the whole village knew the story, and everyone was whispering about Rumour's neighbour.

Before very long, the neighbour heard what was being said about her. She was deeply hurt and very upset that such a dreadful and false story about her was swirling around in the village. She wondered who could have spread the story. She told everyone she knew that it wasn't true. But still many chose to believe what they had heard. Distraught and broken-hearted, the neighbour became ill. A very short time later, she packed up her belongings and moved away to another village.

Eventually, Rumour learned that the story he had spread was not true. He was filled with regret at having spread such a lie. So he went to the wisest person in the village to find out what he could do to repair the damage he had caused.

"Go to the butcher and buy a chicken," the wise woman said. "On your way home, pluck its feathers. Place them one by one along the road through the village."

Rumour was disappointed by this advice. It made no sense. He decided he would follow it anyway, since the woman would say nothing else.

The next morning, the wise woman approached Rumour. She had new instructions for him. "Today, walk along the road and gather the feathers you left there yesterday and then come and see me."

Rumour went off to look for the feathers, but could not find a single one. Of course, he thought, the wind has blown all the feathers away.

He searched until red stained the evening sky, and managed to find three tattered, dusty feathers stuck in a shrub along the roadside. He returned to the wise woman and held them out to her.

"Ahh," said the wise woman. "It was easy to scatter the feathers on the road. But was it possible to gather them again? That's what gossip is like. It takes no effort to spread tales and lies, but once gossip spreads, you can never recall it or undo the wrong it caused."

1. RESPONDING TO THE FABLE

a. Why does Rumour spread information about his neighbour?

b. What lesson does Rumour learn? How does he learn it?

c. What do the feathers represent in this fable? Explain the effectiveness of this **symbol**.

d. It would have been faster for the wise woman to simply give Rumour the answer to his question. Why, in your opinion, didn't she do that?

e. What are rumours? How and why do they get started?

f. Have you ever been the subject of a rumour? How did you feel? How did it affect your self-image?

> A **symbol** is a person, place, thing, or event that is used to represent something else. For example, a rainbow is often used as a symbol of hope.

S T R A T E G I E S

2. WRITING A FABLE

A *fable* is a short story that usually teaches a lesson. With your class, discuss the lesson in "Feathers in the Wind." In your opinion, is the lesson an important one? Explain.

Decide on a moral lesson that you think is important for children to learn, for example, "It's wrong to be greedy." Write a fable based on this lesson. Remember that fables are very short and often include animal characters with human characteristics. However, you could choose to follow the model of "Feathers in the Wind" and feature a human character with a name like "Greed" or "Vanity."

Revise and edit your fable until you're satisfied that it will interest and entertain a younger audience. Practise reading it aloud.

Read your fable to younger students. Remember to use gestures, sound effects, volume, and tone effectively.

SELF-ASSESSMENT: Ask the audience to state the lesson of your fable. If they can't, consider how you can make the lesson clearer and then rewrite your work.

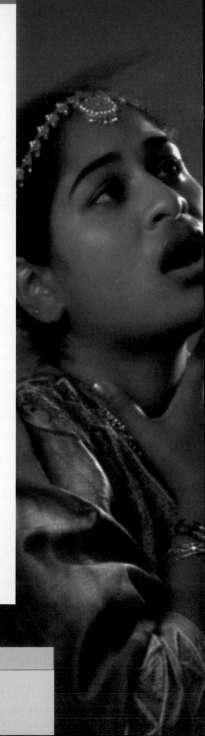

How Feel I Do?

Poem by Jim Wong-Chu

your eyes plead approval
of each uttered word

and even my warmest smile
cannot dispel the shamed muscles
from your face

let me be honest
with you

to tell the truth
I feel very much at home
in your embarrassment

don't be afraid

like you
I too was mired in another language
and I gladly surrendered it
for english

you too
in time
will lose your mother's tongue

and speak
at least as fluently
as me

now tell me

how do you feel?

GOALS AT A GLANCE

■ Analyse the message of a poem.
■ Examine punctuation in poetry.

I Lost My Talk
Poem by Rita Joe

I lost my talk
The talk you took away.
When I was a little girl
At Shubenacadie school.

You snatched it away:
I speak like you
I think like you
I create like you
The scrambled ballad, about my word.

Two ways I talk
Both ways I say,
Your way is more powerful.

So gently I offer my hand and ask,
Let me find my talk
So I can teach you about me.

1. RESPONDING TO THE POEMS

a. Why do you think Jim Wong-Chu called his poem "How Feel I Do?" What does Rita Joe mean by the title of her poem "I Lost My Talk"?

b. The speakers in both poems share similar situations but they feel differently. In your own words, explain what each is saying.

c. Which poem do you prefer? Why?

d. What kind of school do you think "Shubenacadie school" is? What information in the poem makes you think so?

2. POET'S CRAFT ANALYSE MESSAGE

Poets choose their words very carefully. They rely on the sound and the impact of every word to carry the message they wish to convey. What is the message of each poem? How do the poets use words effectively? Record the answers to these questions in your notebook.

SELF-ASSESSMENT: Review the poems in your writing portfolio. How could you improve your choice of words to better reflect your message?

3. LANGUAGE CONVENTIONS EXAMINE PUNCTUATION

With your class, discuss Jim Wong-Chu's use of punctuation. What punctuation marks has he used? Where has he used capital letters? What effect does this have on the reader?

In your notebook, rewrite "How Feel I Do?" in prose form, with the "correct" punctuation and grammar. Share your writing with a partner. Discuss whether or not the prose form has the same effect on the reader as the poem does.

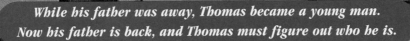

*While his father was away, Thomas became a young man.
Now his father is back, and Thomas must figure out who he is.*

A Hero's Welcome

SHORT STORY BY BARBARA HAWORTH-ATTARD

I left a pail of milk cooling in the summer kitchen for Ma, scraped a chair up to the table, and began loading my fork with scrambled egg. Food halfway to my mouth, Jenny began shrieking, "There's a strange man coming up the lane, Ma!"

We all rushed over to the window, Ma, Harry, and I, and peered out over Jenny's brown curls.

"That's no man, that's your father," Ma said. She drew back slowly from the window, her face working, deciding its expression. She quickly crossed to the stove and broke three eggs into a bowl. "Thomas. Pour your father some coffee," she ordered, beating the yolks streaky yellow into the clear whites.

And that was it. No band, no marching parade, just my father walking down the rutted lane in the cool dawn.

GOALS AT A GLANCE

- Discuss characterization in a story.
- Write a friendly letter.

59

I was barely eleven when he left our farm west of London, Ontario in 1941 for the war in Europe, and a man of almost fifteen when he returned in late November of 1945.

I poured a second cup of coffee and shoved it across to my father sitting opposite me, in the chair I'd sat in for the past four years. He was shorter than I remembered, but that could be because the years had left me several centimetres taller.

Ma slapped more bacon on his plate and he nodded his thanks and suddenly it was like he'd sat there every morning. I opened my mouth to ask a question, but Ma shook her head in warning and I stayed quiet.

Harry and Jenny stared at him until I began to wonder if he'd think he'd grown a third arm or something. Harry was five when Dad went away and Jenny nearly two. She thinks she knows Dad but she really only knows him through our stories.

Finally he pushed his empty plate away and stared at each of our faces in turn. "Is it the weekend?" he asked. The first words out of his mouth.

We shook our heads.

"Thursday, Dad," Jenny said. I could tell she was trying out the word *Dad* on her tongue, seeing how it fit.

"Holiday is it?"

Again we shook our heads. I didn't understand what he was getting at.

"Well then, you're all going to be late for school if you don't get moving."

My mouth fell open. When James McKinley's father came home they had a big welcome back party for him. But our Dad...near four years he'd not seen us and he wanted us out of the house.

He pushed back his chair and stood. "While your Ma fixes the lunch pails, we'll take a walk around the farm, Thomas."

I hurriedly shrugged my arms into my jacket and ran down the porch steps after him. He stood for a moment, perfectly still, looking out over frost-stubbled fields glowing amber beneath the slanting, early morning sun. We walked to the barn and swung back heavy wooden doors that creaked their protest.

"Could do with some oil on those hinges," he said.

He stopped to pat a cow on the rump. "All milked?"

I nodded.

"You didn't take time to clean the stalls though."

"Harry and I do it after evening milking," I mumbled. I wondered if he remembered my letter to him telling of the last calving and how Ma and I had been up all night.

He walked the length of the barn, leaned over, and ran a hand along the blade of the mower. "This here's got rust on it. You have to take care of equipment if you expect it to run right."

Anger flushed my face. I wanted to tell him how I worked late into the night after school all September and October bringing in the oats and barley, mowing the grasses, then doing homework with eyes so heavy-lidded the black print in my textbooks jumped around making it impossible to read. Getting the rust off, well, I left that until winter when things slowed down somewhat. I almost told him this, but Harry yelled it was time for school and nothing was said.

As we walked along the concession road, Jenny told everyone who'd listen how her Dad was back. She used the word Dad so much I began to wonder if she knew any others. Harry tried so hard to be indifferent, but he looked nearly ready to burst and finally did, bragging to the boys walking with us how his Dad would tell him war stories all evening long. I almost told him that I doubted he'd hear a single one but decided there was no point in that. I was glad to see them turn off at the little school and let me walk in peace the rest of the way to the collegiate.

I sat all day staring at chalkboards, teachers, ruled paper, and ink wells, but not seeing them at all. Instead I saw Dad running his hand over the mower blade, pointing to the barn door hinges and the stalls, and remembered the letters I wrote telling him which fields I'd planted, which ones I'd left fallow.

Returning home in the late afternoon dusk, I ran up the lane to the house and quickly traded my school clothes for my working coveralls. Through my bedroom window I saw Ma and Jenny in the back orchard picking the last of the apples for a pie. I clattered down the wood stairs and called to Harry. Rushing into the barn I stopped so suddenly Harry nearly ran up my back. Dad was seated on the three-legged stool milking a cow. My job.

"You boys get cleaning those stalls," he said without looking around.

Harry quickly grabbed a pitchfork, happy to be free of milking. He'd always been afraid of the cows and their restless feet.

I stood a moment then said, "I usually milk while Harry mucks out."

"Milking's nearly finished so you both can do stalls today," Dad said.

"But that's how we've done it every day since you've been away," I told him, surprising even myself with the stubbornness in my voice.

"Well, I'm back now," he said.

Slowly I took the fork and heaved dirty straw into a pile. My father had been my hero. His feet confidently walked the furrows, planting, harvesting. His voice was calm as he settled the horses and cows. I'd followed behind, walking like him and talking like him, thinking out the words before speaking. That's how he was and how I wanted to be.

"Dad," Harry said, "What did you do over in the war?"

"Pretty much what every other soldier did over there," Dad replied.

Harry waited but Dad said nothing more. No heroic war stories for Harry to repeat at school the next day.

"James McKinley's father came home with a chest full of medals," I said, voice shrill. "Five in all. He wore them to town one day. He told us that he fought so many Germans he soon lost count."

Dad raised his head from the milking pail without losing his rhythm and looked at me.

I pretended not to see. For once I was not thinking about my words before I spoke. "They had a big party for him when he came home. A real hero's welcome."

Dad picked up the pail and pushed past me into the dairy. Harry and I finished the stalls and took turns cranking the handle of the separator. Cream into one bottle, milk into another.

After supper Ma told me to empty Dad's bag in the summer kitchen so she could wash his things next morning. I pulled khaki shirts and pants from his duffel bag and put his shaving kit aside, then heard a clanking in the bottom. Metal hitting metal. I up-ended the bag and out fell a medal and then another. By the end I counted eight, three more than James McKinley's father. Hanging on coloured ribbons, they dangled from my fingers, one with an oak leaf and two with silver bars over star-shaped medals. *Pretty much what every other soldier did*. I stood there a long time holding them, then went into the kitchen.

Dad sat next to the stove smoking a cigarette, Jenny leaning against his leg. After a moment he put a hand on her head, stroking her curls. Harry lay on the floor on his stomach, turning the pages of a comic book while Ma darned socks. It all looked so right, Dad might never have been away.

"Where do I put these?" I asked him, holding up the medals.

Harry's eyes went round. "Gosh," he said.

A shadow passed over Dad's face so quickly I wondered if it were just a trick of the light. "Put them on my dresser for now," he said.

I passed through the kitchen to their bedroom and left the medals gleaming in a puddle of coloured ribbon on the dresser. I turned back to the door and Ma was behind me.

"Some men are just like that," she said.

Later that night after the little ones were in bed, I wandered out to the kitchen and saw Dad standing on the back porch. I pulled my jacket on and went out to the woodbox, piling firewood in my arms. I watched the red end of Dad's cigarette move slowly to his mouth and down again, saw white smoke curl up in the black night and wondered how many cigarettes he'd smoked in how many countries. We'd sent enough overseas to him.

"Had a while in Montreal between trains," Dad said, "so I toured around the city a bit. Couldn't believe the amount of stuff in the store windows. Dresses, shoes, chocolate, meat. Same thing in Toronto and I wondered if those people even knew there'd been a war on. Then I get back here, to the farm, and it's changed. You changed. You grew up on me. Harry and Jenny too. Thought I knew that from your letters, but I was wrong."

I said nothing, remembering the letters from Italy, Holland, France, and Belgium.

"Four years," he said. A match flared yellow, lighting his face momentarily as he lit another cigarette. "I got a bit of money coming to me from the army," Dad said. "Do you think Austin Taylor would sell us his flatlands down by the river?"

Us! I set the wood down on the porch and turned the idea over in my mind before speaking. "It'd make good pasture for the cows. We could get more stock," I said. I took a deep breath. "We could do with some equipment too. New tractor would be nice." My heart pounded in my ears.

Dad nodded. "Saturday morning we'll speak to Taylor, then go to the Co-op in town. See what they have." He ground his cigarette out with his foot, splashing red sparks into the night, and went into the house.

1. Responding to the Story

a. How has Thomas changed since his father left? How does he feel about his father's return?

b. Why does Thomas say his father had been his hero? Do you think he feels the same way at the end of the story? Why or why not?

c. What does Ma mean when she says, "Some men are just like that"? Do you agree or disagree? Explain.

2. Reading Discuss Characters

With a small group, analyse the characters in this story. Have each member of the group create a web for one character. Remember to include character traits that are revealed by what the characters think, say, and do, and by what others think or say about them. For each character trait add a quote from the text that supports it. When each group member is finished, discuss the webs and revise them to include any new information.

3. Writing A Friendly Letter

Scan the story to locate references to letters that were sent among the characters when the father was away. What types of information did they contain? Write a friendly letter or e-mail to a parent or other relative. Describe an incident involving someone you know in which you both came to a better understanding of one another.

Self-Assessment: Check your spelling before you send your letter or e-mail. Have you used homophones correctly? Have you consulted a dictionary to ensure correct spelling? Check your punctuation and grammar. Have you used complete sentences? Have you organized your ideas into paragraphs? Have you presented the incident clearly? Make sure you have followed the form of a friendly letter.

Conversation with Myself

Poem by Eve Merriam

This face in the mirror
stares at me
demanding *Who are you?*
  What will you become?
and taunting, *You don't even know.*
Chastened, I cringe and agree
and then
because I'm still young,
I stick out my tongue.

GOALS AT A GLANCE

- Write a personal response to poetry.
- Analyse photographs.

1. RESPONDING TO THE POEM

Can you answer the two questions asked by the face in the mirror?
If you feel you can, then do so in your journal. If you don't feel
ready yet, explain why.

2. VISUAL COMMUNICATION ANALYSE PHOTOS

Catherine Chatterton, a photographer, created this photo and the ones on
pages 8–9 and 56–57. With a partner, examine and discuss these photos
and what they represent. How do they make you feel? Why? How do you
think they were created? Do they effectively represent the selections or the
theme? Explain.

REFLECTING ON THE UNIT

SELF-ASSESSMENT: READING

As you worked on this unit, what did you learn about
• parody?
• point of view?
• message?
• fables?
• symbols?
• developing characters?
In your notebook, list some of the reading strategies you used to help
you prepare for reading or as you read selections.

WRITING LETTER TO A CHARACTER

Which character in this unit would you like to talk to? Why? What would
you tell him/her about yourself? What questions would you ask this
character? Write a friendly letter to the character you've chosen. Share your
letter with a partner, asking him or her to respond in role.

ORAL COMMUNICATION GROUP DISCUSSION

With a small group, discuss further one of the issues raised in this unit,
such as media influences on self-image, or gossiping. Brainstorm
solutions to the problems that are created by this issue. Then share your
response with another group. What conclusions can you draw?

"And what," said the Emperor, "does this poem describe?"
"It describes," said the Poet, "the Cave of the Never-Never."
"Would you like to see what's inside?" He offered his arm.
They stepped into the poem and disappeared forever.

George Barker from "Introduction"

Trails *to* ADVENTURE

TRAILS TO ADVENTURE

Could you guarantee someone else's safety no matter what the circumstances?

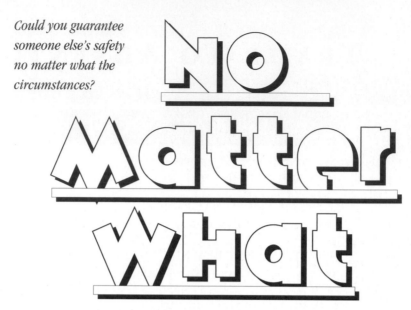

No Matter What

Short Story by Joan Lowery Nixon

I heard the jangling crash of a bicycle being thrown on the front walk and jumped to my feet. I couldn't count how many times Mom and Dad had told my ten-year-old brother Danny, "Don't treat your bike like that! Take care of it." I was in charge of Danny while Mom and Dad were at a sales conference in nearby Midland, so, as Danny burst through the front door and stumbled into the room, I snapped out the same words.

Danny, his dark hair tousled, stared at me through huge, frightened eyes for only a split instant, then whirled to slam and lock the front door behind him. Every freckle on his face stood out against skin so pale it seemed translucent. "Megan," he whispered, "I gotta talk to you."

"Danny! You look awful! What's the matter?" I cried.

Danny didn't answer. He clapped his hands over his mouth and dashed into the hallway. I heard the bathroom door slam and the sickening sounds of violent retching.

I sighed impatiently. It wasn't easy taking care of a ten-year-old brother, not even for a weekend. He didn't like my being in charge and wanted to argue, argue, argue over everything. The last time I had given up—probably too easily.

"You're too young to go to the doctor by yourself," I'd insisted.

"I am not," he'd complained. "Mom made the appointment. It's just a follow-up because of my sore throat, and she promised that I won't be getting a shot." He looked away, a little embarrassed. Everyone in the family knew Danny's fear of needles and shots.

"I can take care of myself," Danny said. "I don't need a bossy big sister to tag along after me."

"It's hot and sticky, and the wind is filled with dust. I can drive you."

"You think you're a big shot, Megan, but you only got your licence a few months ago. Besides, I can ride my bike."

I thought about the street traffic, about Danny getting lost, and about Mom emphasizing my responsibility in taking on this job. But Danny's lower lip stuck out as he said, "If you try to go with me, I won't go," and I gave up.

"Okay," I shouted. "Go by yourself. Who cares?"

Now, everything Mom had told me came back in a king-sized guilt trip.

"Megan," Mom had said, "you're only sixteen. Are you sure you can do a good, thorough, competent job of taking care of Danny, no matter what?"

Impatiently, I'd rolled my eyes. "Relax, Mom," I'd said. "Trust me. I can take perfect care of Danny...no matter what."

How could I know what "no matter what" covered? I realized that even though Danny had complained, I should have gone to his doctor's appointment with him. I hung outside the bathroom door, a glass of water in my hand.

In a few minutes I could hear tap water running and guessed that Danny was probably washing his face, so I knocked lightly at the door. With all my heart I wished Mom was on hand. She'd know what to do. "Is your sore throat worse?" I asked. "Did the doctor give you something that's making you sick? Should I call the nurse?"

The door opened, and Danny leaned against it. He zeroed in on the glass of water and took it from me.

"Sip, don't gulp," I cautioned.

"Megan, stop telling me what to do," Danny said. He took a long, slow drink, then added cautiously, "Don't call the nurse. You might get the wrong one."

"How can there be a right or a wrong one? There are only three nurses."

"Four."

I knew there were only three, but I wasn't going to quibble. "And they all work for Dr. Lee."

Colour began to come back into Danny's face, and I stopped worrying about him, but there were still some things I needed to know.

"What happened to make you sick?" I asked.

Danny's face closed in, as though he were seeing something no one else could share, and a gigantic shudder shook him from the top of his head down to his toes. He began to cry.

I took the glass of water out of his hands, placed it on the floor, and wrapped my arms around him, holding him tightly as tremors shivered through his body. He was terrified of something.

Holding him off, trying to look into his eyes, I asked, "What is it, Danny? What's scaring you?"

He wiped his eyes and nose on one sleeve, leaving a long, wet smear. "An old man came into the doctor's waiting room," he said. "He sat in the chair right across from me." Danny shuddered again, then said, "He's dead."

"Oh, Danny, how awful!" I told him. "How did he die?"

"He was just sitting there. And then the nurse with the dirty laces on her shoes came by."

"Dirty laces? Nurses don't wear dirty shoelaces."

Danny's lower lip trembled, but it rolled out stubbornly. "I know what I saw. Her shoelaces were dirty."

He paused, and I put an arm around his shoulders, pulling him close. "What else did you see?" I asked.

He shivered, but didn't answer.

"Did you see the man die? Is that what's frightening you, Danny?"

Danny pulled back so he could look up in my face. "I didn't know he was dead. I thought he was asleep. Sarah called his name—"

"Sarah? Dr. Lee's receptionist?"

"Yes." Danny took a deep breath. "The man didn't answer, so the woman who was sitting next to him said, 'Wake up, Uncle Frank.' And then she kind of screamed. And then she hollered at the receptionist, 'I think he's dead!'"

Danny had told me his story, yet his body was as tense as a string on Dad's guitar. There was something more that was bothering him. "What else do you want to tell me?" I asked.

Before Danny could answer, the doorbell buzzed loudly, and we both gave a start.

"Don't answer!" Danny whispered and grabbed my arm.

"Don't be silly, Danny. I have to see who's there," I said.

Danny groaned again and dashed into the bathroom, locking the door.

The door buzzed again—this time a long, insistent buzz. I sighed and answered it.

A tall, slender man, with thick brown hair and a smattering of freckles across his nose, stood on our front porch. "Miss Sanderson?" he asked.

"Yes," I said.

"You have a brother named Daniel Sanderson?"

"Danny? Yes."

"Are your parents at home?"

Mom had taught me what to say to strangers. "They're due home any minute."

The man wore jeans, a dark cotton shirt, a jacket, and spotlessly clean white running shoes with cream-coloured laces. He reached into the inner pocket of his jacket and pulled out a small leather folder. He opened it and quickly flashed the contents in front of me. It looked like a business card and a metal badge, but everything happened so fast I couldn't read what was written on either of them.

"Detective Bart Ridgway," he said. "Sheriff's Department. May I come inside and wait for your parents?"

"No," I said. "If you're with the Sheriff's Department, why aren't you wearing a uniform?"

"Plain-clothes detail," he answered. He looked at me for a moment, as though sizing me up, and said, "Is your brother home? I'd like to talk to him."

I didn't budge. "Why should he talk to you?" I asked.

"Because it's important that I contact him before anyone else does," Ridgway said.

"Why?"

Ridgway sighed impatiently. "Okay. I'll tell you what I can," he said. "Have you ever heard of Frank Berkeley?"

"Everyone in town knows about Frank Berkeley," I said.

I'd heard Mom and Dad talking about Mr. Berkeley. According to local gossip, the man was terribly rich. Probably a billionaire. He was in his mid-nineties, and his nieces and nephews were already arguing about the money he was going to leave them. Mom said she heard that one of them was even trying to get Mr. Berkeley to change his will.

Ridgway said, "This morning, because Berkeley had suffered painful leg cramps during the night, his niece Julia took him to see his doctor—Dr. Lee."

"Surely, he didn't die from leg cramps," I said.

"You know that Frank Berkeley's dead." Ridgway gave me a piercing look, and I blushed with embarrassment.

"Yes, Danny told me."

"What else did he tell you?"

"Nothing much. Just that the receptionist called Mr. Berkeley's name and he didn't answer, and his niece tried to wake him up and couldn't." I thought of telling Ridgway what Danny had said about the nurse with the dirty shoelaces, but I changed my mind. It sounded dumb.

"Did your brother happen to mention any unusual circumstances regarding Mr. Berkeley's death? We have reason to believe he saw what took place."

It took a moment for everything he'd said to register. The shock of surprise hit me like a blow to my stomach. "Are you talking about murder?" I asked.

Again the searching look before Ridgway looked at his watch, then back to me. "Please ask your brother to talk to me," he said. "It's very important."

"I'll ask him," I promised and shut the door. Murder? Danny hadn't said anything about a murder. And, yet, I was positive that Danny hadn't told me the whole story. He hadn't had a chance.

Shakily, I walked into the hallway and called, "Danny, there's a policeman here to see you," but Danny didn't answer.

I rattled the knob on the bathroom door. It was locked. "Danny, open up," I said. "You don't have to talk to the policeman if you don't want to, but at least come out of there."

No answer.

I ran to the kitchen and got a small screwdriver—the one Dad had always used when Danny was little and accidentally locked himself in the bathroom. I poked it into the little hole under the handle and jiggled it and the handle until the door opened.

The bathroom was empty, and the window over the toilet was wide open.

"Oh, Danny!" I said aloud, terrified that he had run and I didn't know where he was. "What did you see? What do you know?"

The steadily blowing wind already had deposited a sifting of gritty dust along the sill, so I automatically reached for the bottom of the window to pull it down and close it. But Ridgway's voice stopped me.

"Where's your brother?" he demanded.

I whirled to face him, gasping with fear. "How did you get in? The door automatically locks."

"Those automatic locks are nothing. Fortunately, you forgot to fasten the dead bolts."

"You're with the Sheriff's Department," I said, "so you know that it's not legal to break into people's houses, even for the police."

"This is an emergency," Ridgway said. "I told you. It's important that I reach your brother before anyone else does."

"Important to who? You?" I challenged.

"To your brother," he answered. He looked through the bedrooms until he found the messy room that was obviously Danny's. Ignoring me and my protests, he searched under the bed and in the closet.

Finally, back in the living room, Ridgway faced me. "Do you know where he's gone?"

"No," I sobbed. I was surprised to discover that I'd been crying.

Ridgway opened the door, but I grabbed his arm. "What is this all about?" I asked. "Does it have to do with murder?"

His glance was so sharp that I winced. "Murder?" he asked. "If it was, it's going to be nearly impossible to prove. That's where your brother comes in. He was the only eyewitness to Berkeley's death."

"D-Danny d-didn't say anything to me about a murder," I stammered, but I thought about how terrified he'd been and how I was sure he hadn't told me everything he'd wanted to tell.

"We tried to question him, but he bolted," Ridgway said. He pulled an envelope from his jacket pocket, tore off an end, and wrote a phone number on it. Handing it to me, he said, "If you find Danny, or if he comes home soon, please call this number. It's very important that I hear what Danny has to say."

I'd seen enough cop shows on television to know that this didn't seem right. "Don't you have a business card?" I asked.

"You've got the phone number. That's all that's important," he said. Without another word he strode across the porch and cut across the lawn to his car.

I didn't watch him drive away. Danny's bike was gone, and I had a fairly good idea of where he'd taken it.

As I was about to close the door a marked car from the Sheriff's Department pulled up to the curb in front of our house. Two men in uniform got out, came up the walk, and handed me their IDs.

They gave me plenty of time to read them.

"Is your mother home?" the one named Thomas asked.

"My parents are out of town," I answered.

By this time they stood right in front of me. "Your name, please?" Thomas said.

"Megan Sanderson."

"Do you have a brother named Daniel Sanderson?"

"Yes."

"May we speak to him, please?" the deputy named Scott asked me.

I said, "Look, Danny isn't here. I don't know where he is, but he got scared and took off when your Detective Ridgway came to question him about what he saw in Dr. Lee's waiting room."

"A person named Ridgway questioned him?"

"Bart Ridgway, your detective. But I told you, he didn't get to question Danny. Danny ran away."

They looked at each other. "There's no one in the Sheriff's Department named Ridgway," Scott said. "Suppose you tell us about him."

My stomach clutched as I described Bart Ridgway and told the Sheriff's deputies what we had talked about. Finally, their questions stopped, and I asked, "Who is Bart Ridgway?"

"That's what we're going to find out," Thomas said. "In the meantime, I'd suggest you think of any place your little brother might be hiding and let us know."

I was afraid to put my question into words, but I did it. "Do you think that somebody's after Danny because he might have seen Mr. Berkeley's murder take place?"

Again they glanced at each other before studying me. "Who said it was a murder?" Scott asked.

"Mr. Ridgway," I said.

Thomas gave me a business card. "You can reach us at this number," he told me.

It wasn't until after they'd driven off and I'd locked and bolted the front and back doors, that I realized I was still clutching the scrap of paper with Ridgway's phone number on it. Why hadn't I given it to the deputies?

Shrugging, I tucked the paper into the pocket of my jeans. It didn't seem important now. The only thing I had in mind was finding Danny. And I thought I knew where he might be.

I needed Mom. I needed Dad. I put my hand on the phone, ready to dial the number they'd left for emergencies, but I waited, not knowing what to tell them. I couldn't say, "Come home. A murderer is after Danny. He's run away. I'm going to try to find him." They'd be so unstrung, they'd probably have an accident on the way home.

I shuddered. What could I tell them? Nothing that made sense. I'd have to try to handle this myself, no matter what.

I'd learned about Danny's secret place one day when I'd been practising my driving on traffic-free streets and had wandered into a block north of town in which a builder had planned a community of homes. It was during the oil boom of the early eighties and he'd named his development Brushwood Point. But suddenly the boom had busted, as people said in West Texas. The big companies left town, and with them the employees who could afford large, beautiful homes. Ever since then, three partially built houses on Brushwood Drive have sat alone on oversized lots, ragged and dusty, like sightless, eroding monuments to another world in another time.

I had spied Danny's bike lying on a front walk, so I'd parked Mom's car and done some exploring for myself. In back of the house I'd found a door with a hole cut for hardware that hadn't been installed. The door was ajar, so I'd silently entered. And it was there, in a dim wood-panelled room, that I'd discovered Danny in a fort he'd built out of old lumber scraps.

"How'd you find me?" he'd yelled indignantly.

"If you're going to hide, then don't leave your bike in plain sight," I'd said and laughed. "You've got a good fort here."

"I've even got ammunition," he'd said, and pointed to a pile of dull chrome knobs, and what Dad calls elbow joints for pipes. There were even a couple of showerheads.

"Don't tell anybody, Megan! This is my secret!" Danny had begged me, and I promised I wouldn't. Everyone needs a private place. When I was Danny's age my private place was in a closet with a louvred door. I'd perch on a pile of luggage and play with my dolls in utter contentment, because no one in the whole world knew where I was.

Now, I knew where Danny had gone. He had to be hiding in his fort.

I headed for the garage with my driver's licence and a ten-dollar bill tucked into my hip pocket, and Dad's cellular phone hooked to my belt. I eased Mom's old grey sedan onto the street and forced myself to take off slowly, just in case someone was watching.

Someone was.

I had driven only a block before I realized that I was being followed by a sedan as nondescript as Mom's old clunker. It was staying a good block behind me, so I couldn't get a good look at either the car or the driver. I raised, then lowered, my speed, and the car stayed with me at the same pace. I turned down a block, then down another, and the car followed.

The forgotten, unfinished houses on Brushwood Drive were nearby, so I headed into the parking lot of a large supermarket.

Leaving the car, I walked into the front door of the supermarket and out the back.

A guy who was busy tearing outer leaves off a box of heads of lettuce looked up as I passed by. "Hey! You're not supposed to be here," he said.

"It's okay. I'm leaving," I told him, and walked down the open ramp that led to the alley. I cut through to another boulevard, crossed it, and followed a path through residential streets to Brushwood Point.

There was no sign of Danny or his bike. With trembling fingers I eased open the back door to the house in which Danny had built his fort, and tiptoed inside. As I saw his bike resting against the frame of a kitchen counter, I sighed with relief.

I quietly walked to a spot near the door of the library. The house creaked and snapped in the heat of the day, and I could imagine ghostly figures trailing down the stairs and up my backbone.

Shivering, I whispered hoarsely, "Danny?"

Something crashed near my head, bouncing off the door frame. I picked up a showerhead and yelled, "Cut that out, Danny! It's me—Megan!"

Danny's head slowly rose over the battlements. "Megan!" he cried shrilly. "Get in here! Hurry! They might be coming!"

"*Who* might be coming?" I asked.

"C'mon! Hurry!" Danny insisted.

He visibly trembled with fear, so I quickly leaped over the barricade and crouched down. I dropped the showerhead and put my arms around him.

"You shouldn't have come here. What if somebody followed you?" he asked.

"No one followed me," I said. "I made sure of that."

For a moment I stroked his shoulder and arm, trying to soothe him. Then I asked, "Danny, tell me exactly what you saw in Dr. Lee's waiting room."

"I told you most of it."

"Tell me the rest. You wouldn't tell the Sheriff's deputy, so tell me."

"I couldn't tell him, Megan. The nurse with the dirty shoelaces was there. She pulled me outside. She said she was going to give me just a little shot, and I wouldn't feel a thing. But somebody else was coming."

I held him tightly. "That's when you ran, wasn't it? You must have been awfully scared."

"I was. I didn't want to die, too."

"Did you think that the shot would make you die?"

Danny nodded vigorously. "It made Mr. Berkeley die."

I tried not to show the shock I felt. Quietly, I asked, "Danny, what did you see? How did Mr. Berkeley die? You can tell me."

"He was sitting in his chair, looking at a magazine in his lap," Danny said. "Some people came in the room, and some people walked around, looking for chairs. Sally told everybody that Dr. Lee was running late, and the waiting room was filled with people. A nurse came in with a lot of magazines and handed them out. Then another nurse came in, only she came from outside. She went around behind Mr. Berkeley, and bent over him for just a second. I saw a needle. She gave him a shot in his neck." Danny's voice quavered, and a tear rolled down his cheek. "She saw me watching her. Megan, I didn't want her to give me a shot in my neck, too."

"Of course you didn't," I said. "And she won't. Not ever." I hoped Danny wouldn't hear the fear in my own voice. "What did Mr. Berkeley do after the nurse gave him the shot?" I asked.

"He went to sleep, I think," Danny said. "He put his head down on his chest, and he stopped reading his magazine." He shuddered. "But then the woman with him said he was dead."

"What did the nurse look like?" I asked.

Danny looked up at me, surprised. "A nurse," he said.

"I mean, did she have dark hair? Or blond? Or grey? Was she short or tall? Thin or fat?"

Danny thought a long moment. "She had dirty shoelaces," he said.

I put a finger up against his lips. I'd heard creaking steps at the back of the house.

My heart hammered so loudly in my ears I could hardly hear Danny whisper, "Someone's here."

I glanced around the windowless room. This wasn't a fort. We were in a trap! The steps came closer, and I froze, unable to move.

Bart Ridgway stepped into view and smiled at me. "You were easy to follow," he said. "It's a good thing you found your brother for me."

"Megan, look at—" Danny whispered.

"Now I can take care of him...and you," Ridgway said. His smile grew broader.

Danny clutched my arm, the pressure of his fingers painful. "See...the dirty shoelaces," he whispered.

I took a good look at Ridgway's shoes. His white running shoes were a brilliant, brand-new white, but the laces on his shoes were cream. Up against the white, they did look strange. I guess to Danny's eyes the darker colour seemed dirty.

It was then I noticed the glass syringe and needle that appeared in Ridgway's hand. Danny did, too. I could hear him suck in his breath.

"You were the nurse who injected Mr. Berkeley?" I asked.

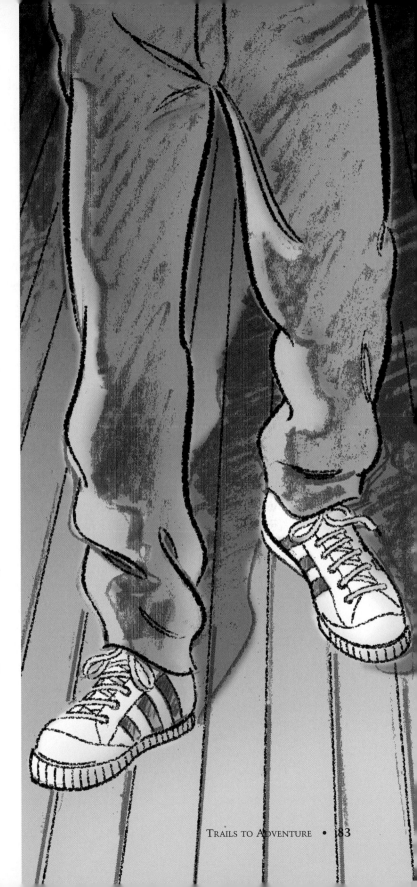

"I was, complete with uniform and wig." He chuckled, looking smug, as though he wanted to brag about himself.

The fingers of my right hand closed around the shower head I'd dropped.

"The will had been changed, and someone wanted to make sure it stayed that way, so they hired the best."

"You're a hit man?" I whispered.

"It doesn't matter who I am," he said. "By tonight I'll be in another state, unrecognizable to anyone in this town, and you...well, you and your brother won't be around either." He raised the syringe. "This will drug you until I decide what to do with you."

I jumped to my feet and threw the showerhead, aiming at the syringe. It was a good hit. The glass shattered, and I could see little pinpricks of blood appear on Ridgway's hand and wrist. He and I both stared as they blossomed like flowers.

"What have you done?" he screeched. He stared at his hand and at the puncture marks where the fluid had entered his body. Then his eyes rolled back and he flopped like a rag doll to the floor.

"Is he dead?" Danny whispered.

"No," I said. "He'll wake up in a few hours." I pulled Dad's phone from my waist and Thomas's card from my pocket and made the call.

I told Thomas what had happened, and where to find us, and said, "The charges are murder, attempted murder, and—oh, yes—breaking-and-entering. Danny and I are eyewitnesses."

Thomas told me that he and Scott were on their way, so I hung up. I glanced again at Ridgway and was awfully glad he was going to wake up in jail.

"Mom," I planned to say, "you asked me to do a good, thorough, competent job of taking care of Danny, no matter what. The *no matter what* was the hard part, but hey, look! I did it!"

1. RESPONDING TO THE STORY

a. Do you think Megan fully understood the responsibility of caring for Danny "no matter what"? Explain.

b. Is the ending of this story believable? Explain.

c. How has the author used the plot devices of chance and coincidence to develop the story? Give two examples.

2. ORAL COMMUNICATION DRAMATIC PRESENTATION

With three or four classmates, plan a dramatic presentation of an important scene in the story. Reread the story, and, together, choose a scene. Write a short script for it, deciding what sound effects, lighting, and props to use. Rehearse and then present it to the class. Remember to use facial gestures and body language.

PEER ASSESSMENT: Ask your classmates for feedback. What strengths do they think your performance had?

3. STORY CRAFT ELEMENTS OF PLOT

This short story contains all of the elements of a good story:

- an *introduction*—gives the setting, describes important characters, and relates an exciting or mysterious event to get the story going quickly
- the *rising action*—a series of events that builds suspense
- a *climax*—when the suspense "explodes" in a final adventure or confrontation
- a *resolution*—explains unanswered questions and ties up loose ends

Find places in the text where these four elements appear, and record them in your notebook. Compare this story's plot to other stories you've read.

4. EDITOR'S DESK ANALYSE DIALOGUE

Dialogue can reveal important information about the characters in a story and can help to move the plot forward. Analyse the author's use of dialogue in "No Matter What." How do conversations between the characters reveal action? What personal traits of the characters did you learn from these conversations? If the story were written without using dialogue, would it be as dramatic? Explain. What did you learn about using dialogue in your own writing?

Song of the Voyageurs

Poem by Anonymous

In the course of the journey,
Subject to sudden mishaps,
Your body soaked to the bone,
Woken before dawn by the birds;
With no rest,
neither night nor day,
With nothing but wearisome work,
Always worrying about the approach of winter
and being beaten by the winds...

Oh! I tell you, comrades,
There is no one on earth
Who endures as much misery as we do
who are married to our work.
As for me, I can't wait
until we get home again.
Never again will I come
to this damned country
which has almost worn me out.

GOALS AT A GLANCE

- Respond critically to poetry.
- Analyse characterization.

1. RESPONDING TO THE POEM

a. Why do you think this poem is named "Song of the Voyageurs" instead of "Poem of the Voyageurs"? What are the similarities and differences between poems and songs? Give some examples of songs that you think might be considered poems.

b. Poems often tell stories. What is the story in this poem? Retell this poem to a partner, paying particular attention to when and where it is set and what happens to the speaker.

c. Where do you think "this damned country" is? What makes you think so? Why does the speaker describe the country this way?

d. What do you know about *voyageurs*?

2. READING ANALYSE CHARACTERIZATION

Reread the poem. As a class, answer the following questions:

- How would you describe the speaker?
- How would you describe the speaker's attitude?
- How does the speaker feel about having adventures?
- What does the speaker want?
- How has the poet created a strong character?
- In what time period does the poem take place?

3. POET'S CRAFT ALLITERATION

This unknown poet uses **alliteration**. Read the poem aloud. Locate examples of alliteration in the text. What sounds are repeated? What effect does this have? Do you think the poet uses alliteration successfully? Why or why not?

SELF-ASSESSMENT: In your notebook, define alliteration in your own words, including an original example of this poetic device.

> **Alliteration** is a series of words that begin with the same sound. For example, *the soft sea wind whistled round the wharf.*

HOW TO

SELECT RESOURCES

Goals at a Glance

• Evaluate resources for accuracy, bias, and relevance. • Locate information.

When you're starting a big research project, choosing the right resources can be the most important step you take. Locating good sources of information quickly can save you valuable time and effort.

Start with a Topic

What topic interests you? What do you want to find out about this topic? Do you think you'll be able to find enough information?

1. Brainstorm a list of questions you'd like to find answers for. Choose one or two that really interest you. For example, if you were interested in voyageurs you might ask "Who were the voyageurs?" and "Where does the word *voyageur* come from?"

2. Create a list of key words about your topic. Start by making a word web of your own knowledge on the subject.

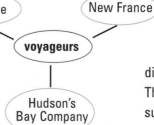

Choose the Right Resources

Where do you look for answers? The three most important resources are:

People

People—such as friends, teachers, librarians, parents, and elders—are excellent sources of information. You might find experts in your community, on the Internet, or through referrals.

Plan five or ten questions for an interview. Avoid asking questions that lead to simple yes or no answers by asking questions that seek to clarify or provide more information. If you want more than just the facts, ask for your interviewee's feelings and opinions as well.

Reference Materials

Start by checking out general sources, such as encyclopedias or other reference books. Then look at more specific sources, such as books, magazines, and

PROCESS

newspapers. Catalogues and indexes can help you identify possible resources. Search the table of contents and index for your topic and key words. Does the publication contain good illustrations or photos that you can use?

If you're not sure whether an article or chapter will be useful to you, read the first paragraph or two, or skim the first sentence of each paragraph. Keep only those resources you think will be most helpful in answering your questions.

Electronic Sources

Consult the Internet when you need up-to-date information, want to contact an expert, or need opinions or information from a variety of people.

Use more than one search engine. Try a variety of key words and phrases. (A search for "voyageurs" will find many unrelated things that happen to contain that word, whereas "New France, voyageurs" will yield more useful results.) Videos and other non-print media provide information in audio and visual forms (documentaries, recordings of songs, etc.). Don't overlook these great sources.

Evaluate the Resources

Ask these questions for each resource:
- Is it *recent*?

  Use the most up-to-date information available. The copyright date is usually printed on the first pages of a book, and is on the front of newspapers, videos, and magazines. A Web site's home page should state when it was last updated.

- Is it *accurate*?

  Who wrote or created the resource? The most reliable sources include museums, universities, scientific organizations, well-known publishers, and other institutions.

- Is it *objective*?

  Are all sides of the topic presented? Is the information unbiassed? If the information comes from a person or group that is trying to persuade you to hold a certain point of view, it may not be a good resource to use.

- Is it *relevant*?

  Does the information fit your topic? Is it easy to understand? Does it provide the right amount of detail? Make notes as you search. Be sure to include full information about the source: title, author, publisher, place and date of publication, and page number. Share information about the best sources with your classmates.

Self-Assessment

- ❏ Did I choose a topic that had enough information available on it?
- ❏ Did I define my topic as a question?
- ❏ Did I locate a variety of reliable resources?
- ❏ Did I check my resources for bias?
- ❏ Did I select relevant information?
- ❏ Did I acknowledge the sources of my information?

PROCESS

In this folk tale, a brother and sister follow the same path, but have very different adventures.

The Water of Life

FOLK TALE
BY KAY STONE

Once there was a land so barren that in some places only stones seemed to grow. A brother and a sister lived there, as poor as anyone else, but managing to stay alive from one day to the next. Though they had little between them, they did have one very precious thing. This was a tree unlike any other tree, a tree that bloomed in winter.

When all the other trees had lost their leaves and stood bare against the winter sky, this tree began to put out its first new green leaves; then it grew one perfect blossom that bloomed on the highest branch at the top of the tree, and this flower slowly became a perfectly formed fruit that glowed softly like the winter sun.

"Isn't our tree wonderful?" said the brother each year. And the sister would answer, "Yes, as wonderful as the earth itself."

On the first day of each new year, when the fruit was ripe, the brother and sister would take it down, divide it, and eat it, and the rest of their year would be filled with joy. This didn't mean they had no troubles; but their sorrows did not overwhelm them.

GOALS AT A GLANCE

- Analyse illustrations.
- Analyse the use of the colon.

One year everything changed. The tree did not bloom that winter. It put out no new leaves, no blossoms, no fruit. The brother and sister stood in the snow at the base of the tree, looking up, not knowing what to do. As they watched, a strange bird came flying down out of the blue sky and settled on the highest branch. It began to sing so beautifully that at first they listened only to the music, silent with wonder. Then the sister thought she could hear words echoing in the melody.

"Brother, listen to the words," she said. "The bird is singing about our tree." So they both listened, and in this way they heard that their tree had stopped blooming because they had not shared the fruit with anyone else. It would not bloom again unless they found one cup of the Water of Life and brought it to the tree.

"If you do that, year after year the tree will never stop blooming from that day on," sang the bird.

"Where is that water?" demanded the brother. "I'll go and find it and bring it back here."

The bird sang that the Water of Life was in a well on the top of the mountain on the far side of the great forest. When the song ended, the bird flew away, disappearing into the blue winter sky.

"I'll go," said the brother confidently. "You stay here and take care of the tree."

"No," said the sister, "I want to go with you. There's nothing I can do here for the tree if what it needs is the Water of Life." The brother grumbled because he wanted to do it by himself; but he had to agree, so the two set off together.

They walked farther than they'd ever gone in their lives, and after a long time they came to the great forest. There, beside the path at the very edge of the woods, they saw a red fox crouching, gnawing on a small white bone.

The fox looked up at them and said politely, "Where are you going? Not many come along this road. It's very dangerous, you know."

"We've come to find the Water of Life," the brother answered brusquely, never having spoken to a fox before.

"And do you know where that is?"

"Of course."

"Do you know where it lies?"

"Of course I know. It's at the top of a mountain beyond this forest."

"That's what the bird told us," the sister said courteously.

"Yes, that is true. You are absolutely correct. And do you also know that when you walk on the stones that lie on the path leading almost to the top of the mountain, do you know that those stones will speak to you? They will insult you and they will flatter you, and they'll even cry; but no matter what the voices say, go on. Listen but do not stop, for if you do you will become one of the stones."

They were surprised to hear this, and thanked the fox, then set off into the great dark woods. They walked on and on, until at last they came to the end of the forest and stepped out into the bright sunlight. They could see a mountain covered with evergreen trees, and a wide path of stones that wound up through the trees almost to the top of the mountain.

"The fox was right," the brother said eagerly, and he ran through the snow to the base of the mountain.

"Remember the stones," called his sister, but it was too late. He'd already started to climb up the mountain path. The very first stone he stepped on spoke to him.

"Stop!" it called out.

He went on, calling back, "I'm not stopping for you!"

When he didn't stop, the stones began to insult him. They knew just what to say to make him angry. "Hey! You'll never get to the top," one called out, and another yelled: "You're silly, no sense at all." The stones laughed derisively as he moved over them. He was very angry as he listened to them but he went on. Finally their words made him so furious that he forgot the words of the fox.

He stopped. He became one of the stones lying on the path.

By now the sister had come to the first stone of the path and heard it call out: "Stop!" but she remembered the words of the fox and went on. When she didn't stop the stones began to insult her, calling out in different voices: "You silly girl, do you believe in talking foxes?" And others yelled: "Do you really think you're smarter than your brother?" She heard them but went on, and even when she heard her brother's voice among the stones she kept walking up and up, sorry that she was now alone.

When she didn't stop, the stones began to flatter her, saying all kinds of wonderful things, telling her that she must be very special to have come so far.

"Please, stop and tell us your secrets so we can be as wise as you are," they called. She heard their words and was tempted for a moment; but then she went on because the fox had warned her, and she trusted the fox.

At last the stones began to wail and cry out to her in pitiful voices: "Oh please! Stop! Please don't leave us here like this, all alone! We have been lying here for so long. Oh stop, please stop!"

She heard their unhappy voices, and now she really wanted to stop and help them; but she remembered the words of the fox. If she stopped now she wouldn't be able to help them or anyone else. So she willed her feet to move over the weeping stones, one step at a time, up and up, with their sad voices calling out behind her as she went on. Finally the path ended, and as she stepped off the very last stone it shouted: "Don't go up there! You'll die up there!"

But it was too late. She left the path and climbed higher, and at last found herself at the top of the mountain. The whole world was at her feet, spread all around her. It was so wonderful that she almost forgot that she'd come to the top of the mountain to find the Water of Life. She pulled her gaze back from the wide world and looked down at her feet. There she saw the stones of an ancient well, the well of the Water of Life. A small silver cup stood on the edge of the well.

She reached down to take the cup in her hands. But as her fingers touched the cup she heard a deep hissing sound; the earth under her feet began to tremble and shake, and then the well was filled with a deep roaring, like the sound of a great storm approaching. Before her startled eyes a great golden dragon rose up from the well, towering above her.

It spoke in a voice of deep thunder, "Why have you come here?"

"For the Water of Life," she stammered, "only one little cup for the tree."

"One cup, you say? One cup is much more than you think. But I will allow you one cup—if you will do something for me."

"What could I do for you?" she said, her voice full of the fear she felt.

"You can polish the scales on the top of my head until each one glows like the sun. If you do that, I will give you one cup of the Water of Life."

"But how can I do that? I have nothing," she stammered.

"You have two good hands, and that's all you need."

She looked down at her ordinary hands and, with nothing else to offer, she agreed to touch the dragon.

The dragon bent down his great golden head and she began to polish the scales, each one carefully, until each golden scale glowed like the sun. When she finished, the dragon lifted his great head and hissed slowly: "One cup, and take care how you use it."

As the great golden dragon sank back down, the well filled up with surging water. The sister seized the silver cup and filled it to the brim, turned quickly, and started back down the mountain.

When she came to the first stone, the one that had warned her not to go further, she tripped. A single drop of water fell from the cup onto the stone. Before her eyes that stone turned into a human being. They looked at each other, then she looked at the water in the cup.

She put her finger in, took one drop of water, and touched the next stone with the water. That stone, too, became a human being.

And the next...

And the next...

And the next...

She noticed that the water in the cup did not diminish, and then she understood the dragon's words. One cup was more, much more, than she thought. She went down the mountain path, touching each of the stones with one drop of precious water.

Each stone took its own human shape again, and they were all filled with joy. But no one was happier to see her than her own brother. They hugged each other gratefully, and then, followed by all the others, they carried the cup filled with the Water of Life back through the great forest, past the red fox who greeted them, back along the path that led to the tree. As all the people gathered in a great circle and watched, the sister and the brother held the cup together and poured out the precious water at the base of the tree.

As the water sank slowly into the earth, the tree began to put out new leaves, and then blossoms, exactly enough for all the people who were there. As they watched, each of the blossoms turned into a perfect round fruit that glowed like the winter sun. The sister and brother divided all the fruit and shared it with every person there, and each who tasted it found that their new year was filled with joy. This did not mean they had no troubles; but their sorrows did not overwhelm them.

And because they did that, year after year the tree has never stopped blooming, from that day to this.

1. RESPONDING TO THE FOLK TALE

a. This tale involves the Water of Life and a Tree of _____. Complete this statement with an appropriate noun. Explain your word choice to a partner.

b. Using a dictionary, find out the meaning of *tenacity*. Use this word in a sentence that describes this story or a character in it.

2. READING ANALYSE CHARACTERIZATION

With a partner, discuss the brother and sister in "The Water of Life." Compare them, giving examples from the story that illustrate their similarities and differences. Do you think Kay Stone has created convincing characters? Why or why not? What techniques has she used to develop her characters?

3. VISUAL COMMUNICATION DRAGON IMAGES

Reread the passage in which the dragon rises from the well. With your class, discuss the image on page 95. Do you think the artist has drawn the dragon effectively? Why or why not? What would you have done differently, if anything?

In a small group, research and compare a variety of dragon images in fairy tales, picture books, comics, novels, movies, or video games. How are dragons characterized in these media?

4. LANGUAGE CONVENTIONS COLON

Scan the folk tale and locate each sentence that uses a *colon* (:). What does the colon represent? In your notebook, list possible reasons why the author might have used them. For what other purposes might writers use this punctuation?

*Da Trang, the hunter,
has special abilities
that lead him
in and out of trouble.*

Da Trang

VIETNAMESE FOLK TALE
BY TONY MONTAGUE

LONG AGO AND FAR AWAY, DEEP IN THE RAIN FOREST OF
VIETNAM, there lived a hunter whose name was Da Trang.
Every morning Da Trang took his bow and his quiver of arrows
and followed the same trail to go hunting. One day, as he passed
beside a great banyan tree, he was distracted by a bird up in the
branches and came within a footfall of stepping on not one but
two bright green and highly venomous snakes! They were
twined around each other. With lightning reflexes, Da Trang
drew his bow to shoot.

But he did not shoot. He just stared at the two snakes, and
the snakes stared back, unblinking, unmoving. And the longer
Da Trang gazed down at the deadly creatures, the more his fear
gave way to fascination. He was overwhelmed by the intensity
of their colour, the intricacy of their markings, the brilliance
of their sheen, and the grace of their movements, as slowly the
two snakes began to uncoil from each other. For what seemed
a long time, Da Trang stayed transfixed by their beauty; at last
he took a step backwards, walked around them, and continued
on his way.

GOALS AT A GLANCE

- Analyse the use of suspense.
- Write a folk tale using the selection as a model.

The next day, as he passed beside the banyan tree, there were the two snakes once again. And once again Da Trang stood, mesmerized by their extraordinary elegance and beauty. Now every day, as Da Trang followed the trail through the forest to go hunting, he stopped to admire the emerald-green snakes that had come to live beneath the tree. Not only was Da Trang no longer afraid of them, he admired them, he respected them, he even began leaving offerings of food for them. Da Trang took these serpents as his allies.

One day, many weeks later, as he approached the banyan, Da Trang heard the sound of a furious struggle and saw a huge cobra attacking the two green snakes! At once Da Trang drew his bow and fired. The arrow cut through the cobra's hooded neck and it slithered off into the forest, pursued by one of the green snakes.

But its companion lay dead on the ground. Da Trang picked up the beautiful, smooth-skinned creature, now drooping lifeless from his hands, and tears welled in his eyes. He, the hunter who had always feared and hated snakes, was crying for one now. Da Trang buried the emerald snake beneath the banyan tree and placed forest flowers on its grave. Then he went home to his cabin, greatly saddened. He had lost his two allies. One was dead, and the other had fled.

That night Da Trang had the strangest of dreams. He dreamed that the surviving green snake came up to his cabin, into his cabin, up onto his bed, and came sliding up to where his head lay upon his pillow. With its little tongue it licked Da Trang's ear, and whispered to him: "Thank you, hunter, thank you for all the kindness you have shown to me and to my dead companion. And for your kindness I have a gift."

From its mouth the snake produced a silvery pink and grey pearl; and, with flickering tongue, it carefully placed the little object beside Da Trang's head.

"Next morning, before you go hunting, put this pearl in your mouth and keep it beneath your tongue. Guard it carefully and tell no one. Thank you, thank you for your kindness."

Then the bright green snake was gone.

At dawn, when Da Trang awoke, he could remember every detail of the dream. As he lay thinking about the snake's mysterious words and its gift, he noticed something on the pillow beside him. It was a little shimmering pearl! The snake had told Da Trang to put it in his mouth before going hunting, and to keep it beneath his tongue— so he did.

The first animal that Da Trang chanced upon that day was a wild pig. But his arrow missed, and the pig ran off to hide. As Da Trang was stalking through the underbrush, he passed beneath a tree. Perched on a branch above him were two crows. They were talking to each other in their language, and Da Trang could understand every word that they said!

"Kraar! Kaa! D'you think that hunter will be able to find the pig?"

"Kraar! No way. His eyesight isn't any good—not like a bird's."

"But his hearing is pretty good these days," Da Trang called out. Not only could he understand the two birds, he could speak to them as well! Such was the magic of the pearl beneath his tongue.

The crows nearly fell off their branch.

"Kraar rwakh! He's talking to us in our language!"

"Yes," replied Da Trang, "yes, I can speak your language—and if one of you will show me where the pig is hiding..."

"Then what? Then what?" croaked one of the crows eagerly.

"Then after I shoot and kill it, I will leave you the parts that I do not want."

So the crow led Da Trang to where the pig had gone to ground. This time the hunter's arrow did not miss the mark. Da Trang slit open the pig's belly, drew out the entrails, and left them on the ground for the crow.

"Gnaak! Kaa! Kaa! This is good, this is very good!"

"Yes, it is good. And I propose that from this time forth we should hunt together. You lead me to the game, and I'll leave you all the parts for which I have no use. What do you say?"

"Kai! Kai! I say yes!"

Thus it was that Da Trang became the most successful and the most famous hunter in all of Vietnam—thanks to the snake's magic pearl that enabled him to understand and to speak the language, not just of crows and other birds, but of all creatures. And of course he never revealed to anyone the source of his extraordinary powers.

But one day, after Da Trang had shot and killed a wild pig and left the entrails as usual for the crow, another bird came along and stole them. When the crow arrived, there was not a trace.

"Kraaa! Kraagh! That hunter! He's cheated me! I always knew he would!"

The angry bird flew off to find Da Trang.

"Kragh! Graak! What about my share of the hunt?"

"I left it on the ground for you—as I always do."

"No! There was nothing. You cheated me!"

"That's not true."

"You're a cheat—and a liar."

"Hey!" said Da Trang, becoming angry in turn. "Don't ever call me that."

"Gnaak! Liar! Liar! Liar!"

Da Trang reached for his bow and, pulling an arrow from his quiver, he fired at the crow...but missed.

The crow seized the spent arrow in its claws and flew off, croaking furiously.

"Kaagh! Kaagh! You'll pay for that! You'll pay dearly for that!"

The next morning, in the river that flowed through the capital of Vietnam, beside the king's palace, a corpse was discovered— with Da Trang's arrow stuck through it! Soldiers came and pulled the body from the river, and pulled the arrow from the body. Such was Da Trang's fame that they knew at once it was his arrow. So Da Trang was arrested, taken to the city and thrown in jail, accused of murder. No one would believe his protestations of innocence, and how could he explain? Even he did not understand...the crow...the arrow...

As he sat in his tiny prison cell, staring gloomily at the wall, Da Trang noticed a column of ants climbing in great haste. Now Da Trang could speak the language of all the animals—the smallest as well as the largest—so he called out to the leading ant:

"What's all the hurry?"

The ant stopped and replied, "A flood. There's a big flood coming. Do as we do—head for the hills!" and it pressed on.

Da Trang shouted to the jailer, "Guard! Guard! Take me to the king, I beg of you! I have news, urgent news! It's a matter of life or death."

So Da Trang was brought before the king of Vietnam. On his knees he pleaded: "Your majesty, do not ask me how I know what I know, but believe me. The river is about to rise and burst its banks. The whole city will be under water, and many, many of your people will drown—unless everyone leaves at once for higher ground."

The king considered a long time. At last he spoke: "Prisoner, I don't know whether to trust you or not. But I cannot risk the lives of my subjects. So we will leave. However, if this turns out to be some desperate last-minute ploy by which you think to save your skin, you will die tomorrow, at dawn."

But it was true. No sooner had the king gathered all his people and left for the surrounding hills than the river rose up and burst its banks, and floodwaters submerged the entire city. Many thousands would have died, but, thanks to Da Trang, no one drowned. The king was deeply grateful to him.

"Not only do I release you from prison and believe your story about the crow and its wicked ways, but you clearly have extraordinary abilities. I need them in the service of my kingdom, and I hereby name you, Da Trang, my chief counsellor."

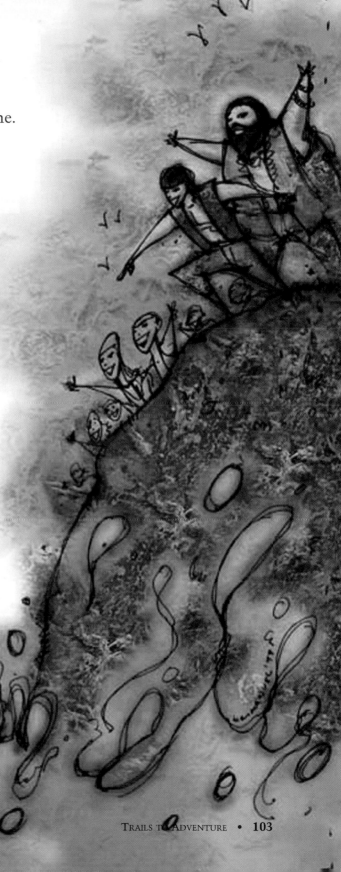

So it was that Da Trang the hunter became the most powerful person in all of Vietnam, besides the king, of course. And so it was that Vietnam became a very strong and very rich country. For Da Trang knew things no one else could possibly know. He knew when enemy armies had invaded the kingdom, he knew where they were, he knew how many they were—because the birds told him, the insects told him, the horses told him, the snakes told him. He knew when the floods and the storms were coming. He even knew when the earthquakes were coming. The animals know these things before we do and they told him everything. And Da Trang never once revealed the source of his powers—the shimmering pearl that he kept day and night beneath his tongue.

But one day the king had to visit one of the islands off the coast of Vietnam. As always the chief counsellor travelled at the king's side. It was the first time that Da Trang had been to the seashore.

He was amazed by all the strange and wonderful creatures that he found there and that—when the king wasn't looking, of course— he conversed with.

While Da Trang and the king were being rowed out over the shallow waters to board the royal ship, Da Trang heard the strangest of voices beneath the waves. He peered down and saw a family of squids. The adult squids were singing lullabies to the baby squids!

It was so weird and so wonderful—so bizarre, so beautiful—that Da Trang began to laugh, to laugh uncontrollably. He couldn't help himself. He threw back his head and the pearl fell out of his mouth and into the sea!

Appalled, Da Trang leaped from the boat into the shallows and began desperately churning the waters. "Your majesty! Bring soldiers! All your men! Please! They must help me."

"But what is it you have lost?" asked the astonished king.

"A pearl, a little pearl. It's very valuable. You can't know how valuable it is!"

Dozens of men waded out into the shallows and churned the waters with Da Trang in search of the pearl—but they found nothing. Da Trang waited until it was low tide and he wandered all over, plunging his hands down into the sand and sifting the grains through his desperate fingers. But he found nothing.

The following day Da Trang continued his search. But he found nothing. He searched every day for a week, every week for a month, every month for a year, for two, for ten, for twenty years. But he found nothing. Da Trang stayed by the seashore for the rest of his life, searching. He never gave up hope, but he never found the pearl again.

Buddhists believe that after we die we may be reborn on earth—although not necessarily as human beings; more often and more likely we return as animals. And the Vietnamese say that the restless spirit of Da Trang did indeed return, and is to be found to this day in those little crabs that live on the seashore between high and low tide and that we in the West call "hermit crabs."

In Vietnam they are called "Da Trang crabs," because the people believe that in these tiny creatures is the spirit of the hunter. With their one huge pincer they seem to be digging, but they're not digging, they're searching, searching among the hundreds, the thousands, the hundreds of thousands, the millions, the billions, the trillions of grains of sand for the pearl, the pearl that Da Trang lost, the pearl that the snake had given him, the pearl that once had given him the power to understand and to speak the language of all the animals.

----

1. RESPONDING TO THE FOLK TALE

a. What is the setting of this tale and why is it important?

b. What features of this selection make it clear that it's a folk tale?

c. How does Tony Montague create **suspense** in this story?

d. What are the good and bad consequences of having this pearl?

> **Suspense** is a feeling of tension, anxiety, or excitement resulting from uncertainty. An author creates suspense to keep the reader interested.

2. ORAL COMMUNICATION RETELLING

In your notebook, jot down the major events in this story. Use these notes to help you retell the story in your own words to a partner. Together, work on a modern version of this traditional story. How will you create suspense? Present your story to a small group.

3. LANGUAGE CONVENTIONS SERIAL COMMAS

Read the following passage from the story aloud:

> ...the intensity of their colour, the intricacy of their markings, the brilliance of their sheen, and the grace of their movements...

The author has created phrases with a parallel structure and has used serial commas to divide each phrase. This creates a poetic effect in the story. The author is used to telling this story to a live audience. What other phrases in "Da Trang" sound poetic when read aloud? How does the punctuation help to create a poetic effect?

S T R A T E G I E S

4. WRITING A FOLK TALE

Reread the opening paragraphs of both "The Water of Life" and "Da Trang." How do the authors capture the reader's interest?

Use one of the following phrases to begin your own short tale:
- Long ago and far away, deep in the...
- Once there was a land so...

Where and when will you set your tale? What will your hero be like? What journey will your character(s) go on? What adventures will unfold? How will you create suspense in your tale?

SELF-ASSESSMENT: As you proofread your work, check your punctuation. Have you used colons and serial commas correctly and effectively?

It began as a road to riches, ended as a trail of broken dreams, but led many on the adventure of a lifetime!

Iron Trails to Adventure

Newspaper Article by Catherine George

Climb aboard, folks. We're off on a trip into history. Gold Rush history.

You're aboard the White Pass and Yukon Route, a narrow-gauge rail line that traverses the coastal mountains between Skagway, Alaska, and Lake Bennett, B.C. The trip over the White Pass summit is considered one of the world's most spectacular train rides for its heart-stopping scenery and almost-perpendicular climb.

The 64-km journey traces the historic "Trail of '98," one of the daunting routes that took thousands of gold-seekers from the staging grounds at Skagway to the gold fields of the Klondike in Canada's Yukon Territory.

You're seated in vintage parlour cars from the 1890s, trimmed in wood and brass, with potbellied stoves, old-time lamps, and all. The only thing different from Gold Rush days is the diesel engine that's pulling us this day. But if you happen to be here on select dates in the summer months, you'll be towed by refurbished Steam Engine No. 73, the last White Pass steamer, re-introduced to the WP&YR line in 1997.

Skookum Jim

Tagish Charlie

Today's train trip will be a breeze, nothing at all like what the Stampeders, as they were known, experienced in their mad struggle over the St. Elias Mountains more than a century ago. On foot. And in the heart of the northern winter.

ALASKA

Dawson

YUKON
TERRITORY

Gulf of Alaska

Whitehorse

Fraser — Lake Bennett

Skagway

Juneau

NORTHWEST TERRITORIES

Great Bear Lake

Great Slave Lake

Yellowknife

PACIFIC OCEAN

BRITISH COLUMBIA

Prince Rupert

Inside Passage

Prince George

ALBERTA

Grande Prairie

Edmonton

Calgary

KEY

0   100 200 300
kilometres

Vancouver

Victoria

thirst for gold. And those who made it as far as Lake Bennett still had another 650 km of treacherous rapids and whirlpools, swarms of mosquitoes, and dense forest to conquer before reaching the gold fields at Dawson.

It's said the stampede to the Klondike attracted the best and worst of men and women. For a few precious golden flakes, they were willing to suffer unspeakable hardship, risking life and limb, betraying their friends and their families. Because gold was everything, gold was all.

As you'll soon realize, the White Pass and Chilkoot crossings were the toughest test of all for those with the unquenchable

It's hard to believe that the most convenient gateways to the Yukon were here at Skagway and nearby Dyea (now a ghost town). They were the easiest access to the inhospitable wilderness routes over the Chilkoot and White Passes and they became boom towns overnight when word got out that gold had been discovered on Rabbit Creek (later named Bonanza Creek) near Dawson in the summer of 1896.

Prospectors George Carmack, Skookum Jim Mason, and Tagish Charlie are credited with the discovery, though no one really knows which of them actually discovered the nugget that set off the greatest gold rush the world has known.

With the trio isolated in the wilderness and freeze-up coming, word of their discovery didn't reach the outside world until the following summer when Yukon miners loaded with gold started arriving in the ports of Seattle and San Francisco. At a time of deep economic depression, sensationalist journalism told of Yukon rivers flowing with gold, setting off the biggest mass migration of gold-seekers in history.

More than 100 000 headed for Alaska and the Yukon Territory: accountants, dancers, shop clerks, dress-store owners, labourers, bankers, journalists, gamblers, and gangsters. Katherine Ryan from New Brunswick was one of the first women to climb the trail into the Klondike, seeking adventure and riches. She later became the first woman to join the North West Mounted Police.

Those with gold fever arrived in Skagway on ships and pretty well anything else that would float, most of them ill-prepared dreamers. Few had any idea where the Klondike was or what lay ahead in the more than 700 km of harsh wilderness between the coast and the gold fields.

All they had was grit and a determination to reach Lake Bennett in time for the spring ice break-up. There they could fashion boats and rafts to take them down the Yukon River to the Eldorado concealed in the remote reaches of the Yukon.

Shortly after you depart the Skagway train depot, look out to your right. You'll see Gold Rush Cemetery, burial place for some of Skagway's early residents, the most notorious being swindler and con artist Soapy Smith. Soapy never got as far as the gold fields at Dawson. Instead, he got rich mining the pockets of the cheechakos (greenhorns) who began arriving in Skagway in the summer of 1897.

Soapy's lucky streak eventually ran out when he was shot dead by local resident and hero Frank Reid in 1898. Reid later died of his wounds in the shootout and both are buried here in Gold Rush Cemetery.

Skagway today is a touristy little town of restored board-walks, false-front souvenir shops, and old-time saloons, and is a popular stop for the cruise ships plying the Inside Passage in spring and summer. In fact, most passengers aboard the WP&YR are on excursions off the cruise ships.

It's said that Soapy made the Red Onion Saloon his last stop before his shootout with Frank Reid. These days it's a popular stop for sourtoe cock-tails.

We'll climb 873 m on our 32-km trip up the "golden stairs" to White Pass summit. It takes us about an hour and a half. But for many Stampeders it took days, weeks, even months, often as many as 40 trips back

---

Some of the more famous adventurers include:

- Nellie Cashman, who opened a restaurant in Dawson City and then a grocery store in Fairbanks. She operated many claims on Nolan Creek and was still travelling 563 km by dog sled to tend them when she was 78.
- "Big Alex" McDonald from Nova Scotia, who was known around the world as the "King of the Klondike" because he operated and owned so many claims.
- Martha Purdy Black, who staked an extremely rich claim on Excelsior Creek, and after the Gold Rush continued to live in the Yukon. In 1935 she was elected a Member of Parliament.
- William Ogilvie, Ottawa's official surveyor in the Klondike, who had a reputation as an honest and scrupulous man who could not be bribed, no matter how big the gold nugget!

---

and forth through sleet and snow, carrying the ton of supplies that was required in order to cross into Canada.

They carried supplies, day and night, up and down, over what many of the sour-doughs described as "the meanest 33 miles (53 km) in history." And the North West Mounted Police were there at the summit to see that each and every Stampeder adhered to the rules.

There's a famous moment captured on film—once seen, it's forever etched in the memory—of a long line of people, backs horribly bent from the weight of their packs, struggling single file through the deep snows toward a narrow mountain pass. One powerful image, in black and white, tells the poignant story of the world's last great rush for gold.

These days hikers, much better prepared, challenge the scenic trail of glaciers, waterfalls, and steep grades in summer, but the majority of visitors are passengers on the WP&YR as it wends its way through forest and mountain tunnels and clickety-clacks across trestles spanning deep gorges.

Belching smoke and clanging steel, the WP&YR follows portions of the trail that was carved by the gold-seekers so long ago. Remains of abandoned cook stoves, old boots, and picks are still evident, as are stone cairns marking graves of unfortunates who perished on the unforgiving trail.

At Mile 17.5 we cross over Dead Horse Gulch where some 3000 pack horses, overworked and overburdened, met their terrible end. They "died like mosquitoes in the first frost" was how author Jack London put it. Remains of their bleached bones can still be seen on the rutted trail.

At the summit, halfway to Lake Bennett, the American and Canadian flags fly side by side at the boundary line where the North West Mounted Police checked the fortune-seekers' supplies. If they didn't have enough grubstakes to survive a year in the inhospitable North, they were turned back.

Word of the Gold Rush had spread quickly. The *London Times'* colonial reporter, Flora Shaw (Lady Lugard), travelled from London to the Klondike in 1898 and helped spread the word about the fortunes being made. Also in London, a group of venture capitalists obtained rights to build a rail line over the mountains from Skagway. But, after surveying the terrain and experiencing the weather conditions, Sir Thomas Tancrede declared it couldn't be done. That was until Canadian rail contractor Michael J. Henley convinced him that with enough dynamite he could blast a road to anywhere.

THOSE ADVENTUROUS STAMPEDERS

Some of the most interesting stories to come out of the Klondike Gold Rush focus on the courageous women who risked everything, including their lives, to struggle over the pass and fight for their share of the gold and the glory. One out of every ten Stampeders was a woman. The women worked just as hard as the men, and faced as many, if not more, hardships. Imagine trying to climb the pass wearing the typically long woman's dress of the time, with a corset making every breath difficult! Many women abandoned their traditional attire in favour of more sensible trousers, and faced the insults of men.

Klondike Kate

In 1897, Belinda Mulrooney heard about the Gold Rush and sold her dress shop in Juneau, Alaska. She bought fabric and hot water bottles, and carried them to the Klondike, where she sold her goods at a 600% profit. She stayed on to open a restaurant, hotels, and a construction business.

Kathleen Eloisa Rockwell, or "Klondike Kate," helped support her family by joining a travelling song and dance troupe headed for the Klondike. Kate became famous for her "flame" dance. She wore a red dress with more than 2000 m of chiffon that she swirled, much to the delight of the prospectors.

Belinda Mulrooney

Against all odds, Henley did accomplish the impossible. Construction began in the spring of 1898 and by the summer of 1899 the narrow-gauge line had reached Lake Bennett. It took just over two years and $10 million to complete the line from Skagway to Whitehorse, an engineering marvel at the time.

Ironically, by the time the railroad was completed, the stampede to the Klondike had pretty much fizzled out.

Through the early part of the century the little line continued to carry passengers, freight, and mail in the North. It was chief supplier for the construction of the Alaska Highway during World War II, but hard times had forced it to suspend operations by 1982.

Oddly, it was the cruise industry that revived the rail line in 1988. And, instead of bringing gold out of the Yukon, the White Pass trip brings it in, in the form of tourist dollars.

From White Pass Summit the train makes its noisy descent into the spruce- and aspen-covered Canadian landscape, then rolls through lunar-like terrain that is as close to desert as you'll find in Canada. It makes a whistle-stop at Fraser, B.C., where passengers can continue by coach on the Klondike Highway to Whitehorse.

Last stop: Lake Bennett at Mile 40.6, the end of the Chilkoot and White Pass trails where more than 30 000 Stampeders built a tent city in the winter of 1897–1898 waiting for the thaw. The forests were stripped bare as a flotilla of more than 7000 makeshift boats were constructed and launched. It is said more died on the treacherous Yukon rivers than died crossing the Chilkoot and White Passes.

And it's claimed that of the 40 000 who made it to Dawson only 300 found their fortune. Even so, many stayed on, captured by the spell of the Yukon and changing the North forever.

1. RESPONDING TO THE ARTICLE

a. What elements of the 1890s journey attract you? Which do not?

b. If it were possible, which version of the Gold Rush trail would you prefer to travel: 1890s or the present? Explain.

c. Choose one of the people mentioned in the article. With a partner, discuss this figure's life and accomplishments.

S T R A T E G I E S

2. RESEARCHING ORGANIZE INFORMATION

Locating relevant information and organizing it are important research skills. Divide a page from your notebook into four squares, giving each a heading (for example, geography, building of the railroad, impact of the Gold Rush, and notorious personalities). Reread the article and jot down the vital facts, recording information in the appropriate square.

What subheads do you think would help readers to better understand the article? Where would you place them?

SELF-ASSESSMENT: What benefits are there in organizing your information in these ways? How can this information be used in future writing?

3. MEDIA ANALYSE ROLE OF MEDIA

Reread this article and discuss with a partner the role the media played in the Gold Rush. Searching the Internet or using the library, locate and read some of the actual newspaper reports from the Klondike Gold Rush.

Imagine that you are a reporter in the summer of 1896. Write a sensational article for your local newspaper about the discovery of gold. Include a headline aimed at exciting your readers. Draw a picture or find a photo to help illustrate your article.

What do you know about Harlem—
a neighbourhood in New York City?

Harlem

Poem by Walter Dean Myers

Images by Christopher Myers

They took to the road in Waycross, Georgia
Skipped over the tracks in East St. Louis
Took the bus from Holly Springs
Hitched a ride from Gee's Bend
Took the long way through Memphis
The third deck down from Trinidad
A wrench of heart from Goree Island
A wrench of heart from Goree Island
To a place called Harlem

They brought a call, a song
First heard in the villages of
Ghana/Mali/Senegal
Calls and songs and shouts
Heavy hearted tambourine rhythms
Loosed in the hard city
Like a scream torn from the throat
Of an ancient clarinet

GOALS AT A GLANCE

■ Respond critically to the poem and images.
■ Prepare a choral reading.

A new sound, raucous and sassy
Cascading over the asphalt village
Breaking against the black sky over
1-2-5 Street.
Announcing hallelujah
Riffing past resolution

Sometimes despair makes
The stoops shudder
Sometimes there are endless depths of pain
Singing a capella on the street corners

And sometimes not.

Sometimes it is the artist looking into a mirror,
Painting a portrait of his own heart.

Place, sound,
Celebration,
Memories of feelings, of place

A journey on the A train
That started on the banks of the Niger
And has not ended

Harlem.

---

1. RESPONDING TO THE POEM AND IMAGES

a. How do the poet and artist feel about Harlem? What makes you think so?

b. Which line in the poem do you find the most effective? Which image? Why?

c. Are there any words or references in the poem that you don't understand? Discuss these with your class. On a map, try to locate the places mentioned in the poem.

2. ORAL COMMUNICATION CHORAL READING

This poem has a wonderful rhythm. With a small group, prepare a choral reading of "Harlem." Discuss how you will read each line—quickly, slowly, loudly, quietly, happily, or sadly. Present your choral reading to the class.

You never know who you might meet when you're….

On the Road

Short Story by Joanne Findon

April 23, 1854

The weather has improved these last few days and I believe that I can now begin my journey. The road is still soggy, but passable.

Mother has been even more strict with me than usual, and made me do all the washing yesterday. I worked from first light until dark, and felt I should die with weariness. Mother is curt with me so much of the time that I fear my soul will wither within me if I do not go away. I am certain of the rightness of my decision.

Sarah M. Bonney

April 23, 1994

Hi Jess! What a hole this is! I'm dying of boredom! There's nothing to do here—it's way out in the bush and the nearest town is 30 km away. Of course, there's no bus, and no bike I can borrow. So I'm stuck here in this house with Mom and Grampa and Gran, who is sure taking a long time to die. Mom is on my case all the time about how I should be more "understanding" about what everyone's going through. Give me a break! Gran is a meanold thing, I've never liked her. And I have to leave all my friends to come to this wasteland!

If I could just get to St. Andrews I could get a bus to Fredericton, or Saint John. Remember Melissa Hardy who moved away last spring? She lives in Saint John now, I think. Maybe I could go stay with her for a while.

Answer me, Jess! I don't care if you have nothing to say—I'm dying out here! Check your e-mail every hour!

Sarah   :(

April 24, 1854

I shall start out tomorrow morning. Mother has given me permission to attend the church prayer meeting at Whittier's Ridge and to stop at Aunt Martha's by the way for dinner first. She does not know that I shall never reach the church. I shall be in St. Andrews before my absence is noted. Then to Mr. Charles to borrow money. I am certain he will lend to me, for the sake of Father's friendship.

Oh, how difficult it is to keep secret my passion to be gone from here! Sometimes I feel I shall burst from its pent up fury! Not two hours ago Mother asked me to darn a mountain of stockings. I worked by the pitiful light of the candle, and all the time I wanted to scream out, "I shall soon be free to follow my Muse, away from this drudgery!" But I held my tongue.

I shall be like Jacob in *The King's Highway* and make my way in the world and return home in glory, to the admiration of all. Mr. James Gardiner believes that I have a "deep well-spring of talent"; those were his very words when he visited me after publishing those first poems in *The Sentinel*. Mother and Father were unimpressed by his praise; I know they think I am a silly, romantic girl who ought to banish these notions of being a writer from her head. One day they will see how mistaken they are.

April 24, 1994

Dear Jess,

Thanks for your message! Thank God they have phone lines out here! I'd die without this modem! Mom knows I'm using her computer a lot, but she doesn't know why.

Thanks for Melissa's phone number. I'll call her later when the doctor's here and they're all down in Gran's bedroom. I already snuck a call and found out about buses to Saint John. I have *got to get out of here!* The tricky part is getting to St. Andrews, where I have to get the bus. It's 30 km! I've never walked that far in my life, but I'll have to give it a try. Although there isn't much traffic around here—it's like everybody's waiting to die, not just Gran! Mom says it hasn't changed much here in 150 years and I believe it.

Gotta go—Mom thinks I'm doing homework.

Sarah

April 25, 1854

Dear Diary,

This is the last time I shall write on your clean white pages. You are too large to take along on my journey. I can find no way to hide you in my clothing, and Mother would be suspicious if I set off for the church with you tucked beneath my arm! So farewell, and wish me Godspeed. I trust you will not hold it against me if I replace you in Boston, once I am settled.

My heart is filled with steady resolve. I am on my way at last.

Sarah M. Bonney

April 25, 1994

Jess—I'll phone you when I get to Melissa's. Mom thinks I'm in the spare room reading my great-great-grandmother's diary. Mom says she was a "real rebel" when she was young, but I bet back then *anyone* who was different was called a rebel. She was probably as much of a grouch at 15 as Gran is at 75—always telling everyone what to do, always thinking she's the only one who's right about anything.

Anyway, I'm going to sneak out the back door. Hope these boots hold out!

:)   Sarah

April 25, 1854

I have had the most extraordinary experience! So strange I can barely put it into words. Exhaustion presses upon me, yet I cannot sleep. How shall I describe what happened? I...

Mother has seen my candle here in the corner and will wonder why I am up, scribbling madly...

April 25, 1994

Jess—I know it's midnight and you're not going to read this till tomorrow—but the weirdest thing happened to me!

I guess you figured out I'm back at Gran's, not at Melissa's. I started out, just like I said, got a ways down the road, and met somebody—a girl about my age—and then she—we talked and then we had a fight—and then she was gone! And now I'm sitting here staring at this stupid hat and wondering...

I'm not making sense. Need some sleep. Catch you tomorrow when my head's in gear.

Sarah

April 26, 1854

I write this with shaking hand, squinting to see by the thin light that seeps through our one window, wrapped in my warm cloak, and huddled on the floor by the bed. It is very early. I pray that the scratching of my pen does not wake Lucy and Lizzie beside me. Sleep eludes me, but I must write. How else will I understand?

I set out as planned, stopping at Aunt Martha's on the way. She was very kind, fed me buckwheat cakes and chatted cheerfully, suspecting nothing. I walked on, crossing Bonney Brook for (as I thought) the last time in years. When I reached the turning for Whittier's Ridge I walked straight on, meaning to continue to St. Andrews. But—and I cannot write this sensibly—as I walked on I suddenly noticed a person beside me. Just that—she was not there, then she was there, dressed in clothing so strange that I halted and stared. I say *she*, because I came at length to understand that it was a girl who accompanied me; but this was not immediately clear. I thought at first that this person was a boy, for he wore britches fashioned of some deep blue cloth, and a short jacket fitted to the upper body, made of an unfamiliar material. The hair was cropped very short, but baubles dangled from the ears and the voice was high and melodic, like a girl's.

"Hi," said this person, and I realized that I had been staring at her with inexcusable rudeness. I flushed deeply, and endeavoured to redeem myself. Her unfamiliar word I interpreted as a greeting.

"Good afternoon," I said. "Forgive me, but I have not seen you in these parts before. I assume you are a traveller?"

"I'm just here visiting my Gran," she said. "Actually, my Mom dragged me out here to visit her. I didn't want to come. I'm from Trawno."

"Trawno! Where is that?" I asked. I have met a number of strangers over the years, from New York and Boston, and even a man from Montreal. But this place was unknown to me.

She gave me a peculiar look which suggested that she thought me dimwitted. "In Ontario, of course. Don't you learn anything in school?"

All the while, she was chewing on something which could only be tobacco. This gave me a great shock, for in this community chewing the weed is considered a most unsavoury habit, even among menfolk. This, combined with her rude and condescending manner, made me ill-disposed toward her.

"We are too few in number here to afford a proper school," I said— with undue haughtiness, I admit to my shame. "Our parents teach us at home as best they can."

Her eyes widened at this. "You're kidding! I thought everybody had schools, even out here in the boonies! But like, you can read and stuff, right?" I am trying to record her exact words, but they were often so peculiar that I was unsure of their meaning.

How ignorant she must think us! I straightened my shoulders, and answered, "Yes, of course. We learn to do sums, and study something of geography and history, through whatever books come our way. My brother Albert brings back weeklies from Maine, and many of these contain excellent reading material."

"Oh...great," she said. Her face showed puzzlement, although I could not think why. I had spoken clearly.

"Where are you headed?" she asked then.

I replied that I was bound for St. Andrews.

"Hey, me too. We can walk together," she said. "By the way, my name's Sarah."

"Sarah is my name as well," I said slowly. I had to remind myself that Sarah is a common name.

We talked—ah! Father has risen to do the milking, and beside me Lizzie stirs...

April 26, 1994

Jess—I'll try this again. That girl—I can't stop thinking about her. One minute I'm walking along by myself and then I notice that the pavement's run out and the road is dirt. It's actually a spooky road—I never saw a single car go by, and the only person I saw was some old guy working in a field. And *then*—there she is beside me, like from nowhere. Dressed in really funky clothes—I mean, she's wearing this brown dress that looks like it's made of burlap, way down below her knees, and clunky workboots as if she's going out logging or something. And some sort of blanket around her shoulders instead of a coat. And a crazy little straw hat on her head. All I could see of her hair was a long dark braid down her back. A real pale face, no make-up on. She's maybe around my age—hard to tell.

I ask her where she's going and she says St. Andrews. I say, "Hey, me too. We can walk together." She looks at me kind of weird then, but she doesn't say no.

I tell her I'm going to get the bus to Saint John. She frowns and looks at me really odd, and says "bus?" like she's never heard the word before. And I say, "Yeah, there's one every day at 4:30, non-stop. I phoned and checked." She doesn't say a thing, just shakes her head and looks away. Shy? Stupid? I don't know.

So I ask her why she's going to St. Andrews and she says she's going on from there to Boston to start a new life as a writer!! Can you believe that? I couldn't help it—I started laughing so hard I thought I'd bust a gut. A writer!

She glares at me and starts walking faster.

"Hey, come back!" I say, and run to catch up. "I'm sorry, okay? I just never heard anyone say that before! I mean, where're you going to get the money to live on your own?"

She says, "I shall borrow from Mr. Charles. Father has built four fishing boats for Mr. Charles. He will lend to me, I am sure." This is how the kid talks, I swear.

Then I go, "You're sure he'll lend you money? Did you call ahead and ask?"

And she frowns again. "Call?" she says. "I could not call. St. Andrews is 18 miles away!"

"I mean phone. Don't you have a phone?" But she just clams up at that. Go figure.

Jess—Mom's coming upstairs.

Later. S.

April 26, 1854

It is much later, dear Diary. The butter is done and at last I have a few moments to myself.

The girl I met on the road had a strange, cocky air about her. I have not met anyone like her before. She used words I have never heard from people hereabouts. I expect this is how they talk in Trawno.

She said she was going to St. Andrews to "catch a buss" to Saint John. I did not understand this, but she looked at me with such fierce eyes that I was afraid to ask what she meant. But O, Diary, I should never have told her about my plans! She laughed out loud, without even trying to hide her mirth! I was humiliated! Mother and Father would never do this, no matter what their true thoughts. Even brother James, who thinks himself very smart just now, would never mock me so to my face!

I did not think the girl at all pretty, and her clothing was most unbecoming. I just must help Mother settle little Mary...

April 26, 1994

Jess—Where was I? Oh yeah, the girl asks me if I have money for my journey, and I tell her I have about thirty bucks, and her eyes bug right out. I don't know why she's so impressed by that, but I say "It's enough to get me to Saint John, and maybe grab a burger in St. Andrews first" and she looks at me funny again. Does she think that's too much? Not enough? Who knows.

Then I say, "So you're running away from home too?" And she looks all surprised and flustered, and then looks away and finally nods. When I ask her why, she says, "Mother and Father are so dreadfully strict with me. I am the eldest girl and must help with the heavy work all day long, and have no time to write. I cannot live this life of drudgery!" Then, get this—she says, "I fear the mews will abandon me if I continue this way!"—whatever *that* means!

But the part about heavy work sounds pretty bad, so I say, "Sounds awful. You'll be better off away from them."

"And you?" she asks.

I go, "Mom's been on my case lately for not being the darling daughter she thinks I should be, especially around Gran when she's so sick and everything, but I guess I have it pretty good compared to you."

"Your grandmother—who is she?"

"My Grandma Craig. I think her first name's Martha."

She frowns, and says, "I do not know of any Craigs in this neighbourhood—only in Chamcook and St. Andrews."

"Lives just back there. The blue house with the old cars in the front yard. Those are Grampa's; he used to collect them, now they just sit there and rust."

She frowns again, then she asks suddenly, like she's been saving it up for a while, "Why are *you* leaving?"

So I tell her about Gran lying there dying of cancer, and about watching Grampa moon around the house like a lost dog, and about Mom pulling me out of school so we could be here, even though there's *nothing* to do, and how I've always hated Gran and the way she always thinks she's right about everything, and how I just don't want to be here *at all*. And the more I talk the more she looks at me all horrified, like I'm some kind of monster.

And then she goes, "How can you leave your mother at a time like this? It is your duty to stay and help—we all must face death as best we can, and we cannot expect it to be pleasant!"

She's sounding a lot like Gran when she says this, and it makes me really mad, so I say, "Hey, wait a minute! What about you? You're leaving home when it sounds like there's lots that needs doing! What'll your parents do without you? And did you tell them where you're going? If they're anything like my mom, they'll be going crazy when they find out you're gone! So don't give me this garbage about *duty*!"

We've stopped in the middle of the road by this time, and we're standing there yelling at each other.

"You are the most unmannerly girl I have ever met!" she shouts. For someone so small and thin she has a big voice.

"And you are the bossiest, snobbiest little so-and-so *I* have ever met!" I scream. We stand there, breathing hard, staring each other down.

She turns away first and starts walking on real fast. So I do too. We don't talk, we just walk, both of us boiling mad, down that rough, muddy road. After a while I notice the sky's clouded over and the wind's come up. And wouldn't you know it, I've left my scarf back at Gran's.

She's walking so fast I can barely keep up, even though it's pretty rough in spots. The mud is seeping into my boots. I could've sworn this part of the road was paved when we drove here the other day.

Anyway, we come to this place where the road dips down into a bunch of dark trees. The wind is really strong now. We passed the last farm ages ago, and it's really *spooky* here. We both stop, just stop dead in the middle of the road. Good thing there's no traffic.

She just stares at that road disappearing into the woods and...

April 26, 1854

Peace at last, with Mary sleeping like an angel. I shall write until this miserable stub of a candle burns out. Mother and Father are sorting seeds for planting.

I resume my account. I fear we had a terrible fight, this strange Sarah and I. She reproached me for leaving my family when I am most needed; yet her own reasons for setting off on her journey were vain and selfish! She had no apparent plans, no sense of a higher calling such as I have; only a deep dislike of her grandmother and a discontentment with home life. She seemed not to have the vaguest notion of what she would do when she reached Saint John. And yet when I pointed these things out to her, she flew into a rage and screamed at me like a banshee!

I tried to walk on alone, but she followed, and we stumped along in wrathful silence for perhaps a mile. Then I noticed a glowering sky to the south; a chill wind sprang up, clattering through the bare branches of the maples by the road. A noisy black cloud of crows descended on the field to our left, and I began to feel uneasy.

I have not often travelled this stretch of the road. We had passed the last of the Clarence farms some time ago, and reached a place where the road descends a hill and disappears into the gloomy shadows of a tamarack wood. I imagined walking through those dark shadows, and my heart froze with terror.

I stopped short, suddenly overwhelmed by a sense of the utter folly and madness of my attempt.

"What am I trying to do?" I cried out, blinded by a rush of tears. I feared the girl would laugh at me again, for sobbing so, but she did not. She had halted as well, and as I stole a look at her face I saw that her eyes were wide with fear.

"How much further to St. Andrews?" she asked me in a very small voice.

"Very far—miles and miles," I told her.

She shook her head and spoke as if to herself. "Even if I do make it to Melissa's, I can't stay there forever. Mom'll come and get me and drag me back here."

I wiped my tear-stained face with my handkerchief and looked at her. "I must be on my way," I said. My voice was shaking.

"You're going home?" she asked.

"No—I must go on to where I am expected," I said.

"I'm going back to Gran's," she said. Her voice was also shaking. This surprised me greatly, for until a few moments ago her manner had been self-confident, and even aggressive.

I held out my hand to her. She shook it solemnly. For a moment we stood silently, joined only by our two hands and our locked gaze. Then I pulled away, and crossed the road. I climbed over the fence of the first field on my left and pushed through the tangle of bushes there, intending to cut across the farms diagonally and so reach the Whittier's Ridge road further on. But one of the branches caught at my hat, and I turned to see the wind lift it in the air and blow it back toward the road. I thought I heard Sarah's shout, but when I reached the fence she was gone—and so was my new straw hat, so dearly bought with the maple sugar I made last month! How could both Sarah and my hat have disappeared so quickly?

I reached the church just a little late. Not a soul asked me why.

Oh Diary, why do I feel so alone now?

My candle is spent, and so am I.

April 26, 1994

Jess—sorry we got cut off—Mom picked up the phone downstairs. Like I was saying—when we got to this wooded place we both chickened out. She started *bawling*, if you can believe it! But then I got to wondering if maybe this wasn't the greatest idea. I mean, I should at least wait until I can get a ride into town.

"You going home?" I asked her.

"No," she says, "I am going on to where I am expected." Whatever that means. And then she holds out her hand to me, all serious and formal, and I shake it. Her hand was warm and strong, and rough like Gran's. I took one long look at her face then. Piercing grey-green eyes and a firm little jaw. Not someone I'd want to tangle with very often, I'll tell you. But maybe a friend—maybe.

Then she pulls away and starts off across the road. "Hey!" I shout. "What's your last name?"

"Bonney," she says. "I am Sarah Martha Bonney."

And then she climbs over the fence and jumps down into some bushes on the other side. Two seconds later I see something pale flying through the air—it's her straw hat, caught by the wind. It comes sailing right at me, and I catch it before it hits the ground. "Hey, wait! Your hat!" I yell, and run after her. But when I get to the fence, she's gone. Just like that! Disappeared! I climb up onto the fence and wave the hat above my head, calling her name, but there's no sign of her. But you know what? This is what really freaked me—when I get back to the road, it's *paved*! I *know* it was dirt just a second ago—I *know* it! How else did I get all this mud in my boots?

Too weird, Jess. Do you believe in ghosts?

So I'm back at Gran's. Mom never asked me where I'd been, and I'm not going to tell her either. Although I can't hide this stupid hat from her forever. Actually, I tried it on and it looks pretty cool on me. Maybe I'll keep it—if I don't see Sarah again.

I've been thumbing through that old diary Mom wants me to read. There might be something here after all—Mom says there's a part where great-great-grandma talks about how she ran away from home in 1854. Might be interesting.

Catch you later.

Sarah

April 29, 1854

Dear Diary,

I have thought and thought, and have decided that that other Sarah was not a ghost. Strange—although I disliked her, I also found her intriguing. She has the greenest pair of eyes I have ever seen.

I must remember to ask Mother about this Mrs. Martha Craig. Perhaps Sarah found my hat on the road. I would not mind seeing her again.

I will make my journey some day, but I see now that a fifteen-year-old girl is not perhaps well-suited to making her way in the world alone.

Mother has been kinder to me since my little adventure. Does she suspect? Of course, I shall never tell her.

Sarah M. Bonney

- -

1. RESPONDING TO THE STORY

a. The two Sarahs are very different, yet they are remarkably similar. If the time travel episode hadn't ended, do you think the girls could have become friends? Explain your opinion.

b. If each Sarah could learn one thing from the other, what should it be? Explain how both characters would benefit from this new knowledge.

c. What do you think it would be like to encounter someone from the past? What three questions would you ask the person you met?

d. They say that running away ultimately solves nothing. Do you agree? Support your opinion in a paragraph.

2. ORAL COMMUNICATION GROUP DISCUSSION

Although they lived over one hundred years apart, both teens were frustrated by similar circumstances. In a small group, discuss the following:

- What were the causes of their frustration?
- Do you think these are common complaints for most teens?
- Can you relate to their problems?

Explain your views.

SELF-ASSESSMENT: In a discussion with your classmates, do you listen to their opinions? Do you ask them questions to find out more about what they're thinking? How do you demonstrate respect for their ideas, especially if they are different from yours? How do you support your opinions?

3. LANGUAGE CONVENTIONS HOMOPHONES

Identify the **homophones** in the story that added to the miscommunication and misunderstanding between the two Sarahs. Choose a set of homophones and use them in a sentence that shows the correct meaning of each word. You may find it helpful to keep a list of common homophones and their meanings in your writing journal.

Homophones are words that are pronounced alike but are spelled differently, for example, *to*, *two*, and *too*. Homophones can easily be confused in speech and in writing.

4. STORY CRAFT STYLE

This story is told entirely through e-mail messages and diary entries. Examine the writing of both girls and compare their writing styles from the perspective of form (diary versus e-mail) and language (differences in tone and vocabulary).

Choose one of the entries in the story and rewrite it in the language of the other Sarah. What did you have to change?

Which style do you prefer? Why?

Empty Fears

Poem by Brian Lee

What's that? — Coming after me, down the street,
With the sound of somebody dragging one foot
Behind him, who pauses, who watches, who goes
With a shuffle and mutter
From the wall to the gutter
In the patch where the light from the lamps doesn't
   meet . . .

Oh . . . it's only a bit of paper — a hollow brown bag
Open-mouthed, like a shout — a bit like the face
Crumpled-up, of someone who's going to cry,
Blown on the wind, from place to place,
Pointless, and light, and dry.

Who's that? — Watching, from the upstairs windows
Of the house where the hedge grows right back to the
    door,
Where the half-drawn curtains droop and discolour
And a yellow bulb burns away
And the milk's on the step all day —
Somebody lives there, no one comes or goes . . .

Oh . . . it's only an empty coat on a hanger
That sways in the draught like a man who depends
On only one thing — the something inside
That's holding him up, waiting for friends
He writes to, but no one's replied.

What's that? — Whispering, where the fence round the lot
Sags like a fading hope: the gate just here twists
On its hinge like a bird's broken wing
And shrieks as you look, and see:
Nothing, where all the shops used to be,
People coming and going where now they are not . . .

Oh . . . it's only the breeze, that's fretting itself
Amongst the stiff thistles, each standing alone,
Upright, all winter, dead, but not gone . . .

But if it's only these things, what blows
Through me, to make me afraid, who knows?

1. RESPONDING TO THE POEM

a. Why do you think the poem is called "Empty Fears"? Create another title that would convey the same message and mood.

b. Have you ever experienced a situation similar to the one in the poem? In a small group, describe both your feelings and physical reactions as the situation unfolded.

c. In your notebook, retell this poem as a story.

2. ORAL COMMUNICATION DEVELOP A MONOLOGUE

Reread the poem and think about how it is similar to a **monologue**. Choose one of the following and develop a short monologue for it:

- a topic on which you have a strong opinion
- a topic on which you can give some advice
- a topic about which you are very knowledgeable

With a partner, discuss your topic. Ask your partner to make notes. Use these notes to write a first draft. Remember to make the monologue sound natural and convincing. Have fun with it! It's your turn to speak your mind.

> A **monologue** involves one character either thinking aloud or speaking to himself or herself in an informal, conversational style. A good monologue often includes contrasting moments of calm and energy. When delivering a monologue, remember to use different tones, volumes, and pauses.

3. MEDIA PRODUCE A VIDEO

With a small group, use the situations described in the poem to develop a scene from a movie. Select your "star," camera, sound, and lighting crews, set designer, and costumer. Rehearse your scene. Use a video camera to record your presentation.

GROUP ASSESSMENT: Watch your video and discuss with your group how you could improve the scene. What did you do well? What would you change the next time?

4. LANGUAGE CONVENTIONS RHETORICAL QUESTIONS

Speakers sometimes ask questions to which they don't really expect answers. These are called *rhetorical questions*. Find two examples of rhetorical questions in the poem. Why do you think people use them?

Out of This World

MAGAZINE ARTICLE
BY ANDREW PHILLIPS
AND SARAH GREEN

Scan the title, photos, captions, and subheads in this article and predict what it will be about.

KEEPING IN TOUCH

This is ground zero, the holy of holies of the American space program. The flight control room at Johnson Space Center in Houston is instantly familiar from a dozen movies and a thousand newscasts. The banks of computer terminals, the three giant screens up front, the digital clock counting down to the next mission—this is where Earth talks to Space. If something goes wrong and an astronaut has to deliver the fateful message, "Houston, we have a problem," this is where it comes in.

GOALS AT A GLANCE

- Prepare and take part in a debate.
- Recall and summarize information.

Canadian astronaut Chris Hadfield is the key link between the ground and astronauts aboard the space shuttles that are the pride and joy of NASA, the National Aeronautics and Space Administration. As NASA's chief **cap**sule **com**municator, or CAPCOM, he is the person who talks to the shuttle—and who represents its crew to the scores of anxious officials below. Hadfield was in the CAPCOM chair the evening of Thursday, May 27, 1999 as the shuttle *Discovery* lifted off from Kennedy Space Center in Florida on a mission to dock with the spanking new International Space Station 400 km above the Earth. Aboard was Julie Payette of Montreal, the biggest star Canada has put into space in years.

A Wonder of the World?

Their destination was the space station—or at least the parts that had already been bolted together. By any measure it is a staggeringly complicated undertaking that will be one of the marvels of the engineering world once it is completed. Sixteen nations are involved. More than 100 major components must be taken aloft aboard 45 flights and assembled in the pitiless environment of space. Astronauts will have to make at least 160 space walks—a high-risk part of any mission—totalling 960 hours. The finished product will be 108 m long and weigh 472 tonnes—vastly greater than anything ever put into orbit. Payette compares it to "assembling a whole cruise ship in the middle of an ocean during a storm," and that may be underestimating the challenge.

This space station will contain six research laboratories and a total space equivalent to the interior of two jumbo jets—all orbiting the Earth every 92 minutes and 24 seconds.

To the true believers at NASA, this is the modern-day equivalent of building the pyramids or the great cathedrals of Europe. "What did the Egyptians or the Romans do?" asks Hadfield. "They let people do things that were just on the cutting edge of technical and human capability. And we are just now capable of leaving Earth. As far as significant events in history go, this is huge."

It was while watching the 1970s *Apollo* missions in suburban Montreal that 10-year-old Julie Payette first dreamed of becoming an astronaut.

Payette—fascinated by astronauts, their spacesuits, and the bumpy travel in lunar vehicles—grew up devouring space magazines and even pinned up a picture of astronaut Neil Armstrong in her bedroom.

"I wanted to be like them," Payette said recently. "I wanted to be an astronaut."

On a Cape Canaveral launch pad on Thursday, May 27, 1999— amid a thick haze of smoke and the deafening rumble of the engines on the space shuttle *Discovery*—Payette, now 35, realized her childhood dream.

"I think people had tears in their eyes," said Payette's friend

Suzanne Fortier, vice-principal of research at Queen's University, who was among 350 Canadians in Florida for the launch. "It's just extraordinary. You have a sense not only of a vessel taking off, but...you know there are people in there and Julie is in there. It's taking off with all her work and her dreams."

Julie Payette, Canadian astronaut

The liftoff also propelled Payette into history. She's the eighth Canadian in space, the second Canadian woman, and the first astronaut from this country to board the International Space Station, floating some 400 km above the Earth. She's also the youngest Canadian astronaut.

Nicknamed Ms. Fix-It for the 10-day mission, Payette was also the choreographer of a 6-hour space walk to transfer equipment and supplies to the station.

But it was not solely Payette's place in history that turned the Montreal native into the *Discovery* mission's media darling.

Payette speaks six languages, including Russian, and over the years the electrical engineer has built an impressive résumé in her lifelong drive to be an astronaut.

She is also a gifted singer and musician, a triathlete and skier, a scuba diver and licensed pilot, trained to take a Tutor plane—used by the famed Snowbirds—on solo flights.

After secondary school, Payette crossed the ocean to attend the International College of the Atlantic in South Wales and returned home to graduate with a bachelor of engineering from McGill in 1986 and a master of applied sciences at the University of Toronto in 1990.

Engineering professor Ursula Franklin said she has "very warm memories" of Payette's years at the university.

"We knew whatever she chose to do, she would do well... She has a lot of life ahead of her. This is a very major achievement, but I'm sure this isn't going to be her defining moment." ◆

1. RESPONDING TO THE ARTICLE

a. Explain Chris Hadfield's comparison of the space station to the Egyptian pyramids and the cathedrals of Europe.

b. What do you think are Julie Payette's personal qualities that contributed to her being chosen for the astronaut program?

c. Why do you think the author has described space as a "pitiless environment"?

d. You have won a seat on the first flight into space for members of the public. Will you accept it? Explain why or why not.

STRATEGIES

2. ORAL COMMUNICATION DEBATE AN ISSUE

Hold a class debate on the following topic: "The money spent on space exploration and research would be better spent in improving life on Earth." As you prepare and then debate, remember to

- think about your opinion and the position you'll be taking
- review the facts in the story
- work co-operatively with others on your team to develop three points that support but do not repeat each other
- summarize your information and position
- prepare a persuasive argument that is about two minutes in length
- memorize and practise delivering your argument
- speak persuasively, slowly, and clearly
- listen carefully to everyone's points, especially the opposing team's
- prepare your *rebuttal* (your response to the opposing team's points)

SELF-ASSESSMENT: Did you present a convincing argument? In your rebuttal, did you respond to the opposing team's points, or did you just restate your own case? What part of your debate could have been improved?

3. READING RECALL INFORMATION

As NASA's publicity officer, you will be meeting the press to inform them of the mission that will be taking Julie Payette and her teammates to the space station. In your notebook, list the facts of the article in point form and in order of their importance, so that you can clearly and quickly share the information with the reporters.

REFLECTING ON THE UNIT

SELF-ASSESSMENT: ORAL COMMUNICATION

As you worked on this unit, what did you learn about
- preparing monologues?
- preparing and presenting a debate?
- retelling stories?
- choral reading?
- sharing information, ideas, and opinions?

WRITING ADVENTURE STORY

In a small group, discuss the writing formats in this unit and how each told a story. Which format did you think was the most interesting? Explain. Use this format to develop your own tale of adventure—one you have had, or one you wish you've had.

VISUAL COMMUNICATION CREATE AN ILLUSTRATION

With your class, discuss the images in this unit. Which did you find the most appealing? How was this image created?

Look through your writing portfolio for a story that needs an illustration. Use the same method as the artist whose work you've admired to create an image for this story.

POETRY

Greatness

I would be the greatest poet the world has ever known
if only I could make you see
here on the page
sunlight
a sparrow
three kernels of popcorn
spilled on the snow.

Alden Nowlan

BENEATH THE INK

POEMS FROM

WEST COAST RHYMES

Many of the Haida people live on Haida Gwaii/ the Queen Charlotte Islands. These two Haida poets make a strong statement about their home.

Rainlight

Poem by Jenny Nelson

Walking in the rainlight,
wet lace and palelight,
deep within the circle
            of a
misty late o'night.

breath caught with seasmell
hair hung with rainstar
wrap me round with seaweed
or I may float away.

GOALS AT A GLANCE

■ Respond critically to poetry.
■ Compare the poems.

gather all my longings
and wrap them up in seafoam
put them in a paper boat
and let them sail away.

Haida Gwaii

Poem by Jaalen Edenshaw

Forest snap, crack, quiet
Beachspray, breakers, cold
Ocean, wetdeep, fishy
Muskeg, ploddy, damp, full
All part of Haida Gwaii.

POET'S CRAFT ANALYSE POEMS
In a small group, take turns reading the poems
aloud. Discuss and compare the images,
setting, mood, and message of each.
What words have these poets created?
Discuss the images these new words
bring to mind. Develop a comparison
chart for the two poems, including this
information. Share and compare your
chart with another group's.

GROUP ASSESSMENT: How did we
work together as a group? What would
we do differently if we worked
together again?

Robertson Davies, a well-known Canadian author and university professor, gave this speech on poetry to graduating students.

Hear
Every Word

SPEECH BY ROBERTSON DAVIES

Get yourself a good anthology of poetry, and keep it by your bed. Read a little before you go to sleep. Read a little if you wake up before the alarm goes off. Read a little if you wake up in the night. When you are idle during the day—on public transport, or at a committee meeting—let your mind dwell on what you have read. One book will last you a long time. Indeed, it may last you a lifetime, but I hope you may acquire more books of poetry as time goes on. Read, not as people tend to read fiction or history, to get to the end of the book, to have the reading over with, to be able to say "I've read that." No; reread. Read until you find that you are reading the poem without actually looking at the words. Hear every word in your head. Do not skim; do not read quickly, any more than you would play a piece of music absurdly fast on your hi-fi, simply to get it over with. Read, listen to, and savour the words, and the sense.

GOALS AT A GLANCE

- Paraphrase a piece of writing.
- Analyse transition between paragraphs.

Oh yes, the sense. Because that is what poetry is. It is the distilled good sense or emotion of someone especially gifted in wisdom of some sort. Modern poetry has turned its face against rhyme and metre, which are two of the most vivid evidences of poetry. So be sure you read some of that poetry which was written before the modern austerity took command. Read it even if you don't agree with what it says. Read it even if you think it is saying something obvious. Read it because it feeds your Innermost Self, enlarges it, keeps it alert, refreshed, and in good order, so that it never allows you to sink into despair or dullness, or some fashionable stupidity. Poetry is part of the sustenance we take on board for the long voyage of life. Don't imagine it is easy, and don't give up when you find that it is hard. Tussle with the difficult things, and in the end they will reveal their meaning to you, and that meaning may help you over many a difficult place. ◆

1. RESPONDING TO THE SPEECH

a. According to Robertson Davies, how might one book of poetry last a lifetime?

b. How can a person read "without actually looking at the words"?

c. In this speech, Robertson Davies pleads with his audience to read poetry. Were you swayed by his words? Why or why not? Identify the words or phrases that you found to be the most convincing.

d. Why does Robertson Davies think we should read poetry? How does he think poetry can affect our lives?

2. WRITING PARAPHRASE

How does Robertson Davies feel about poetry?

Paraphrase paragraphs two and three of this excerpt. Jot down the main ideas first. Compose your paragraphs. Edit your writing for clarity. Have you accurately communicated the author's ideas? Ask a partner to read your work and compare it to the original. Make any necessary revisions.

> When you **paraphrase** a piece of writing, you restate the author's ideas in your own words. A good paraphrase will reflect your own writing style as well.

PEER ASSESSMENT: Share your writing with a classmate. What two strengths does your partner notice? What suggestions does your partner have for improving your work? What is most helpful to you about this feedback?

3. WRITER'S CRAFT PARAGRAPH TRANSITIONS

Reread this speech and discuss in small groups how Robertson Davies has formed his paragraphs. How does he present ideas within a paragraph? How does he move from one paragraph to another? What effect does this have? How could you use Davies' techniques of paragraph transition in your own writing?

*Have you read other poems by this
famous poet? What do you remember
about them?*

Voice *of a* Poet

Poems by Langston Hughes

Formula

Poetry should treat
    Of lofty things
Soaring thoughts
    And birds with wings.

The Muse of Poetry
    Should not know
That roses
    In manure grow.

The Muse of Poetry
    Should not care
That earthly pain
    Is everywhere.

Poetry!
    Treats of lofty things:
Soaring thoughts
    And birds with wings.

GOALS AT A GLANCE

- Analyse the rhythm of poems.
- Create a biography using media techniques.

Helen Keller

She,
In the dark,
Found light
Brighter than many ever see.
She,
Within herself,
Found loveliness,
Through the soul's own mastery.
And now the world receives
From her dower:
The message of the strength
Of inner power.

1. RESPONDING TO THE POEMS

a. Reread one of these poems and think about its meaning. Tell the poem in your own words to a partner. Discuss whether or not you agree with what the speaker is saying.

b. Langston Hughes was a famous African-American writer who created poems that showed "the diversity of emotions, thoughts, and dreams that he saw common to all human beings." Discuss this statement with a small group.

2. POET'S CRAFT RHYTHM

With a partner, take turns reading the poems. Each has a strong **rhythm**, which you may hear when the work is read aloud. Has the author used rhythm effectively? Explain your answer. Together, reread "West Coast Rhymes." How are their rhythms different?

> **Rhythm** is the arrangement of beats in a line of poetry. The beat is created by the accented and unaccented syllables of the words in the line.

3. MEDIA BIOGRAPHY

Assume that you are a producer responsible for creating a short TV documentary on the life of Langston Hughes (or another poet you

admire). Where will you find information about him? What will you include to make his story interesting? How will you use his poems within the documentary?

In a small group, research Hughes' poetry and his life. Decide what information is relevant to your purpose. Then write a one or two-page outline in which you detail your ideas for creating a documentary. Use this information to develop a storyboard. Share your storyboard with another group, asking for feedback.

PEER ASSESSMENT: Ask this group to rate your proposed production using the following criteria:

- captures interest
- follows a logical order
- presents facts in an entertaining way

Concrete
Poem by
May Swenson

Came a Beauty

Unconscious
came a beauty to my
wrist
and stopped my pencil,
merged its shadow profile with
my hand's ghost
on the page:
Red Spotted Purple or else Mourning
Cloak,
paired thin as paper wings, near black,
were edged on the seam side poppy orange,
as were its spots.

I sat arrested, for its soot haired
body's worm
shone in the sun.
It bent its tongue long as
a leg
black on my skin
and clung without my
feeling,
while its tomb stained
duplicate parts of
a window opened.
And then I
moved.

RESPONDING TO THE POEM

In a *concrete poem*, the poet uses the physical arrangement of the words on the page to help describe a subject or to express ideas or feelings. What shape is the author representing here?

Rearrange the text as straight lines of verse. Do the words in this format create as strong an image as the structure? Give reasons to support your opinion.

155

Dreams of the Animals

Poem by Margaret Atwood

Mostly the animals dream
of other animals   each
according to its kind
> (though certain mice and small rodents
> have nightmares of a huge pink
> shape with five claws descending)

: moles dream of darkness and delicate
mole smells

frogs dream of green and gold
frogs
sparkling like wet suns
among the lilies

red and black
striped fish, their eyes open
have red and black striped
dreams   defence, attack, meaningful
patterns

birds dream of territories
enclosed by singing.

Sometimes the animals dream of evil
in the form of soap and metal
but mostly the animals dream
of other animals.

There are exceptions:

the silver fox in the roadside zoo
dreams of digging out
and of baby foxes, their necks bitten

the caged armadillo
near the train
station, which runs
all day in figure eights
its piglet feet pattering,
no longer dreams
but is insane when waking;

the iguana
in the petshop window on St. Catherine Street
crested, royal-eyed, ruling
its kingdom of water-dish and sawdust

dreams of sawdust.

1. RESPONDING TO THE POEM

a. The phrase "There are exceptions" divides the poem into two parts. Each has a distinctly different mood. Describe the mood in the first and then the second part of the poem.

b. What do you think is the "evil in the form of soap and metal"?

c. What is the message of this poem?

d. Identify two images in the poem that you particularly like. Explain to a partner why they appeal to you.

2. VISUAL COMMUNICATION ANALYSE ILLUSTRATION

With a partner, discuss the illustration that accompanies the poem. Does it help you to appreciate the text? Explain. What is the mood of the illustration? Does it echo the mood of the poem? How do you think the artist created this mood?

Choose the phrase from the poem that appeals to you the most. Create or find a painting or a photo to represent these words. Share your work with the class and explain the meaning of your illustration.

SELF-ASSESSMENT: How does your work effectively represent the overall mood of the poem?

3. LANGUAGE CONVENTIONS HOW TO READ A POEM

Do you find reading poetry difficult? If so, there may be a very simple explanation. Poets sometimes break the conventional rules of grammar in order to create a unique atmosphere in their writing. This is known as *poetic licence.* For example, poets may choose not to use punctuation. This can make it difficult for readers, because punctuation marks help us to understand a text.

To read a poem, look carefully at its structure. Are words and lines put together in a certain way? Are there extra spaces between words or lines? Are indents used? All of these can indicate that the poet may want the reader to pause.

Margaret Atwood plays with punctuation in this poem. For example, she uses the colon twice. With your class, discuss how the colon (:) is used. Describe where and how Atwood uses this punctuation mark. Is this effective? Why or why not? What would you have done differently?

Haiku

by Various Artists

The autumn cicada
Dies by the side
Of its empty shell.
Joso

The long long river
A single line
On the snowy plain
Boncho

No oil to read by...
I am off to bed
But Ah!...
My moonlit pillow
Basho

You stupid scarecrow!
Under your very stick-feet
Birds are stealing beans!
Yayu

GOALS AT A GLANCE

■ Analyse the traditional form of haiku.
■ Write a haiku.

Poems in Your Pockets

Article by Karen Lewis

It's easier than you might think to become a poet. To write a poem, you need a pencil, paper, and your imagination. Poems take many different forms. For example, haiku poems originated centuries ago in Japan and consist of only seventeen syllables.

Here are some ideas to help you write your own haiku. For inspiration, choose an object that is hiding in your pocket or your room. Or wander outside until you find a special rock. Fine poems have been sparked by things as ordinary as a piece of concrete! Hold your object or rock. Feel it, smell it, listen to it. Does it have a story to tell? Maybe it has special powers? What does it dream about?

Close your eyes for a moment to let your imagination warm up. Pick up your pencil and let your ideas flow onto the paper. Experiment with word sounds that you like. "Rock" sounds different from "opal" or "pebble."

If an image or idea in your poem surprises you, you can use it more than once in the poem. Feel free to write wherever your ideas take you, adding details, colours, sounds, and shapes.

Haiku consist of seventeen syllables in three lines arranged 5-7-5. Take this poem, for example. The syllables are separated by dashes:

    1 2   3   4   5
Syc-a-more-leaves-fall
       1   2   3   4 5 6   7
While-skate-board-does-a-back-flip
    1   2   3 4   5
New-scratch-on-her-face.

—Anonymous, America 1990s

To create a haiku, sit quietly with a scene in front of you: your yard, a park, your window. What catches your interest? Write a few words to describe the scene. Arrange your words to follow the 5-7-5 pattern, or come close. Some modern haiku ignore these rules. Try a variety of words to create similar images. Poppies, tulips, or plum blossoms are all flowers, for example. Traditional haiku reflect the poet's personal response to something about nature.

When you are finished, you might have a collection of haiku inspired by the same scene. Haiku are fun to illustrate, especially with ink and watercolours. Whatever you write about, your poem will be a special piece of yourself.

----

1. RESPONDING TO THE ARTICLE AND HAIKU

a. Reread the article. How are traditional haiku formed? Look at the haiku on page 159. Which ones depart from the traditional form? How are they "breaking the rules"?

b. Which haiku do you like best? least? Explain your choices.

2. READING REWRITE A HAIKU

Select a favourite haiku and, in your notebook, rewrite it as a paragraph. Share it and the original haiku with a partner.

3. VISUAL COMMUNICATION CREATE A HAIKU IMAGE

Haiku poems paint vivid images and are often easy to interpret visually. Select a favourite haiku from page 159 or choose one of your own to illustrate. Create a collage, drawing, photograph, or other type of image to represent the haiku. Display your finished piece, including the poem.

4. WRITING Haiku

Try writing haiku. How many syllables are there in your first name? your last name? Use some form of your name to create the first five-syllable line. Compose two more lines to create a haiku that reveals something about you.

SELF-ASSESSMENT: Use the following criteria to assess your haiku:

- correct use of form
- correct number of syllables
- use of imagery
- originality

How successful were you in using these criteria to develop your haiku? Write your response in your journal and use this information as a guideline when writing other haiku.

5. LANGUAGE CONVENTIONS Syllables

When writing poetry it is often important to think about the number of syllables in the words you're using. Syllables affect the beat and rhythm of a poem. Sometimes poets will replace one syllable in a word with an apostrophe, in order to conform to the rhythm they've created or to create a more pleasing sound.

> **...And mamma in her 'kerchief and I in my cap,**
>
> **Had just settled our brains for a long winter's nap,...**

Note in these lines from "A Visit from St. Nicholas" how the apostrophe has replaced the syllable "hand" in the word "handkerchief." Read the lines out loud with the word in full, and think about how the number of syllables can affect the rhythm.

Smokeroom on the Kyle

NARRATIVE POEM BY TED RUSSELL

Tall are the tales that fishermen tell when summer's work is done,
Of fish they've caught, of birds they've shot, of crazy risks they've run.
But never did fishermen tell a tale, so tall by half a mile,
As Grampa Walcott told that night, in the smokeroom on the KYLE.

With 'baccy smoke from twenty pipes, the atmosphere was blue,
There was many a "Have another boy," and "Don't mind if I do."
When somebody suggested that each in turn should spin,
A yarn about some circumstance, he'd personally been in.

Then tales were told of barrels bent to shoot around the cliff,
Of men thawed out and brought to life, who had been frozen stiff,
Of bark-pots carried off by flies, of pathways chopped through fog,
Of woodsman Bill who barefoot kicked the knots from a 12-inch log.

GOALS AT A GLANCE

■ Identify the rhyming pattern.
■ Write and tell a tall tale.

The loud applause got louder when Uncle Mickey Shea,
Told of the big potaty he growed in Gander Bay,
Too big to roll through the cellar door, it lay at rest nearby,
Until one rainy autumn night, the pig drowned in its eye.

But meanwhile in the corner, his gray head slightly bowed,
Sat Grampa Walcott, 83, the oldest of the crowd.
Upon his weatherbeaten face there beamed a quiet grin,
When someone shouted "Grampa, it's your turn to chip in."

"Boys leave me out," said Grampa. "Thanks, don't mind if I do,
Well all right boys, if you insist, I'll tell you one that's true.
It's a story about jiggin' squids I'm goin' to relate,
It happened in Pigeon Inlet in eighteen eighty-eight.

Me, I was just a bedlamer, a-fishin' with my dad,
And prospects for the summer were lookin' awful bad.
The caplin scull was over, it hadn't been too bright,
And here was August come and gone and nar a squid in sight.

Day after day we searched for bait, till dark from early dawn,
We dug up clams, and 'cocks-and-hens,' till even these were gone.
But still no squids, so in despair, we give it up for good,
And took our gear ashore and went a-cuttin' firewood.

One day while we was in the woods with all the other men,
And wonderin' if we'd ever see another squid agen.
Father broke his axe that day, so we were first ones out,
And as we neared the landwash, we heard the women shout.

'Come hurry boys, the squids is in.' We jumped aboard our boat,
And hurried out the harbour, the only crew afloat.
But soon our keel begun to scrunch like scrapin' over skids,
'Father,' says I, 'we've run aground.' 'Me son,' says he, 'that's squids.'

Says he, 'The jigger! heave un out,' and quick as a flash I did,
And soon as it struck the water, twas graffled by a squid.
I hauled it in and what d'ye think? Just as it crossed the rail,
Damned if there wasn't another squid—clung to the first one's tail.

And another clung to that one, and so on in a string.
I tried to shake 'em loose, but father said, 'You foolish thing,
You've got something was never seen before in Newfoundland,
So drop the jigger, grab the string and haul hand over hand.'

I hauled that string of squids, till the boat could hold no more,
Then hitched it in the risin's and started for the shore.
The crews were runnin' from the woods, they'd heard the women bawl,
But father said, 'Don't hurry boys, we've squids enough for all.'

He give the string to Jonas Brown till he pulled in enough,
Then Jonas passed the end along to his neighbour Natty Cuff.
From stage to stage that string was passed, throughout the whole night long,
Till dawnin' found it on Eastern Point with Uncle Billy Strong.

Now Uncle Billy quite thoughtfully before he went to bed,
Took two half hitches of the string round the grump of his stage-head.
Next mornin' Hartley's Harbour heard the news and up they come,
In trapskiff with six pair of oars to tow the string down home.

When Hartley's Harbour had enough the followin' afternoon,
The string went on from place to place until it reached Quirpon.
What happened to it after that I don't exactly know,
But people say it crossed the Straits and landed in Forteau."

Yes, tall are the tales that fishermen tell, when summer's work is done,
Of fish they've caught, of birds they've shot, of crazy risks they've run.
But never did fishermen tell a tale, so tall by half a mile,
As Grampa Walcott told that night, in the smokeroom on the KYLE.

----

1. RESPONDING TO THE NARRATIVE POEM

a. Describe the sights and sounds in the smokeroom. What do you think a smokeroom is?

b. When does this poem take place? Why do you think so?

c. The story seems believable up to a point. When do you suspect that the storyteller is beginning to exaggerate the facts?

d. Why do you think this is called a "narrative poem"? Read it again and list the features that you think a narrative poem should have. How does "Smokeroom on the Kyle" differ from other poems that you've read so far in this unit?

e. Discuss with a partner any words or phrases in this poem that you didn't understand.

2. POET'S CRAFT RHYMING PATTERN

Rhyme is the repetition of the same sound, usually at the ends of words. In traditional poetry, the words at the end of each line in a stanza rhyme with each other. For example, "done" rhymes with "run" in the first stanza of this poem. This is called the rhyming pattern. "Smokeroom on the Kyle" has an *a a* **b b** rhyming pattern in every stanza. What is the effect of a regular rhyme scheme? Does it make the poem easier to read? harder? Read it aloud, concentrating on how the words sound and the lines rhyme.

Reread other poems in this unit and assess the effectiveness of their rhyming patterns. List the different patterns you come across, for example, *a* **b b** *a*, *a* **b** *a* **b**, or *a a* **b b**. The next time you write a poem, use one of the rhyming patterns you've discovered.

3. ORAL COMMUNICATION TALL TALES

This selection is not only a narrative poem, it's also a tall tale. What do you think makes "Smokeroom on the Kyle" a good example of a tall tale?

Think of an experience you've had that would make a good tall tale. How will you exaggerate the facts? How will you add humour? Write your tale in either prose or verse.

Rehearse until you can tell your story smoothly. As you present your tale, remember to

- use your voice effectively
- pause for impact
- vary the volume
- use gestures
- make eye contact with your audience

SELF-ASSESSMENT: Did your presentation go as planned? Were there any surprises? disappointments? What would you do differently next time? How could you improve your tale and your oral presentation?

Song of the Land

GOALS AT A GLANCE

- Respond personally and critically to song lyrics.
- Co-operate with others to prepare a choral reading.

Song Lyrics by Barry Brown

Somewhere there's a land
Where the sun brightly shines
And across the tundra
Slow rivers wind
Where love lives forever
And dreams never die
Somewhere there's a land for you
    and I

Somewhere there's a land
Where the snow softly falls
Elders are cherished
And the past recalled
Where tomorrow is sparkling
In the eye of a child
Somewhere there's a land for you
    and I

It's the song of the land
In the heart of the common man

Raise your voice and join hands
Sing the song of the land

Somewhere there's a land
Where the wind gently blows
We'll raise a family in a home of
    our own
Where people are peaceful and wild
    geese fly
Somewhere there's a land for you
    and I

Somewhere there's a land
Where the sun brightly shines
And across the tundra
Slow rivers wind
Where love lives forever
And dreams never die
Somewhere there's a land for you
    and I

"Song of the Land" appears on Susan Aglukark's CD *Arctic Rose*. Susan Aglukark is an Inuit singer who sings about her people and what it's like to live in the North. Many of her songs are written in both English and Inuktitut.

1. RESPONDING TO THE SONG LYRICS

a. What features of this selection tell the reader that these are actually song lyrics? List the features that you think songs should have and discuss them with your class.

b. Using only one word, describe the mood of this song. What made you choose this particular word?

c. In the song, the speaker sings of both the old and the young. What roles are they given in this culture?

S T R A T E G I E S

2. ORAL COMMUNICATION CHORAL READING

In a group of four to eight students, prepare a choral reading of "Song of the Land." Choose one, or a combination, of the following choral reading techniques:

- in unison—lines read by the whole group at the same time
- antiphonal—selection is divided into parts which are then read by different groups consecutively
- cumulative—selection is divided into parts which are read by groups in a *round*—one group begins and is joined by the second group, which is then joined by another group, and so on
- solo—lines are read by one person

Discuss these techniques and plan your choral reading. What effect or mood do you wish to convey to your audience? How do you think the song should sound? Should it be spoken slowly? quickly? Should your voices be happy? sad? serious? angry? Rehearse until you are satisfied with your performance as a group.

GROUP ASSESSMENT: Use a tape recorder to record and assess your performance. How might your group improve the presentation of this song? Perform the song for the class.

#254

Poem by Emily Dickinson

"Hope" is the thing with feathers—
That perches in the soul—
And sings the tune without the words—
And never stops—at all—

And sweetest—in the Gale—is heard—
And sore must be the storm—
That could abash the little Bird
That kept so many warm—

I've heard it in the chillest land—
And on the strangest Sea—
Yet, never, in Extremity,
It asked a crumb—of Me.

What do you think the phrase "called back" means?

CALLED BACK: A One-Act Play

Script by Christina Ashton

AUTHOR'S NOTE

Called Back by James Conway was a popular book of Emily Dickinson's time. In May 1886, two weeks before she died, she wrote a note to Fanny and Loo (her Norcross cousins) saying, "Little Cousins, Called back. Emily." She borrowed the title of the book to let her cousins know that she was dying.

PRODUCTION NOTES

Script: Direct quotes from Emily Dickinson's poetry, correspondence, and conversations are printed in **bold** type to distinguish them from paraphrased or imagined dialogue.

Stage props: Piano, antique armchair, ladders, brooms, paint buckets

Hand props: Bunch of lilies and commercial snack cake

Stage set: The set is designed for a performance in the classroom, with no special lighting required and items available in any school. For a performance onstage, a spotlight on Dickinson and a backdrop of tall, narrow, heavily draped parlour windows could be added.

GOALS AT A GLANCE

- Analyse characters.
- Present a readers' theatre co-operatively.

Sound effects: The sound of galloping horses offstage, rising and falling

Costumes: Jeans and shirts for the girls; a long white dress and blue shawl for Dickinson

Cast: Frances and Louise: Thirteen-year-olds on summer vacation; Emily Dickinson

Time: The present, late afternoon

Setting: Parlour of the Dickinson home. The house is closed to the public at the moment for cleaning and repairs. The room is empty except for one small antique armchair centre stage; a piano at stage right; a ladder, brooms, and paint buckets strewn around.

At rise: Frances and Louise enter from stage left, arguing. Frances carries a commercial snack cake, which she nibbles from time to time.

FRANCES: We shouldn't have broken in here!

LOUISE: We didn't *break* in. Somebody left the kitchen door unlocked.

FRANCES: *(looking over her shoulder nervously, nibbling at the cake)* It's spooky. Let's go.

LOUISE: It's not spooky. This is a famous historic site, the home of one of our greatest poets. We have the whole place to ourselves. Let's snoop around. *(crosses right)*

FRANCES: No. I still think—

LOUISE: Shhh!

FRANCES: What?

LOUISE: I think I hear someone coming from the main hall. *(takes another step right looking offstage)* Who are you?

DICKINSON: *(offstage)* **I'm Nobody! Who are you?/Are you—Nobody—Too?/Then there's a pair of us!** *(appears carrying a bunch of lilies; short, with thick reddish hair combed back from her face; wears a long white dress and a blue shawl)*

LOUISE: *(backing toward Frances, who is frozen beside the chair)* It's her!

FRANCES: Wh-Who?

LOUISE: Emily Dickinson, of course! Who else? This is her house. That's her poem! *(to Dickinson)* Uh, there's three of us, actually—with you, that is—I mean—

DICKINSON: **These are my introduction.** *(advances, offering lilies to girls, who are too stunned to move)* No? Well, perhaps later then. *(lays lilies on piano, perches on edge of chair like a child, facing audience)* **Don't tell! they'd advertise—you know!** *(scolding)* **How dreary—to be—Somebody!/How public—like a Frog—/To tell one's name—the livelong June—/To an admiring Bog!** *(to girls)* But you must tell *me* your names.

LOUISE: I'm Lou-Louise, and this is my friend, Fra-Frances.

DICKINSON: Fanny and Loo—just like my little Norcross cousins. I shall call you "little cousins." Please do sit down, little cousins. *(Relaxing a little, the girls sit at Dickinson's feet. Dickinson looks around sourly at the ladder and brooms.)* Housecleaning! **It is a prickly art**. Little cousins, are you from Cambridgeport, as my cousins were?

Louise: No. We flew here from Philadelphia.

DICKINSON: Flew? Have people sprouted wings like angels?

How delicious! *(disbelieving)* You flew, indeed. You must be poets like myself with such imagination.

LOUISE: Oh, no, ma'am. Never like you. And we flew in a—a kind of, well, machine. I guess you haven't heard—

DICKINSON: **The Only News I know/Is Bulletins all Day/From Immortality.** But I did visit Washington, D.C., and Philadelphia once. I went by train. **I like to see it lap the Miles—/And lick the Valleys up—/And stop to feed itself at Tanks—/And then— prodigious step...**

LOUISE: *(interrupting)* **Around a Pile of Mountains—/And supercilious peer/In Shanties— by the sides of Roads—/And then a Quarry pare...**

FRANCES: *(interrupting)* **To fit its Ribs/And crawl between/ Complaining all the while/In horrid—hooting stanza—/Then chase itself down Hill—**

ALL THREE: *(in chorus)* **And neigh like Boanerges—/Then— punctual as a Star/Stop—docile and omnipotent/At its own stable door—.**

DICKINSON: *(applauding)* So you read my poems!

LOUISE: Well, not all of them.

You wrote an awful lot.

DICKINSON: Ah, yes, I did. One thousand seven hundred seventy-five, to be exact, or so I am told. I never counted them. Do you read many books, little cousins? My father **buys me many Books—but begs me not to read them—because he fears they joggle the Mind.**

FRANCES: Yeah, my dad is always taking away books he says I shouldn't read.

LOUISE: *(to Frances)* I don't think she means those kinds of books. *(Frances shrugs and nibbles at the cake.)*

DICKINSON: *(leaning forward to peer at the cake with distaste)* What is that, all wrapped in clear crackling stuff?

FRANCES: This? Oh, it's a snack cake. It comes all wrapped like this from the store. Want some?

DICKINSON: Oh, I think not, little cousin. *(brightly)* My father always insisted my baking was best. In truth, I was very good at it, and very precise in how I did it.

LOUISE: Miss Emily, I've got to ask. Why did you shut yourself off from the world? Everybody wants to know. A lot of people make guesses, but nobody knows for sure. Why did you,

if you don't mind my asking?
DICKINSON: *(disgusted)* People. **They talk of hallowed things aloud, and embarrass my dog.** *(girls giggle)* I preferred writing to people over meeting them face to face.
LOUISE: Your letters are very famous now, and your poems. You could have been famous before you—you—uh, went to the other side.
DICKINSON: Perhaps. But I was a shy bird, you know, a little phoebe. **I was a Phoebe— nothing more—/A Phoebe— nothing less—/The little note that others dropt/I fitted into place—/I dwelt too low that any seek—/Too shy, that any blame—/A Phoebe makes a little print/Upon the Floors of Fame—.**
FRANCES: But you made a big print. Even kids like me know some of your poems.
DICKINSON: Perhaps I might have had more fame then, but **Because I could not stop for Death—/He kindly stopped for me—/The Carriage held but just Ourselves—/And Immortality.** *(Offstage, the sound of galloping horses, becoming louder. Dickinson rises and starts right.)*

LOUISE: Oh, don't go!
DICKINSON: But I must. **Since then—'tis Centuries—and yet/Feels shorter than the Day/I first surmised the Horses' Heads/Were toward Eternity—.** *(exits right; off- stage calls out)* **Little Cousins, Called Back.**
(The sound of galloping rises, then fades.)
LOUISE: No! *(follows Dickinson)*
FRANCES: *(panicky)* Louise, don't do that!
LOUISE: *(returning sad and confused)* She's gone—just like that.
FRANCES: *(swallowing last of cake)* Wow! "What I Did on My Summer Vacation." Who'll believe it? I don't believe it myself.
LOUISE: Believe it. *(takes lilies from piano, hands them to Frances, who sniffs them)*
FRANCES: These are freshly picked! They weren't here before Emily came in.
LOUISE: They sure weren't. And they weren't **Called back** either. She must have really wanted us to have them.
(As the stage darkens, the girls bury their faces in the lilies.)

1. RESPONDING TO THE SCRIPT

a. What or who is a "Phoebe"?

b. What do you think the words "He kindly stopped for me" mean?

c. Christina Ashton cleverly weaves historical facts with modern fiction in this one-act play. With a partner, discuss how she accomplishes this.

d. Why does the author use the poet's own words (in **bold**) in her play? Is this effective? Explain.

2. READING ANALYSE CHARACTER

In the script, the characters' personalities are revealed mainly through their words (what they say) and their actions (what they do). With a partner, discuss what you know about each character, and how you gained that knowledge. In your notebook, complete a character chart like the one below.

Character	Words	Actions	What Is Revealed
Emily Dickinson			
Frances			
Louise			

3. ORAL COMMUNICATION READERS' THEATRE

Working in groups of four, develop a readers' theatre presentation of this script. Think carefully about the character you are reading. How is she feeling? What is she thinking? Will you need any props or costumes? Gather these things together. As you present, use your body language and voice to reveal mood. Remember to co-operate with your group members in order to successfully present a readers' theatre.

GROUP ASSESSMENT: If you were to do this activity again, what performance changes would you recommend to your group, and why? How would you improve your own performance?

HOW TO

WRITE POETRY

Goals at a Glance

● Develop strategies for writing poetry. ● Use language and sound in poetry.

Poetry is a very flexible type of writing. It can express feelings, describe observations, recall experiences, explore ideas, celebrate rhythm, and play with sound. Below are some suggestions to help you write poetry with ease.

Start with an Idea

Turn any of your ideas—any at all—into a poem. The subject doesn't have to be unusual or profound, it just has to be something you care about. Here are two effective strategies for developing ideas into poems:

1. Analyse a poem that you like. Write your poem using the same pattern of lines, stanzas, and rhythms.

2. Write something in prose first. Next, take out every word that is not necessary to express the meaning. Work with the words and phrases that are left.

The Language of Poetry

Every word counts in a poem. Your job as a poet is to select the best words and put them in the best order. Nouns should be specific, verbs should be vivid, and every word should be necessary. Sometimes a poet even creates words to help describe an experience. Descriptions should be detailed enough for a reader to be able to experience the poem through the senses.

If you're having trouble finding the right words, try making a comparison. Connect two things that are not usually connected. Consider the following options:

● **Simile**—use *like* or *as* to compare.
  "frogs/sparkling like wet suns"

● **Metaphor**—represent one thing as something else.
  "The long long river/A single line"

PROCESS

- **Personification**—give human qualities to a thing or idea.

  "And sore must be the storm"

- **Hyperbole**—use exaggeration for effect.

  "Of men thawed out and brought to life, who had been frozen stiff."

The Sound of Poetry

In poetry, the sound of the words is just as important as the meaning. Read your poem aloud and adjust the language until it sounds right. To create stronger images and a pleasing sound, use any of these devices:

- **Alliteration**—repeat the same first sound in a group of words.

  "scrunch like scrapin' over skids"

- **Onomatopoeia**—choose words that echo, or imitate, the sound they name.

  "snap, crack"

- **Repetition**—use the same words, phrases, or lines more than once.

  See "The Base Stealer"

- **Rhyme**—place rhyming words at the ends, or in the middle, of lines.

  See "Formula"

- **Rhythm**—arrange the stresses, or beats, in a line. These stresses can be placed at equal time intervals, but they do not have to be.

  See "Song of the Land"

- **Consonants**—select soft consonants like *s, m, n, l,* and *r* to create a gentle sound; use hard consonants like *b, p, d, t,* and *k* to create a harsh sound.

  "the soul's own mastery"

  "Forest snap, crack, quiet"

Break the Rules

A poem is a poem because the writer says so. Experiment. You can create a form that suits your own mood and purpose.

Poetry does not have to follow the usual rules for punctuation. You can use line breaks and spaces between words to show the reader where to pause. You may even choose not to use any punctuation at all. Line breaks can also be used to create rhythm, or to form shapes on the page. Experiment with different line breaks, and read each arrangement aloud. Choose the one that works best.

Self-Assessment

Use the following questions as a guideline as you read your poem aloud:

- ❏ Have I used the best words? Are they in the best order?
- ❏ Does the sound of the words suit the mood of the poem?
- ❏ Could I break the lines in a better way?
- ❏ Have I used original and interesting comparisons?
- ❏ What changes can I make to improve my poem?

PROCESS

The Base Stealer

Poem by Robert Francis

Poised between going on and back, pulled
Both ways taut like a tightrope-walker
Fingertips pointing the opposites,
Now bouncing tiptoe like a dropped ball
Or a kid skipping rope, come on, come on,
Running a scattering of steps sidewise,
How he teeters, skitters, tingles, teases,
Taunts them, hovers like an ecstatic bird,
He's only flirting, crowd him, crowd him,
Delicate, delicate, delicate, delicate—now!

1. RESPONDING TO THE POEM

a. How does the poet realistically describe what it's like to steal a base? Support your answer with words from the poem.

b. Who is speaking in this poem? Give reasons for your answer.

c. What action do you think occurs with the word "now!"?

2. LANGUAGE CONVENTIONS VIVID VERBS

A *verb* is a word that expresses an action or a state of being. A *vivid verb* is a colourful or strong action word, such as *streak, glide, pounce,* or *topple*. List, in order, the verbs used in the poem. Do you think the poet has chosen vivid verbs to describe the action? Explain your answer. Discuss the poet's choice of words with a partner.

3. WRITING USING SIMILES

The poet uses **similes** to help us picture what the base stealer looks like in action. Find examples of similes in the poem. With a small group, discuss their effectiveness.

Think about comparisons that might be made between other animals and athletes. Write a poem of your own. Include strong similes and vivid verbs. Remember, a good simile is not too direct or obvious. It leaves the reader thinking about and visualizing the comparison being made.

Post your poem on the school's Web page, or publish it in a class or school newspaper. Add a drawing or photo that illustrates one of your similes.

SELF-ASSESSMENT: Review the similes you've used. Is it clear what is being compared? Have you created strong images for the reader? How effective are your comparisons? What challenged your thinking during this activity?

> A **simile** is an image created by linking two quite different things or ideas. For example, *the speed skater was as swift as a summer storm*. A simile is easily identified by the use of the words *like* or *as*.

4. MEDIA PRODUCE A RADIO BROADCAST

Listen to a radio broadcast of a baseball game or some other action sport. How does the sportscaster create excitement using words and voice?

With the sportscast as a model, practise reading this poem out loud. Vary your volume and speed while you read. Decide how you will read the climax. When you are ready, perform the poem for an audience as if it were a live radio broadcast.

School Buses

Poem by Russell Hoban

You'd think that by the end of June they'd take them-
    selves
Away, get out of sight—but no, they don't; they
Don't at all. You see them waiting through
July in clumps of sumac near the railroad, or
Behind a service station, watching, always watching
    for a
Child who's let go of summer's hand and strayed. I
    have
Seen them hunting on the roads of August—empty
    buses
Scanning woods and ponds with rows of empty eyes.
    This morning
I saw five of them, parked like a week of
Schooldays, smiling slow in orange paint and
Smirking with their mirrors in the sun—
But summer isn't done! Not yet!

GOALS AT A GLANCE

■ Analyse the use of personification.
■ Write a poem.

305

1. RESPONDING TO THE POEM

a. Describe the narrator's attitude toward school buses in the summer. Support your statements with evidence from the poem.

b. Certain things we identify with specific seasons or times of the year. List five original examples of objects that remind you of a specific time. Are these pleasant associations for you, or not?

2. POET'S CRAFT PERSONIFICATION

The poet uses **personification** when he compares the buses to people. What human qualities does he give these buses? Do you think the description is effective? Why or why not? What else could you compare school buses to?

SELF-ASSESSMENT: In your notebook, define personification in your own words. Include an original example.

> **Personification** is a special type of metaphor in which a non-human object is given human characteristics or feelings. For example, *the sun smiled down on us.*

S T R A T E G I E S

3. WRITING A POEM

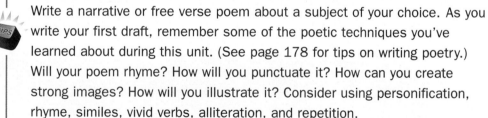

Write a narrative or free verse poem about a subject of your choice. As you write your first draft, remember some of the poetic techniques you've learned about during this unit. (See page 178 for tips on writing poetry.) Will your poem rhyme? How will you punctuate it? How can you create strong images? How will you illustrate it? Consider using personification, rhyme, similes, vivid verbs, alliteration, and repetition.

Ask a classmate to listen as you read your poem aloud. Ask for feedback that will help you write your final draft. As you are reading, listen for awkward lines or words that break the rhythm.

Have you ever wondered how to put your poetic talents to use?

When Hallmark Just Won't Do

A West Coast writer dusts off his poetic licence and sets up shop as a bard for hire.

NEWSPAPER ARTICLE BY ELIZABETH SCHAAL

A few weeks ago Bill Kimmett got an urgent call. The freelance writer from British Columbia was in his home office, cobbling together a magazine piece on exterior house-painting, when a young woman's voice took him from his work.

GOALS AT A GLANCE

- Form and support opinions.
- Analyse and use figurative language.

She'd seen his ad in *The Georgia Straight*—"Poetic Tributes: Celebrate life, love, place, events, or personal vision in poetic words"—and she needed a poem. Fast.

The woman was from Vancouver and, while travelling in Thailand, she'd met a man. Kimmett says, "They were up in the mountains, in a natural steam pool, and it was pitch black. They started talking and all the fireflies came out and that was the only light they had. She wanted to give him something special, so all those things, I put into a poem."

Another woman, in a sentimental mood, wanted an ode to her home in Whistler and the farmhouse in Provence where she'd lived years before: *Rivulets damply run on Whistler trails/As August sweats on the parchment face of Provence*, Kimmett wrote, on specialty paper, and another satisfied customer went home smiling.

As he describes it, Bill Kimmett is surrounded by an ocean of poems. The desk in his house in Lions Bay groans under the weight of the verses, free-form and rhyming, odes, ballads, and haikus he scribbles compulsively about anything and everything.

"In another age I would probably have been the local bard," he says.

For roughly $89, Kimmett will write you a poem to mark any special person, place, or thing, living or dead, and milestones such as birthdays or anniversaries. With careful listening and a client questionnaire ("Are you a dreamer, realist, adventurer, philosopher, other?"), he insists he can get beyond Hallmark sentiments, right into the heart and soul of a person. "The way I express it is, 'Your feelings to my pen.'"

Two years ago, at 52, the bard of Lions Bay took a severance package from his position as an environmental-health director in Vancouver, dusted off his poetic licence, and decided to turn his passion into his living.

"There was never a time when I didn't write poetry," Kimmett recalls from the small coastal community just north of Vancouver. He and his wife raised their three daughters there in a house he built overlooking Howe Sound, Vancouver Island, the mountains, the mist, and the ferries. In winter, he says, "fierce Squamish winds come howling down the mountainside. In summer, after rain, the dew hangs heavy like pearls."

"I write a lot of nature poems as well," he explains.

Born in Ayrshire, in the southwest of Scotland, Kimmett spent his boyhood just miles from where Robert Burns and William Wallace [Braveheart] lived. "When I used to walk through the countryside and see the places they saw, I could always feel this poetic surge in me," he says. "Beyond that, I don't honestly know where it comes from. Growing up, I never knew anyone else who wrote poetry."

Kimmett never studied poetry formally. Instead, he took an environmental-health degree, then set out in pursuit of another life long obsession. "Ever since I was born, believe it or not, I wanted to come to Canada," he says in a soft, Scottish lilt, more a purr than a burr. "When I was 13, I wrote to the RCMP, and they sent me an application form. I remember under 'height,' I wrote 4 foot-10 1/2; 'weight,' 82 pounds. Then I sent it all back to them in my best handwriting. And this is the nice part, which always endeared me to the RCMP, I got a really nice letter back to say that they would keep my letter on file and if I ever came to the country they would certainly reconsider it."

In the drizzle of November, 1969, Kimmett landed in Montreal and, outfitted in blazer, flannels, shirt, tie, Oxfords, and a raincoat, proceeded to hitchhike across the country. "I came to Vancouver with $3 in my pocket. But in life I've always had a strong, optimistic sense that if I think I can do something, I'm not scared of it."

That optimism, or sheer blind luck, preserved him through a hair-raising stretch in the Rockies. "I was actually circled by, I say they were coyotes, but people think they were wolves, and they literally formed a pack round me and followed me along this snow-covered road. But I wasn't scared," he says, still in awe at the memory. "It was almost like a surreal experience."

"So what I would do was stop and make snowballs and throw them, and they would run into the forest. And then as I walked on they would come back out of the forest again and follow me." Eventually they skittered off.

"My life has been poetry since I came here," he says today, his odyssey neverending. "It's almost like a possession. Even sleeping, I find it hard. When I lie in bed at night and look out and see the mist over the mountains, the water glistening in the moonlight, the ferries meandering past, the shadows of the trees on the walls, I can't sleep."

Fortunately, he has an understanding wife. "I no longer drive her nuts by running out and saying look, listen to this, with every single poem I write," he says. She bought him a pen with a tiny light built in so he can write in the middle of the night. After 29 years together, he still woos her with words: *How can I paint the liquid fire/Of sunset trailing tongues on fleeting ocean waves/When all I truly see is you?*

His days he spends as a kind of Poet Laureate for hire, weaving words for other poetic souls.

Business is picking up. *Wedding Bells* magazine has expressed an interest in the idea of personalized poems for weddings, he says. And he's thinking of phasing out his ad in the *Straight* and concentrating solely on his Web page. "It's being designed now, and I've written all the text," he says excitedly, then, catching himself: "Although I'm a poetic soul, I think the Internet is the way to go."

----

1. RESPONDING TO THE ARTICLE

a. Bill Kimmett says, "I could always feel this poetic surge in me." What does this statement mean?

b. Find out the meaning of "Poet Laureate." Do you think that Bill Kimmett should be described as a "Poet Laureate for hire"? Why or why not?

2. ORAL COMMUNICATION FORM OPINIONS

In a small group, answer the following: "How would you feel about receiving a poem from a person, knowing that someone else had written it?" Give three reasons to support your opinion, and share it with the group. Do your fellow group members have similar views?

3. WORD CRAFT FIGURATIVE LANGUAGE

Writers of prose can be just as expressive as poets in their choice of
words and expressions. Find the following expressions in the article:

- "beyond Hallmark sentiments"
- "My life has been poetry since I came here."
- "his odyssey neverending"

Discuss with a partner what they mean and why they are, or are
not, effective.

REFLECTING ON THE UNIT

SELF-ASSESSMENT: POET'S CRAFT

As you worked on activities in this unit, what did you learn about

- reading poetry?
- rhythm?
- writing poetry?
- haiku?
- personification?
- narrative poems?
- similes?
- concrete poems?

VISUAL COMMUNICATION EXAMINE IMAGES

Examine the images for some poems in this unit. Then answer
the following questions in your notebook: Which image do you think most
effectively captures the meaning of the poem it accompanies? Justify your
opinion. Which image do you think is least effective? Why? How would
you change it? Draw or find another that you think works better.

ORAL COMMUNICATION READ ALOUD

With a partner, discuss the poems in this unit, and decide which one you
like best. Read your favourite out loud to your partner. In your reading,
express the meaning you think the poem should have. Listen carefully to
your partner's choice. Have you managed to increase each other's
appreciation of your favourite poems?

TECHNOLOGY

"The world is moving so fast these days
that the man [or woman] who says it can't be done
is generally interrupted by someone doing it."

Elbert Hubbard

TECHNOLOGY

IN OUR WORLD

This mother's gift to her daughter is more valuable than an antique.

A Desk for My Daughter

Memoir by Gardner McFall

When I was nine, and about to enter Grade Four, my mother surprised me by giving me a desk. She bought it for seventy-five dollars at an outdoor auction, and I dimly recall the rap of the auctioneer's gavel, signalling that the circa-1900 fan-front, slant-top desk was mine.

It was oak, a smooth honey colour, stained just dark enough to "look important," according to my mother. The leaf opened to become a solid writing surface. The cabinet held three recessed filing slots, a letter holder, and, in the centre, a space for items like glue and tape. Above that was a drawer, which soon enough held my crayons and collection of seaweed mounted on index cards.

The desk had two larger drawers below that bracketed shelves. At first I put stuffed animals on the shelves and, later, books. On the front, the keyhole's brass plate, which I loved instantly, was fancifully etched with a bird flying up toward a crescent moon and a tree tossed by the wind. And it came with a key that worked. Open or closed, the desk was a marvel. But the most marvellous feature couldn't be seen at a glance, as I discovered the day it was moved into my room.

GOALS AT A GLANCE

- Respond critically to the text.
- Write a memoir.

Seated at it, I removed the small centre drawer from its slip, and, as I did, another drawer fell down from above—a secret compartment accessible when eased down its slanted tracks. Not even the auctioneer had mentioned this secret drawer. I thought my desk was the finest in the world.

From Grades Four through Twelve, I worked at this desk, writing my first poem, reading letters from the friends separated from me by our transient military life, and writing to my father when he was overseas. I filled out my college application on its sturdy leaf, and, more than once during those years, put my head down on it and wept about some now-forgotten matter. For a child in a Navy family, pulling up stakes every two years was hard, but my desk anchored me. It became a kind of repository for all my young selves and lives. It was a constant.

Even after I left home twenty-five years ago for college and a career, I still returned to the desk periodically, storing there the mementos that charted my course: college diploma, love letters, a wedding-gift record book, the first magazine that published my poems.

This summer I cleaned the desk out in anticipation of giving it to my eight-year-old daughter, about to enter Grade Three.

This afternoon we are standing outside our apartment building in New York waiting for the desk to be delivered from Florida. All day she has been anticipating its arrival. I hardly know what it means to her; she hasn't ever asked for a desk, but she's as excited as if awaiting her best friend.

When the van finally appears, she leaps up and down, yelling, "Mommy, it's here!" and something inside me leaps, too. The driver, a Jacksonville antiques dealer and family friend, greets us, slides open the door. I see my desk, wrapped in blankets, sandwiched between a highboy and a bedroom bureau. It looks tiny to me, but I know that to my daughter it is enormous.

With my husband's help, the driver manoeuvres it up to our apartment on a dolly. After he's gone and my daughter and I are in her room, the desk in its corner, I put my arms around her and say simply, "My mother bought this for me when I was going into Grade Four, and now I want you to have it, because you're going into Three."

She gives me a gripping hug and bounds off to put her treasures away—pencils in their holder, diary in one of the file slots. She stands the painted bookends made at summer camp on the top ledge. As I turn to leave her to this greatest of pleasures, she calls after me in an emphatic, rather grown-up way, "Now life's getting organized!"

But I know it's herself she's beginning to organize, along with her crayons, markers, sketch pads, and collection of bears soon to be installed on the bottom shelves. Should I tell her about the secret compartment, I wonder, halfway down the hall, and what I kept in it—beach glass, Beatles cards, things too small or precious to be kept anywhere else? Should I point out the key or the little bird flying up to the moon?

I decide not to. I will let her find them and make of her desk what she will. I like to think that one day in the next century, she'll give it to her own daughter and say, "Your great-grandmother bought this desk at an auction. It has many secrets and charms. See how many you can find."

----

1. RESPONDING TO THE MEMOIR

a. Why is this desk important to the narrator?

b. Why is it important for the narrator to share information about the desk's history with the reader?

c. How does the young girl find the secret drawer? As an adult and mother, why does she decide not to tell her daughter about it? Would you have made the same decision? Explain.

d. How does this selection fit in a unit called "Technology: In Our World"?

2. **WRITING** MEMOIR

In this **memoir** the main character reveals to us details of her past that have special meaning. Reread the selection. Note how she describes the desk through personal experiences, thoughts, and feelings. If this piece was written without using language that was personal and meaningful, would it still be considered a memoir? Why or why not?

> **Memoir** is the descriptive recording of a person's own experiences. It is told like a story with *first-person narration* (using the pronouns *I, me, we,* and *us*).

Think of an object that has special meaning to you. It might be a family heirloom, a favourite book, a shirt, a pair of skates, or anything else you treasure. In your notebook, create your own two-page personal memoir by writing about this object. Remember to

- use details to describe it
- include your experiences, thoughts, and feelings
- write in the first-person narrative voice

PEER ASSESSMENT: Ask a classmate to review your work and check your use of the features of a memoir. How did your classmate react to the piece?

See how satire can be used to make a serious point.

Learn with BOOK

Satirical Essay by R.J. Heathorn

A new aid to rapid—almost magical—learning has made its appearance. Indications are that if it catches on, all the electronic gadgets will be so much junk. The new device is known as Built-in Orderly Organized Knowledge. The makers generally call it by its initials, BOOK.

Many advantages are claimed over the old-style learning and teaching aids on which most people are brought up nowadays. It has no wires and no electric circuits to break down. No connection is needed to an electricity power point. It is made entirely without mechanical parts to go wrong or need replacement.

Anyone can use BOOK, even children, and it fits comfortably into the hands. It can be conveniently used sitting in an armchair by the fire.

How does the revolutionary, unbelievably easy invention work? Basically BOOK consists only of a large number of paper sheets. These may run to hundreds where BOOK covers a lengthy program of information. Each sheet bears a number in sequence, so that the sheets cannot be used in the wrong order. To make it even easier for the user to keep the sheets in the proper order, they are held firmly in place by a special locking device called a "binding."

197

Each sheet of paper presents users with an information sequence in the form of symbols, which they absorb *optically* for automatic registration on the brain. When one sheet has been *assimilated*, a flick of the finger turns it over and further information is found on the other side. By using both sides of each sheet in this way, a great economy is effected, thus reducing both the size and cost of BOOK. No buttons need to be pressed to move from one sheet to another, to open or close BOOK, or to start it working.

BOOK may be taken up at any time and used by merely opening it. Instantly it is ready for use. Nothing has to be connected up or switched on. Users may turn at will to any sheet, going backwards or forwards as they please. A sheet is provided near the beginning as a location finder for any required information sequence.

A small accessory, available at trifling extra cost, is the BOOKmark. This enables the users to pick up their program where they left off on the previous learning session. BOOKmark is versatile and may be used in any BOOK.

The initial cost varies with the size and subject matter. Already a vast range of BOOKs are available, covering every conceivable subject, and adjusted to different levels of aptitude. One BOOK, small enough to be held in the hands, may contain an entire learning schedule. Once purchased, BOOK requires no further cost; no batteries or wires are needed, since the motive power, thanks to the ingenious device patented by the makers, is supplied by the brain of the user.

BOOKs may be stored on handy shelves, and for ease of reference the program schedule is normally indicated on the back of the binding.

Altogether the Built-in Orderly Organized Knowledge seems to have great advantages with no drawbacks. We predict a big future for it.

1. RESPONDING TO THE ESSAY

a. What is the author's opinion about learning information from books as opposed to "electronic gadgets"? Do you agree or disagree with this opinion? Explain.

.b. How has the author used **satire** to express his point of view? Is this an effective way for the author to make a point? Support your opinion by jotting down three examples of satire from the essay. Share these with your class.

> **Satire** is a type of writing that uses humour and irony to point out what is wrong with an organization, person, or society.

c. In your notebook, create a chart comparing learning with books and learning with computers. Work with a partner to generate ideas. Summarize your conclusions in an oral presentation to the class.

2. ORAL COMMUNICATION FORMAL DEBATE

In groups of three, organize and hold a formal debate on the following topic: "Books will always be used in our society as a source of learning and entertainment." You will need to select two debaters, a chairperson, and a panel of judges from the class.

For tips on debating, see page 142. Remember that a successful debate requires you to express your beliefs in a straightforward manner.

SELF-ASSESSMENT: Do you think you presented your ideas convincingly? In what ways might you have improved? Write your observations as a journal entry and refer to it the next time your class holds a debate.

3. LANGUAGE CONVENTIONS ACRONYMS

The essay states, "The new device is known as Built-in Orderly Organized Knowledge. The makers generally call it by its initials, BOOK." This is an example of an *acronym*, a word formed from the first letters or syllables of other words. They are used frequently in English. How often do you and your classmates use acronyms? What are they? What do they represent?

With a partner, brainstorm a list of familiar acronyms. Beside each one, record a definition and a note on its origin. You may want to consult a dictionary. List other examples that you find in magazines and newspapers, or on Web sites. Share these acronyms, definitions, and origins with your classmates.

It's the hottest way to connect instantly with friends near and far.

Instant Messaging

NEWSPAPER ARTICLE BY LINDA MATCHAN

It's 11:15 p.m. and all is quiet at Ariel Klemmer's house. The home-work's done. The folks are in bed. Even Chip, the pet chinchilla, is down for the night.

But Ariel, 17, is in the family room, hunkered down in front of the computer, where things are just starting to heat up. In their respective homes, the same is true for Eric Hou, Nisha Hirani, Brian Hemond, Casey Sukeforth, and Erica Holland, to name just a few friends Ariel will be "i.m.-ing" tonight.

Instant messaging, an Internet tool that lets computer users have live conversations, is to teenagers of the cyber-generation what the phone was to baby boomers—stupefying parents who can't understand what their kids could be saying to each other for so long, and effectively denying computer access to anyone else in the household.

It's not e-mail, since conversations are held in real time. It's not a chat room, since conversations take place between two people (although several can be held simultaneously, in different windows),

GOALS AT A GLANCE

■ Hold an informal class discussion.
■ Use colons and parentheses.

and messages can only be sent to and from people on the user's own predetermined "buddy list" if they happen to be online at the time.

Instant messaging is more like a written telephone conversation. Or the script of a play. It's real life, for better or worse.

An actual conversation:

Brian to Ariel (who is also talking to Casey): What's up :).

Ariel to Brian: Not much.

(Sound of a door slamming, an America Online gimmick to indicate that someone who is online is getting off.)

Ariel to Eric: Why did Erica leave?

Eric: I dunno, she's done that, like, five times.

Ariel to Eric: Freaky.

Eric to Ariel: Yeah, weird. (He steers the conversation to his plans to get a passport.) My dad says it'll take like 10 days.

Ariel to Eric: Can you pay to get it done right away?

Eric to Ariel: It's $35. That's 3 1/2 Presidential Breakfasts (at Bickford's restaurant) with 3 1/2 sides of toast. I'm too cheap.

◆ ◆ ◆

According to a spokesperson for America Online, which popularized the use of instant messaging, some 432 million instant messages travel across AOL each day, but there are no figures on the age of the senders. (A number of other services, such as ICQ and Yahoo, offer instant messaging, too.)

But it's a good guess, based on interviews with teens, that a large percentage of the users are high-school and junior-high-school students, along with some of their copycat siblings in elementary school.

In the household of the Joyce family, 12-year-old Caitlin has 89 i.m. buddies on her list, while her younger sister Kristin, 9, has (at last count) 82.

"It's like a little party every night," observes Dan Klemmer, Ariel's father.

From a teen's point of view, the advantages are numerous. Instant messaging doesn't make the phone ring and wake up parents. It makes gossip instantaneous. You can talk to several people at once—and surf the Web for a homework project, on a different window, at the same time. (You can also listen to music and eat a bowl of cereal.)

"I actually get a lot of work done while I'm online," says Eric Hou, 18, a senior at Lexington High. "It's not like substantial 10-page essays, but if I have some busy work, I'll do that, like 10 problems in math."

Bopping from conversation to conversation, from window to window, isn't much of an exertion to him. "It doesn't seem to bug me that much," he says. "I've grown up around computers. It's just been, like, this big thing in my life."

Did someone mention a generation gap? "I am usually stunned when someone sends me [an i.m.]," says Sue Cohen, a lawyer and mother of two i.m.-literate daughters. "It's not like when you go to your mailbox and you take a letter out and look at the return address and open it up. Someone knows you're online. That blows me away."

◆ ◆ ◆

Not surprisingly, a network of rules and etiquette has evolved around teenage i.m. use, for example:

• It is important to be considerate of others. Always answer promptly, for fear of being labelled "boring" or of being "cancelled," whereby one user chooses not to get another's messages. Don't overdo visual devices ("I've been said to abuse smiley faces," confesses Erica Holland.).

• Changing your screen names frequently is cool, especially among younger i.m.-ers. "I just, like, get sick of one," says Caitlin Joyce, 12, whose recent screen names have included *shamrock23*, *joycer27*, and *fitchlax1* (a composite of her combined interests in the clothing store Abercrombie & Fitch and lacrosse).

• No thought or observation is too trivial or mundane, for example, "I'm hungry" or "my foot fell asleep."

• Abbreviations, code, and shorthand are encouraged, as in **lol** ("laughing out loud"), **brb** ("be right back"), and **jk** ("just kidding").

• Speed is favoured over precision; proper spelling and punctuation may be disregarded.

◆ ◆ ◆

What is an adult to make of this rapid-fire, minimalist form of socializing?

Parents seem to either love it or hate it. They worry that it's keeping their kids up at night and preventing them from getting their homework done. On the other hand, they always know where their kids are. And it improves their typing skills.

"Kids are under a lot of pressure now," says Ariel's mother, Toby Kaplin. "It's a nice release."

As for the experts, some say that beyond the novelty factor, there are some developmental advantages to this form of socializing.

"Kids really want to have a group identity and connect with kids as part of separating from parents without really separating," says John Suler, a professor at Rider University in New Jersey who specializes in the psychology of cyberspace. "The computer is a nifty solution to that."

Carol Weston, a teen expert and columnist for *Girls' Life* magazine, believes instant messaging is a "less intimidating" form of communication for some teens, eliminating the need for scary eye contact.

On the other hand, instant messaging makes it "easy to feel excluded," says Steve Bennett, who has written extensively about computers and kids, including the book *Plugged-in Parent* (Random House, 1998). "The sad thing is there are kids who just kind of sit there and wait for someone to answer."

And the "emotionless aspect of instant messaging may not, he fears, be entirely benign. "It does not encourage thoughtful reflection," he says. And smiley faces aside, "it's an emotionless form of communication."

NAVIGATING YOUR WAY THROUGH CYBERSPACE
Safety Tips by Janice Turner

Feeling overwhelmed by cyberspace and its potential hazards?

Here are some tips to help you start surfing more safely. They represent a sampling of advice from online service providers, Web safety advocates, police, and school officials.

- Use a code or gender-neutral name. Never give out any identifying information, such as your address, telephone number, name or location of your school, or personal details about your parents or family.

  Listen to your instincts. If someone wants to know detailed or intimate information about you, and you start to feel uncomfortable—don't respond. You are under no obligation to tell anyone online anything—no matter how important, impressive, or persuasive they may sound.

- Chat rooms can be particularly dangerous. The person you are talking to may not be who they say they are (a 16-year-old girl could just as easily be a 40-year-old man). What you say in a chat is entirely public.

- Some Web sites ask for information in exchange for a promotional item or contest entry. Don't provide any details about yourself or anyone else without first checking with a parent or adult.

- An e-mail address can be fake. Don't open e-mail from an address you don't recognize. E-mail can be easily copied and forwarded to others, so if you send personal information to friends, ask them to respect your privacy.

- When you post a message to a newsgroup (bulletin board or forum) you give out your e-mail address. In most cases, what you type is available for anyone to view.

- Never agree to get together with someone you "meet" online without checking with a parent or trusted adult first. If you do meet, do so in a public place—and take a parent with you.

- Don't send anyone your photograph or accept any photos.

- Don't accept a file from a source you don't know extremely well. Some programs, accepted unknowingly (sent to you as a "promotion" or a "game," for example), can give the sender total remote access to your computer.

- Report any harassment or inappropriate messages to your online service provider and to police.

1. RESPONDING TO THE ARTICLE

a. How would you describe instant messaging ("i.m.-ing") to someone who knows nothing about it?

b. Do you think i.m.-ing is an effective and efficient way to connect with friends? Discuss the advantages and disadvantages with a partner. Refer to the information and opinions presented in the article.

c. What are some good rules or precautions to follow when you're i.m.-ing?

2. ORAL COMMUNICATION INFORMAL CLASS DISCUSSION

In the article, Steve Bennett claims that instant messaging can leave some teens feeling excluded. As a class, discuss this. Do you think instant messaging could have this effect on some teens? How might this happen? Explain why you agree or disagree with his viewpoint.

Are there any other statements in this article that you strongly agree or disagree with? Discuss them with your classmates.

3. LANGUAGE CONVENTIONS COLONS AND PARENTHESES

Linda Matchan, the author of this article, uses *colons* (:) to show clearly who is posting each message. She uses *parentheses* [( )] to add any extra information that will make things clearer for the reader. An example from the article follows:

> **Eric to Ariel: Yeah, weird. (He steers the conversation to his plans to get a passport.) My dad says it'll take like 10 days.**

Review the article and locate other examples of colons and parentheses. Then, using a language handbook, find out how to use both of these punctuation marks effectively when writing conversations. Record this information in your notebook. It can serve as a reference for you the next time you are creating dialogue in a story or article.

The Path of Our Sorrow

Poem by Karen Hesse

Miss Freeland said,
"During the Great War we fed the world.
We couldn't grow enough wheat
to fill all the bellies.
The price the world paid for our wheat
was so high
it swelled our wallets
and our heads,
and we bought bigger tractors,
more acres,
until we had mortgages
and rent
and bills
beyond reason,
but we all felt so useful, we didn't notice.
Then the war ended and before long,
Europe didn't need our wheat anymore,
they could grow their own.
But we needed Europe's money
to pay our mortgage,
our rent,
our bills.
We squeezed more cattle,
more sheep,
onto less land,
and they grazed down the stubble
till they reached root.

GOALS AT A GLANCE

■ Analyse rhythm and rhyme.
■ Create a collage to reflect selections.

And the price of wheat kept dropping
so we had to grow more bushels
to make the same amount of money we made before,
to pay for all that equipment, all that land,
and the more sod we plowed up,
the drier things got,
because the water that used to collect there
under the grass,
biding its time,
keeping things alive through the dry spells
wasn't there anymore.
Without the sod the water vanished,
the soil turned to dust.
Until the wind took it,
lifting it up and carrying it away.
Such a sorrow doesn't come suddenly,
there are a thousand steps to take
before you get there."
But now,
sorrow climbs up our front steps,
big as Texas, and we didn't even see it coming,
even though it'd been making its way straight for us
all along.

September 1934

Ride Forever

Song Lyrics by **Paul Gross and David Keeley**

I was born up north of Great Slave, 1898
And I rode near all my life on a ranch near Devil's Gate
And I seen this world about me bend and flip and change
Hey, it feels like rain — it's a thundercloud

I could be a coward but I've seen two world wars
And I lost my son Virgil — my Korean reward
And my Lucy died last summer and you ask me if I cry
Hey, I'll show you tears — they're all over this ground
They're falling from these Blue Alberta skies

Chorus:
But I'm going to ride forever
You can't keep horsemen in a cage
Should the angels call, well it's only then
I might pull in the reins

Now, they tell me I'm an old man, they tell me I am blind
They took my driver's licence, this house ain't far behind
I say: jump back all you big suits you got something wrong
Cause I ain't gone, no I ain't gone

I am still breathing, I still have my pride
And I have my memories — your life it never dies
Like the wind that blows in thunder, like the stallion on the fly
I got it all and I'm standing tall
Underneath these Blue Alberta skies

Chorus Repeat

Now I say to all you old men: don't let yourself be broke
If you think the world's gone crazy and it's scratching at your
    throat
It's time to dust off that old saddle, get it on a horse
Kick up your spurs, we're gonna run like stink
We're gonna tear across these Blue Alberta skies

We're gonna ride forever
You can't keep horsemen in a cage
Should the angels call
Well, it's only then we might pull in the reins

1. RESPONDING TO THE POEM AND SONG

a. What seems to be the overall theme in both the poem and the song? With a partner, try to determine why these selections were grouped together. How do they relate to the unit's theme of "Technology: In Our World"?

b. What is the setting of the poem? the song? What do the settings have in common? How are they different? Explain.

c. Miss Freeland in "The Path of Our Sorrow" mentions the Great War. What war is she referring to?

d. The narrator of "Ride Forever" speaks of his "Korean reward." What is meant by this?

2. ORAL COMMUNICATION RHYTHM AND RHYME

With a partner, read the selections aloud to one another. Remember to read slowly and listen carefully so that the rhythm and rhyme can be heard and felt. In which piece do you hear more rhythm? more rhyme? Which selection do you and your partner prefer? Compare your responses with other classmates.

How do rhythm and rhyme contribute to your overall enjoyment and comprehension of the selections? Write your response in a journal entry in which you record certain lines or phrases that are memorable.

3. VISUAL COMMUNICATION CREATE A COLLAGE

Create a collage of images that connect the two selections and their themes. Use magazine photos, bits of coloured paper, string, natural materials, drawings, or text from the poem or song. Mount the collage on Bristol board or some other equally sturdy material. Then display it for your class, explaining what it represents.

*How can technology help
us save the planet?*

On the Trail
to a
Greener Future

Article by Sue Kanhai

The roads in a big city can assault the senses: horns blow, cars and trucks streak by, and exhaust pipes belch fumes. Thankfully, there are places in the city where we can escape the traffic. Greenery, parklands, and pedestrian and bicycle paths are all evidence of an urban core that retains healthy values. In particular, the presence of people on bicycles— whether going to work or school, shopping, or just out for a spin—is an important sign of a green city.

Commuting by bicycle results in wiser land use, cleaner air, reduced congestion on the roads, and improved lifestyle habits. Health-wise, it's a great way to squeeze regular exercise into a busy schedule. Economically it makes a great deal of sense, as expenses for parking, fuel, car maintenance, and transit fares are saved. Of course, the environment wins too. Since the bicycling season coincides with the worst air quality levels of the year, riding helps to reduce pollution when it is most needed. One caution is necessary though, and it's that cyclists may need to wear air filters if they're travelling the same routes as motorized vehicles.

GOALS AT A GLANCE

■ Respond critically to the article.
■ Exchange ideas in small group discussions.

211

In 1995, *Bicycling* magazine rated North America's "10 Best Cities for Cycling." Three Canadian cities made the list: Toronto (#1), Ottawa (#8), and Vancouver (#10). Toronto was given an "eh-plus" for its impressive blend of programs, ridership, and natural amenities. In Ottawa, parking spaces had to be removed to make room for bicycle racks. In Vancouver, several projects have focussed on accommodating pedestrians and cyclists, and the community has responded enthusiastically. While Canadians are certainly off to a good start, it's just that—a beginning. Statistics Canada's 1996 Census reported that 1.12% of the Canadian population biked to work. (A ridership figure over 1% or 2% is considered "not bad.") While residents of Victoria, B.C., clearly led the way at 4.9%, this was the exception rather than the rule. In fairness, the national statistics are pretty respectable given Canadian weather patterns coast to coast.

Changing established habits can be tough. The best strategy may simply be to make cycling an appealing and accessible option. For example, the Region of Ottawa-Carleton and OC Transpo, the local transportation network, together launched "GreenCommute" in March of 1999. The program aims to promote alternative forms of transportation, thereby reducing automobile traffic and pollution levels. Local businesses can also play an important role. Some companies offer as incentives to bicycling employees:
- shower facilities
- storage lockers
- parking for bicycles
- cash bonuses given yearly to help riders maintain their bikes

If you want to see more bicycles and fewer cars in your town or city, you might:

- Call your local bicycling club and tell them you're interested in bike-advocacy issues.

- Contact your local city council, and let them know that safe, connected, and continuous bicycle paths are important to you.

- Do more than just consider alternative forms of transportation, *use* one. A simple change could mean a healthier tomorrow for both you and your neighbourhood.

1. RESPONDING TO THE ARTICLE

a. Why would local businesses want to encourage bicycling?

b. What do local weather patterns have to do with the number of people biking to work or school?

c. What benefits does this article list about increased bicycle use? Who benefits? With a partner, discuss the advantages and disadvantages of increasing the number of bicyclists on city streets.

d. Why do you think it's so important for more people in large cities to use bikes? Do you think increasing the number of bicyclists in smaller towns, or in the country, is as important? Why or why not?

e. What factors would a person need to consider when choosing to ride a bike to school or work?

2. ORAL COMMUNICATION EXCHANGE IDEAS

In a small group, discuss other tools or technologies that can be used to help the environment. Do any of these have a "down side"? How many of these technologies are you using every day?

Copy the T-chart at right into your notebook. With your group, generate ideas and fill it in. Make sure to support each item you include with a note that explains how it helps or harms the environment. Try to list both negative and positive factors for each technology.

Share your chart with the class. Discuss how people can be encouraged to use "helpful" technologies. Why do you think we continue to use technologies that harm the environment? With your class, draw some conclusions about the use of technology in the modern world.

Technologies That Help the Environment	Technologies That Harm the Environment
• bikes—because biking doesn't use gas or cause pollution	• cars—because cars use gas, cause pollution, and use up other resources
•	•
•	•
•	•
•	•
•	•

A young girl dedicates her life to science, and discovers some of the most important technologies of our time.

A Mysterious Contraption

PROFILE BY AMELIE WELDEN

Irène was surrounded by army doctors, medical equipment, and wounded soldiers. Blood was everywhere, and she could hear the battle raging in the distance over the cries of the sick and dying men around her. But eighteen-year-old Irène Curie was used to these horrifying distractions and focussed her attention on setting up the new machine. The French doctors and nurses at the army hospital wondered what young Irène's mysterious contraption was all about.

When she finished setting up, Irène asked for a patient to volunteer. The doctors and nurses gasped in amazement as the soldier's leg bone magically appeared on the screen before them. They could see completely *inside* his leg—through the skin, the blood, and the muscle—right to the bone. And they could see exactly where the bone was broken. Irène was showing them the radioactive technology she and her mother had been working on—the groundbreaking X-ray machine!

GOALS AT A GLANCE

■ Write an opening anecdote.
■ Use a dictionary to check the meaning of words.

214

Irène Curie was born to Nobel Prize-winning scientists Pierre and
Marie Curie on September 12, 1897, in Paris. Her parents spent
much of their time working, so she and her younger sister were
largely raised by their grandfather, especially after Pierre's death in
1906. Irène was tall for her age and very athletic. Her favourite sports
were biking, skiing, horseback riding, and mountain climbing, all
of which she continued throughout her life. She was a quiet and
thoughtful child who loved nature, poetry, and reading, but most
of all, science. Although many girls were discouraged from studying
math and science at the time, Marie Curie strongly supported her
daughters' education in these subjects.

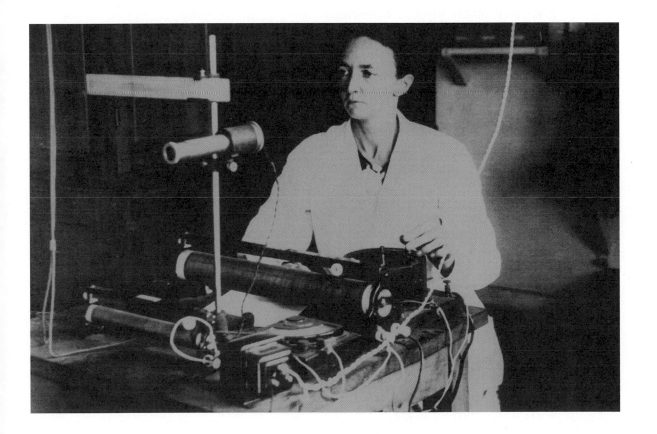

In fact, Marie considered most French schools too narrow in their academic offerings. So she started a co-operative school for her daughters and for eight other children of university professors. The professors themselves taught lessons in art, literature, science, math, English, and German. The co-operative school lasted only a couple of years, though, and after that Irène spent two years at a private girls' school. She later attended the prestigious Sorbonne University in Paris and received her doctoral degree for her studies of alpha particles in 1925.

Throughout her life, Irène was greatly inspired by her mother. Marie Curie was the first French woman to earn a doctoral degree, the first woman to teach at the Sorbonne, and the first woman in the world to win a Nobel Prize (she won two—the first in physics and the second in chemistry). Irène learned a lot from her mother, and they often worked together.

When World War I broke out in 1914, Irène and Marie put together X-ray units for the battlefront. Irène travelled to the French front lines to set them up and teach people how to use them. She showed doctors and nurses how to take X-rays of soldiers' wounds and locate bone breaks and pieces of shrapnel in the images. She then helped surgeons determine the best angle from which to enter the wounds for treatment.

After the war, Irène continued as her mother's assistant at the Radium Institute of the University of Paris. There she met her future husband and research partner, Frédéric Joliot. They married in 1926 and had two children, Hélène in 1927 and Pierre in 1932.

After their marriage, Irène and Frédéric began referring to themselves as the "Joliot-Curies." Together, they conducted ground-breaking experiments and wrote hundreds of reports. In 1934, Irène and Frédéric began experimenting with two metals, polonium and aluminum. Their results led them to a revolutionary discovery—they could create artificial radioactivity! This discovery earned Irène and Frédéric the 1935 Nobel Prize in chemistry. With this award, Irène and her mother, Marie, became the only mother and daughter to both win a Nobel Prize.

Sadly, Marie couldn't share in her daughter's triumph. At the time, no one knew how deadly it was to be exposed to radioactive chemicals. Because of her intense contact with these chemicals in her research, Marie died of leukemia one year before Irène's Nobel Prize was awarded.

After her mother's death, Irène took over the Radium Institute, and Frédéric started work as a scientist at the Collège de France. Irène joined several women's rights groups, speaking out in favour of a woman's right to hold a job *and* raise a family. In 1936, she became one of the first woman cabinet members in France when she was named as the under secretary of state for scientific research. She resigned from her office after only a few months, however, because politics took too much time away from her science.

Irène continued her research, and in 1938 she conducted another groundbreaking experiment. Although she considered her conclusions useless because they did not support what she was working on, later scientists repeated her experiment and realized that Irène had actually discovered *nuclear fission* (the splitting apart of atoms). Her results were analysed by nuclear physicists and laid the crucial foundation for this important area of study.

Irène dedicated her life to her research and continued working in the laboratory until her death in 1956. Like her mother, she also died of leukemia, giving her life for her work. The French government organized a national funeral to honour the life of this great scientist who made some of the most significant scientific discoveries of her time.

----

1. RESPONDING TO THE PROFILE

a. With your class, list some of Irène's scientific accomplishments during the 1920s and 1930s.

b. What career and personal advice did Irène Joliot-Curie receive from her mother? Do you think this helped her achieve great success?

c. What is so unusual about Irène's actions for someone of her age? Do you think it would have been easy or difficult for her to convince the medical teams and soldiers to use the X-ray machine? Explain.

2. WRITING OPENING ANECDOTE

Read the first two paragraphs of this selection. The author has used an *anecdote* (an interesting event or incident) to introduce us to the main character in a way that holds our attention and has great impact. How effective is this technique? Did you want to find out more about Irène based on the opening paragraphs? Explain.

Reread the entire selection and choose another incident that you could use to develop an alternate anecdote. Write your new introduction for the selection based on this information. How does this technique personalize the selection and make it more pleasing to read?

3. WORD CRAFT USE A DICTIONARY

"A Mysterious Contraption" uses many scientific words, such as *polonium* and *nuclear fission*. Make a list of all the scientific words in the text that are unfamiliar to you. Use a dictionary and find their definitions. Then, in the role of Irène, write a diary entry in which you use these words to describe your work at the Radium Institute of the University of Paris. Refer back to the article for details.

Sometimes siblings are closer than they realize.

A CLOSE Match

SHORT STORY BY HELEN DUNMORE

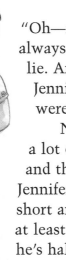

"Oh—is she really your sister?" People are always asking me that, as if I'd bother to lie. And then they look from me to Jennifer. "I'd never have guessed you were sisters."

Nor would I. I used to make up a lot of stuff about being adopted, and that was why Mum and Jennifer were tall and fair, and I was short and dark. But my dad's dark, or at least he was before he went grey, and he's half a head shorter than Mum.

GOALS AT A GLANCE

■ Prepare and write a monologue.
■ Analyse foreshadowing.

219

"It's funny how different sisters can be, isn't it?" That's what my aunts and uncles say. But it's not all that funny for me, because the difference is that Jennifer's got everything. She has long legs that go deep brown in summer, and thick smooth hair that gets blonde streaks in it. She's one of those people who always look right. And she's easy to be with. She doesn't get prickly and hurt and bad-tempered. She doesn't fall out with people. She doesn't get into rages when Mum asks her about homework, or slam her door and knock her best pottery elephant off the shelf and smash it. Jennifer's always done her homework. Sheet after sheet of it, in her beautifully neat round handwriting, handed in on time. Her marks are always good enough, but not too good. Nobody calls Jennifer a keener.

And then there are Jennifer's clothes. Mum's always saying, "I give each of you girls exactly the same clothes allowance. Can you please tell me, Kim, why you never have anything to wear?" Yes, Mum, I can tell you. Because I bought those jeans which would only have fitted me if I'd grown about ten centimetres taller and ten centimetres slimmer. Because I didn't read the care label on my new red top, which was the best thing I ever bought—even Jennifer wanted to borrow it. When it came out of the machine it was a sad red rag, and the two white towels I'd put in with it were sad pink rags. Mum made me pay for them, because they were new, so that was another forty dollars, and now, surprise, surprise, I haven't got anything to wear. Jennifer doesn't spend much on clothes, but she always looks fantastic.

"Where did you get that skirt, Jennifer?"

"Oh, it was in the sale at River Island. It was only ten dollars. It was the last one."

The last one. Of course.

Jennifer does gymnastics, and she's on the school netball team and the school tennis team. I love watching her play tennis. She seems to know just where the ball's going to go, and she's suddenly there with her racket, ready to hit it back. I asked her once how she did it, but she frowned and said, "I don't know." She doesn't even care about winning. If she loses she just shrugs and says, "It was a nice game, anyway."

But Jennifer hasn't been playing much tennis this summer. I wanted to book a court yesterday, but she said, "Not today, Kim. I don't feel like it." She lay sprawled on the grass, with a book beside her which she wasn't reading.

"Are you okay?" I asked. She nodded, and picked up the book and pretended to read it again. She didn't look that great. Later on I was playing CDs in my room when I heard Mum's voice. She sounded really angry. Angry? With Jennifer? I opened the door a crack, and listened.

"I don't ask you to do much, Jennifer, but I don't expect to come in from work and find you haven't cleared the kitchen. You may be on holiday, but I'm not. I expect to have to chase after Kim when it's her turn, but not you."

She was really shouting. I shut the door. I could feel a little secret grin curling over my face. A little later I heard Jennifer clattering the dishes, and the water gushing in the sink.

Things went on like that for a while. It was different from every other holiday. Jennifer didn't go out. When her friends rang she said she was busy. After a while they stopped ringing so much. She lay out on the grass day after day, with a book or a magazine or her radio.

Sometimes she fell asleep for hours. It was so boring. When Mum came home she'd ask what we'd been doing and I'd say I'd been round to Katie's, or I'd been making chocolate brownies or whatever. Jennifer wouldn't say anything. She'd drift upstairs, looking as if she still had the sun in her eyes. Once I came out of the kitchen and I saw her standing halfway up the stairs, quite still, holding onto the banister and staring at nothing.

I thought it was going to go on for ever. Jennifer never even asked what I was doing. I could have done anything I wanted, all those long, hot holidays. But suddenly everything changed. I'd been swimming with Katie and Lisa, but they were going off to have lunch at the local hamburger joint and I hadn't any money, so I came home alone. It was very hot and there was hardly anyone out on the streets. I went in through our back garden gate, and there was Jennifer as usual, sprawled on her back in the sun. But there was something about the way she was lying which was different. And her face looked wrong. It was a dirty-washing-up-water colour.

"Jennifer? *Jennifer!*" She didn't answer. She didn't move. I dropped my stuff on the grass and ran to her. My heart was banging and my fingers were sweaty. I had a horrible feeling that she wasn't ever going to answer. I bent down and shook her shoulder. Then her eyes opened and she looked at me.

"Are you okay? What's happened?"

"I feel funny. I think I fainted. Kim, get Mum."

"Mum's at work."

Jennifer tried to sit up. Her hair was dark with sweat and it stuck to her forehead. She looked awful, as if she was going to be sick.

"Kim, get Mum," she said again, as if she hadn't understood about Mum being at work.

"Okay. I won't be a minute. Listen, just stay there, Jennifer, all right?" I ran across the grass to the kitchen door. If I used the kitchen phone I could still see Jennifer. She looked so bad. She looked...

"Mum! Mum, it's Jennifer..."

That was the beginning. After that it was like a tide coming in. You think you've got plenty of time, because the water's only up to your knees. Then you're thigh-deep, and the waves are pushing you hard. Suddenly the sea's all around you, and then between one wave and the next you lose your footing and when you reach down there's nothing, only deep, cold water. No matter how hard you struggle towards land, you can't get there again.

Everything changed. Mum took Jennifer to the doctor that same evening because she still looked so awful.

"It's probably nothing, but we'll just get you checked over." And she must have phoned Dad, because he came home early too, and cooked fried chicken with rice and peas, and made a lot of jokes which didn't really hide the way either of us felt when surgery time was long over and Jennifer and Mum still didn't come back.

Jennifer was having tests. That's why they'd been so long. Mum looked pale, too.

"What kind of tests?" I asked Jennifer when Mum went upstairs to change.

"Oh. Blood and stuff. He looked at my legs."

"Looked at your legs? What's wrong with your legs?"

"They've got all—" she paused, "bruises on them."

"Did somebody hit you? Is that what's wrong?"

Jennifer smiled, very faintly. "Course not. They just came."

She was wearing her white jeans. Suddenly I realized she'd been wearing jeans or a long cotton skirt for about two weeks. Never her shorts or her swimsuit, even though she was always lying in the sun.

"Show me."

Jennifer hesitated. Then she took a quick look at the door to be sure it was shut, and unzipped her jeans. "There."

There were dark, splotchy bruises on her thighs. She looked down at them, then quickly at me. She looked almost...pleading. As if there was something she wanted me to say.

"They're not so bad," I said. "It was worse when you fell off your bike."

"Yes," said Jennifer quickly. "Yes, it was, wasn't it." And she did up her jeans again, looking relieved.

The next thing was that Jennifer had to go to the hospital for more tests. The blood tests hadn't been too clear or something. Mum and Dad went too, but when they came back Jennifer wasn't with them.

"We dropped her off at Martina's," said Mum. "Peel some potatoes for me, would you, Kim?" She went out of the room and I heard her going upstairs, nearly as slowly as Jennifer had done. I peeled the potatoes, then I thought I'd go up and get my CD player so I could listen to music while I laid the table.

Mum's door was open. I just glanced in, the way you do. I wasn't trying to look or anything. Mum was lying on the bed, her face in her pillow. Dad was sitting beside her, with his arms round her as much as he could. They weren't saying anything, but Mum's back was shaking and I could tell she was crying. I went into my room really quickly and grabbed the CD player and went downstairs.

Jennifer came back very late and went straight to her room. I knocked and after a long time she said, "Come in." Then she looked at me and said, "Oh. It's you."

I fiddled with her light switch. "Are you okay, Jennifer? I mean, were the tests all right and everything?"

Jennifer gave me the coldest, hardest look she had ever given me. "Don't be stupid," she said. I felt myself flush red all over, as if I'd done something wrong.

"How can the tests be okay," Jennifer went on in the same voice, "when they're to find out if I've got leukemia and I'm probably going to die?"

Jennifer did have leukemia. Mum and Dad told me. But it didn't mean Jennifer was going to die. The treatment for leukemia was amazing these days. Most people recovered. I sat there while Mum and Dad told me all the hopeful things about leukemia, and I thought of Mum lying on the bed crying, and I knew she'd guessed too, before the test results came back, just like Jennifer had.

It was a few weeks later that Mum came into my room when I was in bed, just before I fell asleep. I knew all sorts of other stuff by then, that I didn't want to know, about white-cell counts and what was normal and what was Jennifer. Mum and Dad said they'd decided to be completely open with me. Jennifer was going to need a lot of treatment but it was going to work. She'd spent a lot of time

in the hospital already. The only thing Jennifer said was, "If my hair falls out, I'm not going to wear a wig." Then she wouldn't talk about any of it any more.

Mum sat on my bed and crossed her legs. It was nearly dark, but I could just about see her face looking at mine.

"Jennifer needs more treatment," she said. "Dr. Aitchison's told us he thinks the best therapy for her at this stage is a bone marrow transplant." That was the way Mum talked then, just like a doctor herself.

"A bone marrow transplant."

"Yes. You see, if Jennifer could receive some healthy bone marrow which can make new cells for her, she'd have a good chance of making a complete recovery."

"How can she? I mean, she can't have other people's bones transplanted."

Mum sighed, as if I was being deliberately stupid. And maybe I was. The whole thing was so horrible I didn't even want to understand it.

"Just the marrow," she said. "They can take it out of a healthy person's bones, and put it into Jennifer's."

"How?" I asked faintly. Mum hesitated.

"The thing is," she said, "the bone marrow has to be a very close match to Jennifer's. It's no good just anybody being a donor, or her body will reject it. But people in a family are often a very close match. So Dad and I are going to be tested to see if we're good enough..." She was silent for a while, then she added, in a brisk voice as if she was asking me to do the washing-up, "But the best chance of a match is from a sibling."

A sibling. I heard the word as if it was just a word, then I understood. "You mean—a sister?"

"Yes, Kim, there's a very good chance that your marrow might be a close enough match."

My bone marrow! I felt completely sick. "You mean—take out my bone marrow and give it to Jennifer?"

"Not all of it, don't be silly, Kim. Just a little bit."

I notice what Mum doesn't say, as well as what she does. I noticed that she didn't say, *It won't hurt.*

"What do they do?"

"Well, they give you an anesthetic of course, so it's just like going to sleep."

"*What do they do, Mum?*"

"It's quite a simple operation. They just take some marrow from your bone—from your hipbone, it'd be—while you're asleep."

"What with? A needle?"

"Well—yes. A sort of needle. Dr. Aitchison said he'd be happy to talk it over with you, if you've got any questions."

You bet I have, I thought, but I didn't say anything. I hate hospitals, I hate illness, I hate needles, and above all I hate doctors explaining things to me as if I'm about two years old.

"It may not happen. You may not be a close enough match," said Mum.

"No," I said. "After all, look how different we are. People are always saying we don't look like sisters."

◆ ◆ ◆

But we weren't as different as everybody thought. The tests showed that Jennifer and I were more alike than anyone had ever believed. I saw Mum's face go shaky with relief, and Dad turned away and whistled through his teeth, because that was what he did when he couldn't handle us seeing how he felt. Then Mum and Dad were both looking at me. It was a strange, strange feeling. I wanted to say, *Take it away. Don't make it have to happen*. But I knew it was too late for that. Only Jennifer didn't react. She didn't look pleased or anything. She looked as if she was thinking about something else.

Jennifer had to have a lot of treatment to get her ready for the bone marrow transplant. She was in a little room on her own and I wasn't allowed to go in, because of infection getting to her. There was glass at the end wall and I used to wave to her and hold up little notes, but she didn't look terribly interested.

"She's very tired," said Mum. "It's the chemotherapy. Better leave her to rest now." But I noticed that one time when Martina came with us, Jennifer sat right up on her bed and wrote little notes back to Martina. The next day she didn't want to see anyone, not even Mum.

"She's worried about her hair," said Mum. Later on, in the car, I pulled my scrunchie off and my hair flopped round my face, as it always did. I tried to imagine what it would be like if it started falling out when I combed it. I tried to imagine a wig, but I couldn't.

But the next day Jennifer wouldn't see me again, and I stopped feeling sorry for her.

"She's such a brat!" I said to Dad in the car on the way back. He didn't say anything.

"Why should I have holes in my bones and get my bone marrow sucked out, just for a brat like her who won't even talk to me?" I thought Dad would be angry with me, but he just met my eyes in the driving mirror. "I can't give you a reason," he said.

And now I'm in the hospital. It's horrible. They've given me something which has dried up my mouth, and I haven't had anything to drink, and I'm really hungry. And there are people clattering about the whole time, and talking to me as if I'm an idiot. And I still haven't seen Jennifer.

And I'm frightened. I wonder if Jennifer's frightened too? She's waiting, all prepared, just as I am, so that as soon as they take my bone marrow it can go into her. And then, maybe, my healthy cells will take root in her and start to grow. After a while they won't be my cells any more, they'll be hers. They'll start making healthy blood for her, the way they should have done all along.

I can hear wheels skidding and squeaking on the linoleum. I know if I look up I'll see a trolley coming, and yet more people with cloth caps over their heads and big smiles on their faces. This time they haven't come to check on me or chat to me. They've come to wheel me away.

I think of the bruises on Jennifer's legs. I think of her hair. Mum says she shuts her eyes when she combs her hair in the morning. Then she says she doesn't care, she isn't going to wear a wig anyway. People will just have to accept her the way she is. And Mum says, *They will*.

Just imagine, I'm a closer match to Jennifer than even Mum or Dad. But when you think of it, that's the way it ought to be. Your mum and dad get old and die, while you've still got a lot of your life left to live. But your sister doesn't die. She grows up, and goes to work, and maybe gets married, and has kids, and grows old, just the way you do. Your sister stays alive as long as you do, till you're two scrunched-up little old ladies together, laughing at the things you used to do when you were little. *Two old ladies*. Are you listening, Jennifer?

But it doesn't matter if you're listening or not. It doesn't even matter if you don't want to see me. We're as close a match as you can get, and there's nothing in the world either of us can do about it.

----

1. Responding to the Story

a. Describe Kim's relationship with her sister, Jennifer, at the beginning of the story. At what point does the relationship appear to change? What events led to this change?

b. How does the author reveal Kim's feelings about her sister? Is it possible to feel close to someone one moment and not the next? Discuss with your class.

c. Uncles and aunts of both girls comment, "It's funny how different sisters can be, isn't it?" What is ironic about this statement?

d. By the end of the story, is Kim convinced that she is no different than her sister? Does she believe they are "as close a match as you can get"? Support your opinions with examples from the selection.

2. ORAL COMMUNICATION A MONOLOGUE

This story is told from Kim's viewpoint. Jennifer rarely speaks, so we do
not know her innermost thoughts. In the role of Jennifer, prepare and write a
monologue in which you express your true feelings. Talk about your illness and
its impact on your family and friends.

Consider the following suggestions when developing your monologue:

- Use scenes from the story.
- Decide what the character's voice will sound like, and what facial
  expressions or gestures she might use.
- Choose props and sound effects to convey mood and setting.

Write your monologue, rehearse it, and present it to a small group.

SELF-ASSESSMENT: How difficult or easy was it for you to relate to
Jennifer's dilemma? What past experience of your own did you use to help
you relate to this character?

3. READING FORESHADOWING

The author uses **foreshadowing** to warn us that
something unusual might happen to Jennifer.
Reread the story, and, with a partner, locate
examples of foreshadowing in the text. How many
of these hints did you find? Is foreshadowing
a good way to create suspense in a story? Explain.

> **Foreshadowing** is a writing
> device used to give a hint about
> what is to come in the story.
> The hint should not be too
> obvious to the reader or it will
> give away the plot and affect the
> story's suspense.

*An Inuk woman helps
her community
preserve its
language and culture
in changing times.*

Preserving a Culture:
A Conversation with Leah Otak

Biography by Catherine Rondina

On April 1, 1999, the map of Canada changed when the Northwest Territories became two separate territories. The eastern portion is now called Nunavut and the western portion remains the Northwest Territories. Change is nothing new to the 27,000 people who reside there. Over the years, the population of Nunavut—85% of which are Inuit—have learned to adapt to the many changes technology and progress have brought to their society. For many people, these changes have a positive effect on their lives, but the traditional ways of life are quickly being abandoned.

It's this loss of culture and tradition that disturbed members of the Inuit community and moved them to take charge of the changing world around them. For Leah Otak, a native Inuit, it became a personal challenge to try and preserve the traditions and language of her ancestors.

Leah was born into a traditional hunting family in Iglurjuat, a small community on Baffin Island. "We lived in a house made out of sod that my father built by hand," explains Leah. "The houses were built in the fall when the sod was frozen and could be cut into blocks and placed together." Their home was made up of one large room with a big bed on which the family all slept together. "We each had our own sleeping bag, which we would lay across the big bed."

GOALS AT A GLANCE

- Develop a personal essay.
- Investigate the Inuktitut language.

NUNAVUT

On April 1, 1999, the new territory of Nunavut came into being, taking in the central and eastern portions of the Northwest Territories.

This fulfils a long-time dream for Inuit. Nunavut is ruled by a public government representing all of its residents. With Inuit making up 85 percent of the population, they assume their rightful place in Canada's federation and take charge of their own destiny.

The people of Nunavut held the territory's first election on February 15, 1999. Their government assumed political responsibility for the further development of Nunavut April 1, 1999. The Government of Nunavut is democratic, public and responsible, with law-making powers similar to those of the Yukon and Northwest Territories governments.

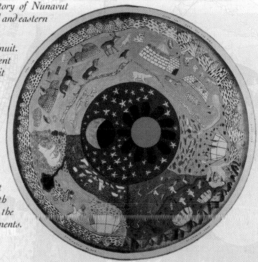

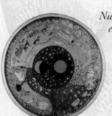

Nunavut is the result of the largest land claim ever settled in Canada. The territory makes up one fifth of Canada's land mass, approximately 2 million square kilometres.

Nunavut means
"OUR LAND"
in Inuktitut, the Inuit language.

http://www.inac.gc.ca

Indian and Northern Affairs Canada   Affaires indiennes et du Nord Canada

Canada

Poster announcing new territory.

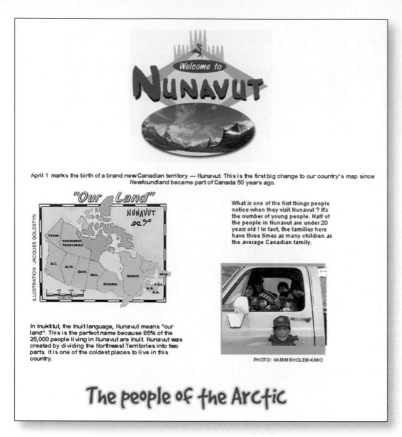

Welcome to **NUNAVUT**

April 1 marks the birth of a brand new Canadian territory — Nunavut. This is the first big change to our country's map since Newfoundland became part of Canada 50 years ago.

"Our Land"

ILLUSTRATION: JACQUES GOLDSTYN

What is one of the first things people notice when they visit Nunavut? It's the number of young people. Half of the people in Nunavut are under 20 years old! In fact, the families here have three times as many children as the average Canadian family.

In Inuktitut, the Inuit language, Nunavut means "our land". This is the perfect name because 85% of the 25,000 people living in Nunavut are Inuit. Nunavut was created by dividing the Northwest Territories into two parts. It is one of the coldest places to live in this country.

PHOTO: KARIM RHOLEM-KIMO

The people of the Arctic

Much of Leah's childhood was spent close to her mother, where she learned traditional sewing methods. "I remember waking up most mornings to hear my mother's sewing stitches," recalls Leah. "She was always sewing skins to make us clothing and we could tell by the sound of the stitches she was putting in what type of animal skin she was working on—that's how quiet it was."

Her father also helped prepare and sew the skins, but it was traditionally the role of the male to hunt and fish for food. "The hunting trips were an exciting time," says Leah, "my older brother would get to go along with the men, who would often be gone for a couple of nights when they were hunting caribou."

Leah and her family spoke the Inuit language Inuktitut. It wasn't until she began school that she was introduced to the English language. In 1960 a school was opened in Igloolik and the children were sent by dog team (a 2- to 3-day trip) to spend the winter there living in hostels and attending school. Separated from their children, many parents decided to come and live in the settlement to be near them. The Otak family, too, moved to Igloolik. There Leah soon learned to speak English, a language her parents would never understand.

It wasn't until Leah was a grown woman, with a family of her own, that events that had taken place began to take their toll on her people. "It was a gradual thing until it just became more and more visible to us," she explains. "We would be out on the land, on ski-doo trips, or fishing, and the elders would use terms that the young people didn't understand. It was like seeing our heritage being lost." That's when Leah and other concerned members of the community decided to take matters into their own hands and find ways to preserve their fading culture.

It began with the discovery of some tape recordings that were made by a university student who had lived with the Inuit. "This fellow was from the outside, and he came up to record the Inuit leadership and he left us the tapes. There was so much vocabulary in it that we got the idea to start recording ourselves," explains Leah.

In 1990 they formed the Igloolik Inullariit Society, an organization of elders that was established to promote and preserve Inuit culture in the Igloolik area. The cassette recordings were their first major undertaking. "We would visit with an elder and ask them to describe a subject, like caribou hunting or a legend," explains Leah. "These elders were born and raised before everyone started to move into the established settlements and were never exposed to another language." Leah is still fascinated by the fact that her people never took notes. All the history has been passed on orally and it is only in the last 100 years that they started to use pen and paper. "The legends followed a very strict rule to not change anything. They are to be told from beginning to end with no alterations anywhere," says Leah. She originally heard the legends from her grandparents and passed them on to her own children, who speak Inuktitut fluently. "Since beginning the oral history tapes, the society now has over 460 hours of recorded history and continues to collect material."

The Inullariit Society also began to encourage language-awareness projects in the community. The group would host special events to raise public interest and allow the community to rediscover its own heritage. The society members would speak about language enhancement at the local school. They adopted an official "Language Week" that promotes the language through games and activities. This takes place each year in conjunction with their "Return of the Sun" celebration in January. "Since we began the language week seven years ago, it has become very popular," says Leah. "At first it was difficult for people to speak Inuktitut, but now almost everyone does."

Another idea the community proposed was to stop mixing the two languages. "We realized that both languages were important to us, but using them together at the same time is what weakened our language in the past," says Leah, whose family follows the rule of never combining the two languages in conversation. The Igloolik people now use one language at a time to express themselves.

All of these extraordinary projects have led to a number of special assignments for Leah. In 1998 she produced a book called *The Arctic Sky* with John MacDonald. In it Inuit legends about the sky, the stars, and star lords are translated, as is information on how to use the stars for navigation. In addition to this, Leah is keeping a journal to record all the words she collects during her interviews with the elders. "Right now I'm just putting them together like a dictionary of terms," she explains. "Someday I hope to put them into vocabulary technique books that describe Inuit traditions."

Leah also hosts her own radio program called *Uquasiliriniq*, which means "talking about our language." Callers of all ages phone in with their questions or concerns about the language. "It's very exciting to do and we get regular callers from the CBC, too," Leah says; she often has elders on the show as featured guests. Her weekly program is one of the most popular shows in the area. With all the positive results from these heritage-awareness programs, Leah, who has been named Director of Culture and Heritage for the new Nunavut government, can't help but feel positive. "The kids, along with the elders, are enthusiastic about the future," she says. "You have to know your culture and your language," she proclaims. "It's the thing that makes us strong."

Some Inuktitut terms and their English meanings:

Inuktitut	English
Ilinniarvik	school
Ilisaiyi	teacher
Siqiniq	the Sun
Ataata	Father
Anaana	Mother
Ikki	cold
Nunavut	Our land

----

1. RESPONDING TO THE BIOGRAPHY

a. Why is it so important for Leah Otak to preserve her Inuit traditions and language?

b. What led to the creation of the Igoolik Inullariit Society? In what projects has the society become involved?

c. Leah Otak believes that preserving the language and traditions of the Inuit culture has had a positive effect on both youth and elders in her community. With your class, discuss why she feels this way, providing specific examples from the selection.

2. WRITING DEVELOP A PERSONAL ESSAY

Do you agree or disagree that it is important for a culture to preserve its heritage? Write a personal essay responding to this question. Use information from the article to support your point of view. Remember to state your opinions clearly. This essay will be added to your writing portfolio.

SELF-ASSESSMENT: What did you base your opinions on? Did you use examples from the selection, other sources, relevant personal experiences, or a combination of all three? Check your work to ensure that you have supported your opinions.

3. MEDIA CREATE A FEATURE ARTICLE

Assume that you are a newspaper reporter interviewing Leah Otak on her appointment to the new Nunavut government as the Director of Culture and Heritage. Based on the information in this selection, write a feature article on her that will appear in your newspaper. Remember to use the *five W's* of newspaper reporting—who, what, when, where, and why. Write your article and display it in your classroom. As an alternative, consider posting it on your school's Web site.

4. WORD CRAFT INVESTIGATE THE INUKTITUT LANGUAGE

Leah keeps a journal in which she collects Inuktitut words during interviews with the elders. Use the Web site address on page 233 to find information on the Inuktitut language. See how many words you can find on this site or others. With a partner, list the Inuktitut words on a chart and write the English equivalents beside them. Compare your chart with another pair's. How different or similar are the Inuktitut words to English?

Goals at a Glance

● Build a content and navigation plan. ● Write content in a style suitable to the Web.

In the professional world, teams of graphic designers, writers, and computer programmers often create Web sites. These teams work together to determine a site's look and feel, its messages, and its sophistication. The process is an ongoing one and costs hundreds of thousands of dollars. However, you can plan, write, and build a personal Web site on your own.

What Do You Like?

Before starting your own site, look at others. The graphic styles and contents of these sites reflect the designer's personality. When surfing, be sure to bookmark the sites that appeal to you, keeping in mind any good ideas you find.

Decide the Contents of Your Site

Web site designers and writers spend a great deal of time and energy in the planning stages of a Web site. You should too. Think about what you want to tell the people who will visit your site and how you want to say it. Remember that a personal Web site is a chance to publish information that is important to you. It can help you to make new friends from afar, get a new job, or publish an online autobiography.

Since everyone in the world will have access to the information posted on your site, be discreet and avoid including too much personal information. You might consider just keeping your Web site on a home computer or on your school's, if possible. Another option is to put it on a floppy disk.

Keep in mind that the Internet is a different medium from books, magazines, television, or radio. Visitors to your site will look for writing that is short, creative, and concise. They will also look for a simple navigation scheme—they'll want to know where they are within the site and will want to be able to get back to the *home page* (the starting point) at all times.

PROCESS

Topics you might consider for a personal Web site are

- About Me
- My Favourite Web Sites
- My School
- My Hometown
- My Favourite Hobbies

You might also want to create a site about a favourite sports team, music group, school subject, or place that you have visited.

Decide Your Site Plan

Web site designers create a chart called the site plan. It shows the content, structure, and navigation. On a blank sheet of paper, draw your site's plan, following the example here. The top square is always the home page.

This page has buttons, or hyperlinks, that the user can click on to get to the other areas or sub-categories of your site. Each sub-category should have links to both the home page and the other sub-categories of the site. For example, if visitors are looking at the "My School" page, they should be able to go directly to the home page or to any of the other main categories.

Write the Content of Your Site

Tackle one subject area at a time. When writing, keep in mind what the site will look like. Be clear, concise, and direct. Plan to include visuals that capture the reader's attention. If you don't "grab" your readers, they'll be off to another site at the click of a mouse!

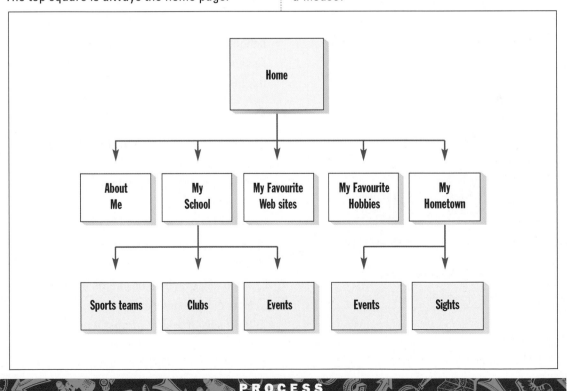

PROCESS

Decide What Graphics to Include

The visual features of your Web site are very important. Include a few key pictures or graphics to enhance your site. However, be aware that too many graphics can leave the site looking cluttered, and can result in a larger file size that will take longer for users to download.

Web sites use two types of graphic files—jpeg and gif. These file types tend to be smaller in size than other formats, making them faster to download.

Include one or two graphics or photos that you've either created or scanned. PaintShop Pro, Adobe Photoshop, Adobe PhotoPaint, or Corel Draw are popular programs you might want to try. Find out from your teacher what is available in your school.

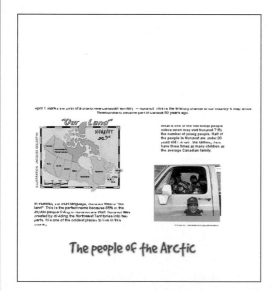

The people of the Arctic

Assemble Your Site

Web pages are built using a language called HTML (Hypertext Markup Language). It uses tags that tell a Web browser how to display a page. The two most common Web browsers used today are Internet Explorer and Netscape Navigator.

Thankfully, many programs exist to help you create sites without having to learn HTML first. These programs let you type in your copy, paste in graphics, and drag and drop these elements to create your pages. Some of the most common programs are:

• Macromedia Dreamweaver
• Microsoft FrontPage
• Adobe Go Live!
• Adobe PageMill

Find out which program is available at your school, or use one that you have at home. Assemble your page. Save it to disk or put it on the Internet.

Self-Assessment

❏ Did I look at other Web sites to find out what appeals to me?
❏ What information did I decide to place on my site?
❏ Did I create a detailed site plan?
❏ How clear and concise is my copy for the site?
❏ What key graphics or photos did I include?
❏ How did I assemble my site?
❏ Did I save it to disk or post it online?

PROCESS

The View from Here

The Great Pyramid
of Khufu [Koo-foo] at Giza

GOALS AT A GLANCE

- Respond critically.
- Examine visuals and captions.

The crowded streets of Mexico City surround the excavated ruins of the Great Temples of Tenochtitlan.

An example of suburban housing patterns of today.

Great Zimbabwe—The Great Enclosure—the largest and most complex structure of Shana society.

A huge eagle-shaped image,
about 30 m long, was built
by the Mississippian people.
This mound can be seen in
Georgia.

The Great Serpent Mound,
located in Adams County, Ohio, was built of clay
in the first century B.C. by the Adena people.
It is about 400 m long and 0.9 m high.

RESPONDING TO THE PHOTOS

In small groups, examine these photos and read the captions.
Speculate as to how these structures were made. Who built them?
Why? What purposes do you think they served?

The Elders Are Watching

POEM BY DAVID BOUCHARD
ILLUSTRATIONS BY ROY HENRY VICKERS

They told me to tell you they believed you
When you said you would take a stand.
They thought you knew the ways of nature.
They thought you respected the land.

They want you to know that they trusted you
With the earth, the water, the air,
With the eagle, the hawk, and the raven,
The salmon, the whale, and the bear.

You promised you'd care for the cedar and fir,
The mountains, the sea, and the sky.
To the Elders these things are the essence of life.
Without them a people will die.

They told me to tell you the time has come.
They want you to know how they feel.
So listen carefully, look toward the sun.
The Elders are watching.

GOALS AT A GLANCE

■ Create an environmental poster.
■ Analyse the use of imagery in a poem.

They wonder about risking the salted waters,
The ebb and flow of running tide.
You seem to be making mistakes almost daily.
They're angry, they're hurting, they cry.

They watch you as you dig the ore from the ground.
You've gone much too deep in the earth.
The pits and scars are not part of the dream
For their home, for the place of their birth.

They say you hunt for the thrill of the kill.
First the buffalo, now the bear.
And that you know just how few there are left,
And yet you don't seem to care.

You said you needed the tree for its pulp,
You'd take but a few, you're aware
Of the home of the deer, the wolf, the fox,
Yet so much of their land now stands bare.

They told me to tell you the time has come.
They want you to know how they feel.
So listen carefully, look toward the sun.
The Elders are watching.

Now, friend, be clear and understand
Not everything's dark and glum.
They are seeing things that are making them smile,
And that's part of the reason I've come.

The colour green has come back to the land.
It's for people who feel like me.
For people who treasure what nature gives,
For those who help others to see.

And there are those whose actions show.
They see the way things could be.
They do what they can, give all that they have
Just to save one ancient tree.

Now I've said all the things that I told them I would.
I hope I am doing my share.
If the beauty around us is to live through this day,
We'd better start watching — and care.

They told me to tell you the time has come.
They want you to know how they feel.
So listen carefully, look toward the sun.
The Elders are watching.

1. RESPONDING TO THE POEM

a. Explain the message of this poem to a partner. Identify who "they" and "you" are in the poem.

b. The poet uses vivid imagery to paint a picture for the reader. What images in this poem appeal to you the most? Why?

c. At the beginning, the speaker's tone, or attitude, is quite serious. Over the course of the poem, it becomes friendlier. What is the reason for this change? Is it believable?

d. How would you describe the structure of this poem? Does understanding the structure help you to interpret the poem? Explain.

e. How do you think this poet feels about "technology in our world"?

STRATEGIES

2. VISUAL COMMUNICATION CREATE A POSTER

This poem has a strong environmental message. Create a poster to raise awareness about an environmental issue in your community. Use photos or drawings, and your own words as well as words from the poem. Think about your message, audience, and purpose. The following steps may help:

- After doing a rough sketch, ask a classmate for feedback about the text and images you've chosen. Use this feedback to develop a second draft.
- Examine your second draft carefully to see how you can change the design for greater impact.
- Develop your final copy of the poster on Bristol board and share it with the class.

SELF-ASSESSMENT: Examine your finished poster. What message does it send? Who is your audience? What is the purpose of your poster? How effectively have you achieved that purpose?

3. POET'S CRAFT ANALYSE IMAGERY

Imagery makes words come alive for the reader. Metaphor, simile, and personification are some of the literary devices that poets use to develop imagery in their work. Imagery can reveal character, create mood, or explain an idea. With a partner, discuss how David Bouchard has used some or all of these techniques in this poem. Make a chart, listing the various types and sources of imagery. Which images are the strongest in this poem?

> **Imagery** is a technique used in description to appeal to the senses. There are many types of imagery, including simile, metaphor, and personification.

REFLECTING ON THE UNIT

SELF-ASSESSMENT: WRITING

As you worked on the activities in this unit, what did you learn about writing or developing

- memoirs
- satirical and personal essays
- monologues
- feature articles
- profiles
- anecdotes
- Web sites
- posters

In your notebook, list some of the key elements that are common to these different forms of writing. How often have you used these elements in your own writing?

WRITING A FEATURE ARTICLE

Interview two or three older relatives or friends about the influence of technology in the workplace during the past ten years. Jot down a few questions to help you start the interviews. Remember to take detailed notes during the conversation. Then write a three-page feature article on technology and the workplace based on the information you gathered. Publish your finished piece in your school newspaper or post it on your school's Web site.

ORAL COMMUNICATION HOLD A DEBATE

In a small group, debate whether or not the Internet and e-mail have increased our abilities to communicate effectively and efficiently with each other. Decide who will be the chair, who will form the opposing sides, and who will sit on the panel of judges. Summarize your conclusions in an oral report to another group. What were the similarities or differences in both groups' findings?

MEDIA *Perspectives*

No Boring Parts Allowed

Poem by Gordon Korman and Bernice Korman

I.

The movie was a thriller;
   I was frozen in my chair;
The city was in ruins —
   there was gunfire everywhere;
The rain came down for six straight weeks;
   the tanks were mired in mud;
A maniac was loose in town;
   the gutters ran with blood.
The hero was in trouble;
   he was hanging by a thread.
There were thirty thousand cannons
   aimed directly at his head.

Below him was the heroine,
   with nitro at her throat.
Their chances of survival
   seemed decidedly remote.
He jumped a measly sixty feet —
   somehow the cannons missed him.
He freed the leading lady,
   they went off and then she — *kissed him?*

      Time out — hang on — hold up!
      By some incredible mischance
      This real artistic action flick
      Turned into a romance!
      It killed the classy things with which
      This movie was endowed,
      And broke my Number One strict rule:
      No boring parts allowed.

II.

The book was fascinating;
    I just couldn't put it down.
A nasty gang of spies was centered
    in this little town.
The author was a genius
    with the deepest bag of tricks.
There had been a hundred murders!
    I was only on page six!
I think it was the car chase
    with the good guys and the crooks
That made me phone to order
    all the author's other books.
A writer of this stature,
    I am quick to emphasize,
Should dry-clean his tuxedo
    to accept the Nobel Prize.
The hero lay in hiding,
    one last bullet in his gun.
There followed a description
    of — *the setting of the sun?*
        I skipped ahead — it was still setting
        After fourteen pages.
        To get through this dumb sunset
        I would have to read for ages!
        The book went for recycling,
        'Cause I have always vowed
        That I would never compromise:
        No boring parts allowed.

III.

I sat awake at two A.M.,
   glued solid to the screen;
It was the greatest TV show
   that I had ever seen.
The Comet-Master, Vorgon,
   went careening past the stars,
Pursued by blaster-demons
   from the government of Mars.

The earth had disappeared,
   and with it, all the human race,
And Vorgon had to find it
   somewhere lost in hyperspace.
At station break I phoned
   to thank the guys at Channel 3.
When I got back, the Martians
   set their guns on "fricassee."
The ship was hit! The hull caved in!
   And things were getting gory,
When Master Vorgon lectured on —
   the moral of the story?

      You interrupt the fighting and
      The killing and the strife
      To have some actor talk about
      The meaning of all life?
      I phoned them back and told them off.
      I'm not ashamed; I'm proud.
      When will these people ever learn?
      No boring parts allowed.

1. RESPONDING TO THE POEM

a. What is the mood of this poem? What words or phrases contribute to it?

b. What is the poet saying about action-adventure movies? Does he have the same attitude towards books? Give examples to support your opinion.

c. People of all ages watch movies or TV shows and read books like the ones described by Gordon Korman. Do these shows or books appeal to you? Why or why not?

d. Why does Gordon repeat the title of the poem within the poem? Is this an effective technique? Explain.

2. MEDIA DRAW CONCLUSIONS

Do people like watching action-adventure movies or reading action-adventure books? With a partner, research the popularity of this genre. You might check a newspaper, magazine, or bookstore for lists of bestselling books. Video stores will have lists of the most popular rentals. How many of the titles fit in the action-adventure category? What conclusions can you draw about the popularity of this genre? Share your conclusions with the class.

STRATEGIES

3. ORAL COMMUNICATION CHORAL READING

With three or four classmates, prepare a choral reading of this poem. As a group, decide how it will be presented—for example, in unison with all group members reading the poem as a whole, or with individual members reciting each stanza separately. Keep the following suggestions in mind:

- Begin and end at the same time when reading in unison.
- Maintain the natural rhythm of the poem.
- Consider which lines or words should be stressed.
- Use your voice to create a dramatic and powerful ending.
- Use music to accompany the poem.
- Practise in front of another group before performing for the class.

PEER ASSESSMENT: Which group recited the poem with the most sensitivity to the mood and rhythm? Were tone, speed, and volume also effective? How does using these techniques lead to a successful choral reading?

HOW TO WRITE A MOVIE REVIEW

Goals at a Glance

- Summarize and describe a movie. • Present an opinion with supporting evidence.

Eveyone loves the movies, but no one wants to waste time and money on a bad movie. As a movie critic, your job is to let the audience know if a specific movie is worth seeing. To be a great critic you should know your audience, be able to state your opinion clearly and concisely, and, most importantly, really love the movies.

Review Styles and Features

Take a look at the variety of movie reviews in newspapers, magazines, video guides, and on Web sites. As you read them, notice the different styles and approaches to reviewing. Three common features in a movie review are
- basic information about the movie
- an opinion on the overall quality of the movie
- supporting evidence to back up the opinion
Other elements of a well-written review include
- a descriptive opening sentence
- the movie title and *genre* (romantic comedy, drama, documentary, and so on)

- the names of the leading actors, producer, director, and sometimes, the cinematographer or writer

At the Movies

Select a movie that you think your readers will want to see. Remember to bring a notebook when you view the movie so that you can make notes either during or shortly after the screening. Jot down the title, the director, the leading actors, and any other pertinent information.

After you've seen the movie, think about your initial reaction to it. Did you like or dislike the acting? Was the writing mediocre or superb? Was the scenery spectacular? Record your responses.

Movie Genres
- Romance
- Comedy
- Drama
- Action-adventure
- Science fiction
- Fantasy
- Horror
- Animation
- Suspense
- Documentary

PROCESS

Writing Your Review

Recall the different types of print and online reviews. Which appealed to you the most? Decide on one style you wish to model. Below are some simple strategies to help you begin writing your review.

1. Your opening sentence should grab the reader's attention by setting the tone and mood of the review. It needs to include a description of the movie as well as your opinion of it. Use vivid adjectives, such as *fast-paced, witty, wild, disturbing, shocking,* or *spectacularly bad.*

2. The synopsis, or summary, of the movie must be brief and concise. It should describe the main action or conflict without giving away the whole story.

3. It isn't enough to say "I didn't like the movie" or "This was the best movie I have ever seen." Reviewers offer evidence to support their personal opinions. Examine why you have such strong feelings about the movie. Ask yourself the following questions:
   - Was the story well-developed?
   - Were the actors believable?
   - Was the movie too long or too short?
   - If it was a comedy, was it funny?
   - Were you entertained throughout the whole movie, or were only parts of it worthwhile?

   If you state that the movie was funny and well-written, give examples of humorous lines. If you claim that the acting was poor, offer reasons. If you have mixed feelings about the movie, sort out what you believe were the good parts and the bad parts. Keep in mind that sometimes it's more difficult to write a review about a movie that leaves you feeling indifferent than one that is simply bad.

4. End with a concluding statement that explains why you liked or disliked it. Did the movie succeed, fail, or simply fizzle? Expressing your personal opinion here is vital, as many readers will determine whether or not to see a movie based on your review.

Self-Assessment

Use the checklist below to assess your review.
- ❏ I researched various types of reviews.
- ❏ I selected a movie that was appropriate for my audience.
- ❏ I watched the movie with a critical eye, examining the writing, acting, cinematography, music, and so on.
- ❏ I recorded my initial reactions to the movie.
- ❏ I informed the readers about the basics of the movie.
- ❏ I presented my opinion and supported it with examples.

PROCESS

How important are heroes?

Here's to You, Joe DiMaggio

Tribute by Paul Simon

My opinions regarding the baseball legend Joe DiMaggio would be of no particular interest to the general public were it not for the fact that 30 years ago I wrote the song "Mrs. Robinson," whose lyric "Where have you gone Joe DiMaggio, a nation turns its lonely eyes to you" alluded to and in turn probably enhanced Mr. DiMaggio's stature in the American iconographic landscape.

A few years after "Mrs. Robinson" rose to number one on the pop charts, I found myself dining at an Italian restaurant where Mr. DiMaggio was seated with a party of friends. I'd heard a rumour that he was upset with the song and had considered a lawsuit, so it was with some trepidation that I walked over and introduced myself as its composer. I needn't have worried. He was perfectly cordial and invited me to sit down, whereupon we immediately fell into conversation about the only subject we had in common.

"What I don't understand," he said, "is why you ask where I've gone. I just did a Mr. Coffee commercial, I'm a spokesman for the Bowery Savings Bank, and I haven't gone anywhere."

I said that I didn't mean the lines literally, that I thought of him as an American hero, and that genuine heroes were in short supply. He accepted the explanation and thanked me. We shook hands and said good night.

GOALS AT A GLANCE

■ Use metaphor and personification in prose.
■ Define words in context.

Now, in the shadow of his passing, I find myself wondering about that explanation. Yes, he was a cultural icon, a hero if you will, but not of my generation. He belonged to my father's youth. He was a World War II guy whose career began in the days of Babe Ruth and Lou Gehrig and ended with the arrival of the youthful Mickey Mantle (who was, in truth, my favourite ballplayer).

In the fifties and sixties, it was fashionable to refer to baseball as a metaphor for America, and Joe DiMaggio represented the values of that America: excellence and fulfilment of duty (he often played in pain), combined with a grace that implied a purity of spirit, an off-the-field dignity, and a jealously guarded private life.

It was said that he still grieved for his former wife, Marilyn Monroe, and sent fresh flowers to her grave every week. Yet as a man who married one of America's most famous and famously neurotic women, he never spoke of her in public or in print. He understood the power of silence.

He was the antithesis of the iconoclastic, mind-expanding, authority-defying sixties, which is why I think he suspected a hidden meaning in my lyrics. The fact that the lines were sincere and that they've been embraced over the years as a yearning for heroes and heroism speaks to the subconscious desires of the culture. We need heroes, and we search for candidates to be anointed.

Why do we do this even as we know the attribution of heroic characteristics is almost always a distortion? Deconstructed and scrutinized, the hero turns out to be as petty and ego-driven as you and I are. We know, but still we anoint. We deify, though we know the deification often kills, as in the cases of Elvis Presley, Princess Diana, and John Lennon. Even when the recipient's life is spared, the fame and idolatry poison and injure. There is no doubt in my mind that DiMaggio suffered for being DiMaggio.

We inflict this damage without malice because we are enthralled by myths, stories, and allegories. The son of Italian immigrants, the father a fisherman, grows up poor in San Francisco and becomes the greatest baseball player of his day, marries an American goddess and never in word or deed befouls his legend and greatness. He is "the Yankee Clipper," as proud as a battleship.

What is the larger significance of Mr. DiMaggio's death? Is he a real hero? Let me quote the complete verse from "Mrs. Robinson":

Sitting on a sofa on a Sunday afternoon
Going to the candidates' debate
Laugh about it, shout about it
When you've got to choose
Every way you look at it you lose.
Where have you gone Joe DiMaggio
A nation turns its lonely eyes to you
What's that you say Mrs. Robinson
Joltin' Joe has left and gone away.

In these days of presidential transgressions and apologies, we grieve for Joe DiMaggio and mourn the loss of his grace and dignity, his fierce sense of privacy, his fidelity to the memory of his wife, and the power of his silence.

1. RESPONDING TO THE TRIBUTE

a. "Here's to You, Joe DiMaggio" is a **tribute**. With your class, discuss how this selection qualifies as a tribute.

b. According to Paul Simon, why is it important to have heroes? Do you think that "genuine heroes" are "in short supply" today? State your own reasons and summarize Paul Simon's arguments.

c. What qualities does DiMaggio have that the author admires? How common are these qualities among people who currently work in politics, sports, or entertainment?

d. How are modern celebrities portrayed by the print or broadcast media? Do you think they are depicted in a fair or realistic way? Explain.

> A **tribute** is an acknowledgment of someone's accomplishments.

2. WRITER'S CRAFT METAPHOR AND PERSONIFICATION

Paul Simon uses **metaphor** and personification to describe Joe DiMaggio. In your notebook, create a chart that is divided into two columns. Reread the selection and jot down under "Metaphor" or "Personification" phrases that demonstrate these literary devices.

Choose two or three of these phrases and model them to describe someone you admire. Share them with the class.

SELF-ASSESSMENT: How easy or difficult is it for you to create original phrases? Check your writing folder. How could you use metaphor or personification in a piece of your own writing? Add your new phrases to your folder and refer to them when next you write an essay.

> A **metaphor** is a writing device in which a word or phrase that usually means one thing is used to describe something else, suggesting that some common quality is shared by the two. For example, *a heart of stone*. Metaphors help to make abstract ideas more concrete, add emotion, and show the writer's feelings.

3. WORD CRAFT DEFINE WORDS

This selection contains many difficult words, such as *trepidation* and *iconoclastic*. Review the selection and list the words that are unfamiliar to you. Can you understand these words based on how they are used in the sentence? In your notebook, create definitions of these words. Then use a dictionary to find out their exact meanings. How closely do your definitions match the ones in the dictionary?

The Radio as Time Machine

Poem by Lorna Crozier

This morning on the radio
Peter talks with a musician.
Five years in Toronto,
she was born in Nova Scotia
where her father
taught her how to play
when she turned three—
her fiddle a sixteenth
the normal size. "Now,"
she says, "it's sitting
on the mantle."
"What would he say," Peter wonders,
"if I asked him
what kind of pupil you were?"
"I don't know."
"Well, put your headphones on,
and let's find out."
"She was a good pupil,"
her father says from Halifax.
"Dad?"
"You should see your daughter,"
Peter says. "She's wearing
a big grin. How come you're
so pleased?"
"It's just so good to hear him."

GOALS AT A GLANCE

■ Participate in group discussions.
■ Write a free verse poem.

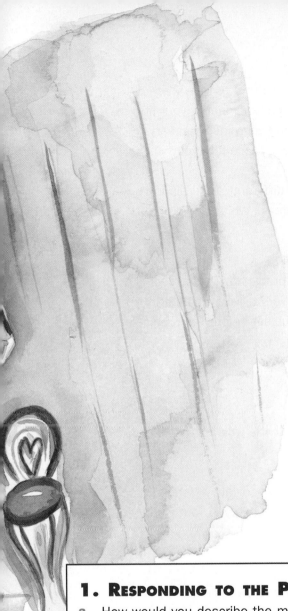

Three years since
my father's death,
I can't help but wish
next time I'm on the radio
Peter will say, "Lorna,
put your headphones on
and we'll ask your dad."
Dad?
Ask him what?
Maybe what he thought
I'd learned from him,
what he thought of me,
—all this time
between us—
even if he had to say
some bad things
with the good,
how I'd be grinning
just to hear
his voice again,
his smoker's cough,
no matter if
the whole country's
listening in.

1. RESPONDING TO THE POEM

a. How would you describe the mood of this poem—happy, sad, or nostalgic? Why?

b. This is a **free verse** poem. Is free verse any easier to understand than a poem that rhymes and has a definite rhythm? Explain.

> A **free verse** poem does not use rhyming words, and may not have a regular rhythm or line length.

c. In what ways does this poem fit with the theme of popular culture and media? Discuss in a small group.

d. What is this poem's message about the importance of radio? As a class, discuss the role radio plays in your lives.

2. WRITING FREE VERSE

Use "The Radio as Time Machine" as a model to write a ten-line free verse poem. Your poem could describe a meaningful moment in your life. Remember that it does not have to rhyme and that your lines can vary in length. Read your finished poem to a classmate. Place it in your writing folder.

SELF-ASSESSMENT: How does free verse sound differently read aloud than a poem that has a strong rhythm or rhyming pattern? Which do you prefer to write? to read?

3. LANGUAGE CONVENTIONS SENTENCE ORDER

Most complete sentences have a subject and a predicate. The *subject* is the main noun or pronoun. The *predicate* is the verb or verb phrase. In English, most statements are formed with the subject before the predicate. This is called *natural order.*

Peter   **talks with a musician.**

Subject   Predicate

...she   **was born in Nova Scotia where...**

Subject   Predicate

Some statements have an *inverted order*, with the predicate before the subject. Using some inverted sentences can create variety in your writing.

Here are   **the books.**

Predicate   Subject

Many questions are formed with the predicate before the subject.

Where are   **your books?**

Predicate   Subject

Most commands or requests have a predicate only, with the subject (usually "you") implied or understood.

Put the headphones on.

Sit down!

Duck!

What happens when a dazed stranger knocks on the door?

Save the Moon for Kerdy Dickus

SHORT STORY BY TIM WYNNE-JONES

This is Ky's story. It happened to her. It happened at her place in the country. I wasn't there when it happened, but I know what her place in the country looks like, and that's important. In this story, the way things look is really important.

There's more than one version of this story. If Ky's younger brothers, Brad or Tony, told you the story, it would come out different. But not as different as the way the Stranger tells it. We know his name now, but we still call him the Stranger. Perhaps you know his version of the story. It was in the newspapers. Well, the *National Enquirer*, anyway.

GOALS AT A GLANCE

- Analyse newspapers and tabloids.
- Use simple sentences for dramatic impact.

Ky's father, Tan Mori, built their house in the country. It's a dome. It looks like a glass ice house, but it's actually made of a web of light metal tubing and a special clear plastic. From the outside you can see right into the house, which Ky didn't like one bit at first, because it wasn't very private. But the house is at the end of a long driveway surrounded by woods, so the only things that can look at you are bluejays, raccoons, the occasional deer, and, from way up high on a hot day, turkey vultures circling the sky.

It wasn't a hot day when this story happened. It was two days before Christmas and there was a bad freezing rain. But let me tell you more about the house, because you have to be able to see the house in order to understand what happened. You have to imagine it the way the Stranger saw it.

For one thing there's all this high-tech office stuff. Ky's parents are both computer software designers, which means that just about everything they do can be done on a computer. Word processors, video monitors, a modem, a fax machine—they're always popping on and off. Their lights blink in the dark.

You also have to know something about Ky's family if you want to see what the Stranger saw when he arrived at their door. You especially have to know that they have family traditions. They make them up all the time. For instance, for the past three years it's been a tradition that I go up from the city for Ky's birthday in the summer, and we go horseback riding. I'm not sure if that's what tradition really means, but it's nice.

It's also a tradition with Ky's family to watch the movie _It's a Wonderful Life_ every Christmas. And so, two nights before Christmas, that's what they were doing. They were wearing their traditional Christmastime nightclothes. They were all in red: red flannel pyjamas, even red slippers. Ky had her hair tied back in a red scrunchie. That's what the Stranger saw: this family in red.

They had just stopped the movie for a break. They were going to have okonomiyaki, which is kind of like a Japanese pizza and pancake all mixed up together with shredded cabbage and crabmeat and this chewy wheat gluten stuff called seitan. This is a tradition, too. Ky's father, Tan, likes to cook. So they watch _It's a Wonderful Life_ and they have this mid-movie snack served with kinpara gobo, which is spicy, and other pickly things that only Tan and Barbara, Ky's mother, bother to eat. But the kids like okonomiyaki.

Tan Mori is Japanese. Here's how he looks. He wears clear rimmed glasses. He's short and trim and has long black hair that he wears pulled tightly back in a ponytail.

Ky doesn't think the Stranger had ever seen a Japanese person up close before. He probably hadn't ever seen someone who looked like Barbara Mori, either. She isn't Japanese. She has silvery blonde hair but it's cut very, very short so that you can see the shape of her head. She's very slim, bony, and she has one of the nicest smiles you could imagine. She has two dark spots beside her mouth. Ky calls them beauty marks; Barbara laughs and calls them moles.

It was Barbara who first noticed the Stranger while Tan was cooking the okonomiyaki and the boys were getting bowls of shrimp chips and Coke and Ky was boiling water for green tea.

The freezing rain was pouring down on the dome, but inside it was warm, and there were little islands of light. A single light on a post lit up the driveway a bit.

"There's someone out there," said Barbara. "The poor man." She went to the door and called to him. The kids left what they were doing to go and look.

He was big and shadowy where he was standing. He was also stoop-shouldered, trying to hide his head from the icy downpour.

Barbara waved at him. "Come!" she called as loudly as she could. "Come." Her teeth were chattering because she was standing at the open door in her pyjamas and cold wind was pouring in.

The Stranger paused. He seemed uncertain. Then a gust of wind made him lose his balance and he slipped on the ice and fell. When he got up he made his way towards the house slowly, sliding and slipping the whole long way. He was soaked clear through all over. He only had a jean jacket on. No gloves or hat. As he approached the house, Ky could see that, although he was big, he was young, a teenager. Then Barbara sent her to the bathroom for a big towel.

By the time she got back with the towel, the boy was in the house, standing there dripping in the hall. Barbara wrapped the towel

around his shoulders. She had to stand on her toes; he was big. He had black hair and he reminded Ky of a bear she had seen at the zoo after it had been swimming. He smelled terrible. His wet clothes smelled of alcohol and cigarette smoke. The kids all stepped away from him. Tony crinkled up his nose, but Barbara didn't seem to care.

"Come in and get warm," she said, leading him towards the kitchen.

I haven't told you about the kitchen yet. Well, there is a kind of island shaped like a kidney with a built-in stove and sink. Since the walls of the dome are curved, all the cupboards and drawers and stuff are built into the island. Lights recessed into the ceiling above bathe the island in a warm glow so that the maple countertop looks like a beach.

Tan was already pouring the Stranger some tea when Barbara brought him over and tried to sit him down near the stove where it was warmest. But he wouldn't sit. Tan handed him a tiny cup of steaming tea. The cup had no handle. The Stranger didn't seem to know what to do, but the warmth alone was enough to make him take it. His hands were huge and strong and rough. The tiny cup looked like it would break if he closed his fist.

He took a sip of the tea. His eyes cleared a bit.

"Dad's in the truck," he said.

"Oh," said Barbara. "Where? We should get him. Tan?"

The Stranger nodded his big bear head in the direction that the truck was, but, of course, you couldn't see it from the house. Ky looked down the driveway, but there is a bend in it so she couldn't see the road.

Tan had turned off the gas under the frying pans and was heading towards the closet for his coat.

"I'll bring him back," he said.

"No!" said the Stranger. His voice cracked a little. "He's okay. He's sleepin'. Truck's warm."

Nobody in the Mori family knew what to do. Tony looked about ready to laugh. Ky glared at him. Tan shrugged and looked at Barbara. "It's not too cold as long as he's sheltered." She nodded and Tan turned the stove back on. The okonomiyaki were ready to flip. He flipped them. The Stranger stared at them. Maybe he thought they were the weirdest pancakes he'd ever seen. It's hard to know what he was thinking. Then he looked around.

"Where am I?" he asked.

"The fifth line," said Barbara, filling his cup. The Mori house is on the fifth concession line of Leopold County.

"The fifth?" he asked. He stared around again. He looked as if he didn't believe it. "The fifth?" He stared at Barbara, who nodded. He stared at Tan. Tan nodded, too. The Stranger kept staring at Tan, at his red pyjamas, his long ponytail, his bright dark eyes behind clear rimmed glasses. "Where am I?"

That's when the fax machine started beeping and the Stranger spilled his tea. Brad got him a tea towel but he didn't seem hurt. He stared into the dark where the computer stuff is. There are hardly any walls in the dome.

The fax machine beeps when a transmission is coming through. Then it makes a whirring sound and paper starts rolling out with a message on it.

The boy watched the fax machine blinking in the shadows, because the lights were not on in the office part of the dome.

"It's just what my parents do," said little Tony. The machinery was still a mystery to him, too.

The Stranger looked at Tan again—all around at the dome. There's a second floor loft but it's not big, so the Stranger could see clear up to the curving roof and out at the rain pelting down. If there had been stars out he could have seen them. He seemed to get a little dizzy from looking up.

"Sit," said Barbara, and this time she made him sit on a stool next to the kitchen island. He steadied himself. To Ky he looked like someone who had just woken up and had no idea what was going on.

By now the fax machine was spewing out a great long roll of paper which curled to the floor. The Stranger watched it for a minute.

"I think we should get your father," said Barbara in a very gentle voice.

"No," said the boy firmly. "He's asleep, eh. We was at Bernie's. You know Bernie?"

But none of the Moris knew Bernie. "Cards," he said. "Celebrating... Christmas..." He looked back at the fax. "What is this place?"

Tan laughed. He flipped two okonomiyaki onto a warm plate and handed them to the boy. "Here. You look like you could do with something warm to eat."

"More to read?" asked the boy. He thought Tan had said more to read.

Tan handed him the pancakes. "Try it," he said.

Ky went and got the spicy sauce. She poured a bit on the pancake and sprinkled some nori, toasted seaweed, on top. The Stranger looked at Ky and at the food steaming under his nose. It must have smelled funny to him. He looked around again. He was having trouble putting all this together. These strange sweet salty smells, these people all in red.

"You never heard of Bernie?" he asked.

"No," said Ky.

"Bernie Nystrom?"

"Never heard of him."

"Over on the..." he was going to say where it was that Bernie Nystrom lived, but he seemed to forget. "Dad's out in the car," he said. "We got lost."

"Not a great night for driving," said Tan, filling the Stranger's cup with more steaming tea.

"Saw your light there," he said, squinting hard as if the light had just shone in his eyes. "Slid right out." He made a sliding gesture with his hand.

"It's pretty icy," said Tan.

"Never seen such a bright light," said the Stranger.

Ky remembers him saying this. It rankled her. He made it sound as if their light had been responsible for his accident. Her mother winked at her.

Tony looked like he was going to say something. Brad put his hand over his brother's mouth. Tony struggled but the Stranger didn't notice. The fax stopped.

"You sure you ain't never heard of Bernie?" he asked one more time. It seemed to matter a great deal, as if he couldn't imagine someone not knowing good ol' Bernie Nystrom.

"Is there someone we could phone for you?" Barbara asked. "Do you need a tow or something?"

The Stranger was staring at the okonomiyaki. "Anita who?" he asked. At that, both Brad and Tony started giggling until Ky shushed them up.

"A *tow* truck," said Barbara, very carefully. "To get you out of the ditch."

The boy put the plate down without touching the food. He rubbed his hands on his wet pants. He was shivering. Barbara sent Brad to get a blanket.

"Could I use your phone?" the boy asked. Ky ran to get the cordless phone from the office area. There was a phone closer, but Ky always uses the cordless.

You have to see this phone to imagine the Stranger's surprise. It's clear plastic. You can see the electronic stuff inside it, the speakers and amplifiers and switches and everything.

The Stranger stared at it, held it up closer to his eyes. That was when Ky thought of all the time travel books she'd read and wondered if this guy was from some other century. Then she remembered that he had come by truck. That's what he'd said, anyway. She wondered if he had been telling the truth. He sure didn't want anyone going to look for his father. Maybe he had been planning on robbing them? But looking at him again, she realized that he was in no condition to rob anyone. She showed him how the phone worked.

"What's your number?" she asked.

"Don't got no number," he said. But he took the phone and slowly punched some numbers anyway. He belched, and a sour smell came from his mouth. Ky stepped back quickly, afraid that he was going to throw up.

The phone rang and rang and no one answered it. Ky watched the Stranger's face. He seemed to fall asleep between each ring and wake up again, not knowing where he was.

"Neighbours," he said, hanging up after about thirty rings.

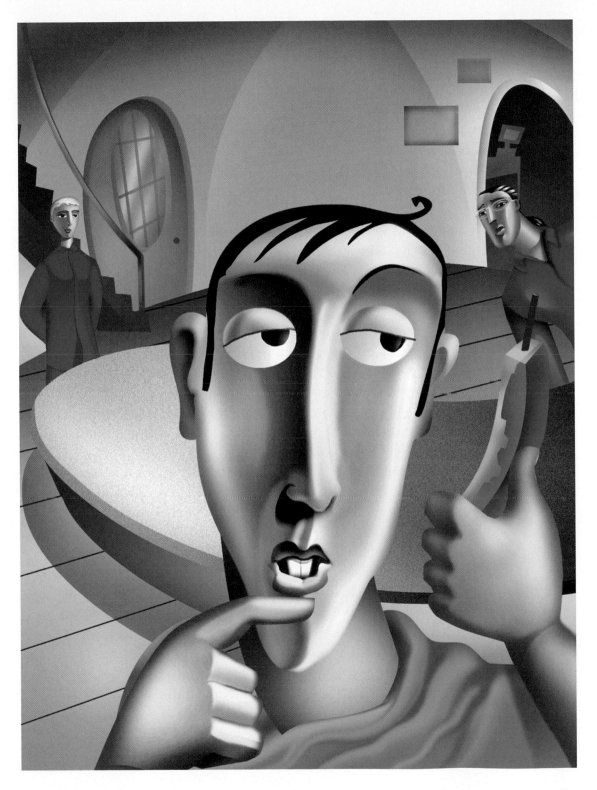

He looked suspiciously at the phone, as if to say, How could I reach anyone I know on a phone like that?

Then he looked at Ky and her family. "Where am I *really?*" he asked.

Brad came back with a comforter and Barbara suggested to the Stranger that he could wear it while she put his wet things in the dryer. He didn't like that idea. But as nice as Barbara is, as small as she is, she can be pretty pushy, and she was afraid he was going to catch pneumonia. So the Stranger found himself without his clothes in a very strange house.

Maybe it was then, to take his mind off wearing only a comforter, that he tried the okonomiyaki. He was very hungry. He wolfed down two helpings, then a third. It was the first time he smiled.

"Hey," said Ky. "It's almost Christmas. You'd better save some room for turkey dinner."

"What?" said the Stranger.

"You'd better save some room for turkey dinner."

The Stranger stopped eating. He stared at the food on his plate. Ky wanted to tell him she was just kidding. She couldn't believe he had taken it so seriously. She was going to say something, but then he asked if he could phone his neighbour again. He still didn't have any luck. But now he seemed real edgy.

Then the telephone answering machine in the office took a long message. It was a computer expert phoning Tan, and he talked all in computerese, even though it was nighttime and two days before Christmas.

The Stranger must have heard that voice coming from the dark side of the dome where the lights flashed. Maybe that was what threw him. Or maybe it was when the VCR, which had been on pause, came back on by itself. Suddenly there were voices from up in the loft. Ky can't remember what part of the movie it was when it came back on. Maybe it was when the angel jumped off the top of the bridge to save the life of the hero. Maybe it was a part like that with dramatic music and lots of shouting and splashing. Maybe the Stranger didn't know it was just a movie on TV. Who knows what he thought was going on there? Maybe in his house there was no TV.

He got edgier and edgier. He started pacing. Then, suddenly, he remembered his neighbour, Lloydy Rintoul.

"You know Lloydy," he said.

Nobody did.

"Sure," he said. "Lloydy Rintoul." He pointed first north and then east and then north again as he tried to get his bearings in this round house with its invisible walls.

"You don't know Lloydy?"

The Stranger, despite his size, suddenly looked like a little lost boy. But then he shook his head and jumped to his feet.

"Lloydy, he's got a tractor," he said. "He'll pull the truck out." He started to leave. "I'll just get him, eh." He forgot he didn't have any clothes on. Tan led him back to his stool. Barbara told him she'd check on the wash. Tan said they should maybe phone Lloydy first. But Lloydy didn't have a phone, either. The people Ky knows in the country all have phones and televisions. But there are people around Leopold County who have lived there longer than anyone and lived poor, scraping out a living on the rocky soil just like their ancestors did.

Maybe the kids were looking at the Stranger strangely then, because suddenly he got impatient. Ky said that he looked like a wild bear in a downy comforter cornered by a pack of little people in red pyjamas.

"I'm gonna get Lloydy," he said loudly. It sounded like a threat. It scared the Moris a bit. Barbara decided to get him his clothes even though they were still damp.

And so the Stranger prepared to go. They didn't try to stop him but they insisted that he borrow a big yellow poncho because it was still raining hard.

Now that he had his clothes back on and his escape was imminent, the Stranger calmed down a bit.

"I'll bring it back," he said.

"I'm sure you will," said Tan, as he helped him into the poncho.

Ky went and got him a flashlight, too. It was a silver pencil flashlight she had gotten for her birthday. She had to show him how it worked.

"I'll bring this back," he said to her.

"Okay," she said. "Thanks."

And then he was gone. He slid on the driveway and ended up with a thud on his backside.

"He'll have awful bruises in the morning," said Barbara.

She called to him to come back. She told him she would call for help. He turned halfway down the driveway and seemed to listen, but his hearing wasn't very good even up close, so who knows what he thought she said. She did mention getting the police. Maybe he heard that. Whatever, he turned and ran away, slipping and sliding all the way. Tan considered driving him, but the ice was too treacherous.

"What are the bets," said Brad, "that we never see that stuff again?"

◆◆◆

They never did. The Stranger never did return the poncho or the flashlight. In the morning the family all went out to the road. There was no truck there. Somehow, in his haze, the Stranger must have found Lloydy Rintoul or somebody found him or his dad woke up and got the truck out. It was a mystery.

Ky tried to find Bernie Nystrom's name in the phone book. There was no listing. The boy had never said the name of his neighbour and they already knew that Lloydy Rintoul had no phone, so there was no way of tracking him down. The Moris didn't really care much about getting their stuff back, though. It was Christmas, after all.

I saw the story in the *National Enquirer* in January. I was in line at the grocery store with my mother, reading the headlines of the tabloids. I enjoy doing that. There are great stories about tribes in Brazil who look like Elvis Presley, or some seventy-five-year-old woman who gives birth to twin dolphins, or families of eight who live in an abandoned filing cabinet. But this headline jumped off the page at me.

TEEN ABDUCTED BY MARTIANS!
*Country boy undergoes torturous experiments
while constrained in an alien flying saucer!
Experts wonder: Who or what is Kerdy Dickus
and what does he want with our moon!*

I don't know why I flipped open to page twenty-six to read the story. I don't know why I paid good money to actually buy the rag. Somehow I knew. And when I showed the picture on page twenty-six to Ky, she gasped.

It was him. There was the Stranger showing the huge bruises inflicted by the aliens on his arms and ribs and thighs. He told of how he had seen a blinding light and the truck had been pulled right off the road by the saucer's powerful tractor beam. He told of how the aliens had hypnotized him and brought him to their saucer. He told of the drugs they had made him drink; how they had tried to get his father, too, but he had stopped them. He told of the weird food they had made him eat and how it had made him throw up all the next day. His mother could attest to his ill health. "I've never seen him so green," she said. "And he's normally such a healthy lad."

It was his mother who had contacted the *National Enquirer*. She read it all the time and she knew it was a story that would interest them.

His father, too, although he had managed somehow to stay out of the clutches of the aliens' hypnotic powers, could attest to the attack on the car. And then—blackness. There were two hours missing out of his recollection of the night. The aliens had obviously zapped him.

"Something ought to be done about this kind of menace!" said the father.

According to the newspaper, the boy underwent several sessions with a psychiatric investigator after the incident. The investigator specialized in AATT: Alien Abduction Trauma Therapy. He put the boy in a deep trance and

interviewed him at length. "Truth drugs" were administered, and all the results concurred: the boy had obviously undergone a close encounter with alien beings. Under the trance the boy revealed some overheard conversation that might, the investigator believed, partially explain the purpose of the aliens' trip to earth.

"This might be a reconnaissance mission." Other experts in the field agreed. "But their long-term goal has to do with our moon and the saving of it. From what? *For* what? It is hard to tell."

One line had become imprinted on the boy's mind. The only spoken part he recalled vividly from his close encounter.

"Save the moon for Kerdy Dickus."

"Perhaps," said the psychiatric investigator, "there is some alien purpose for the boy remembering this one line."

The article went on to give a pretty good account of the aliens, what they looked like, what their flying saucer looked like. But you already know all that.

◆ ◆ ◆

I had heard about the Stranger from Ky. That's how I somehow recognized the story in the *Enquirer*. The next time I saw the Moris, I showed them the paper. But after they had all laughed themselves silly, we talked about it a lot.

Should they try to find the Stranger, now that they knew his name? Even without a phone, they could easily track him down. Should the paper be contacted, so that the truth could be known? What about the psychiatrist who specialized in AATT? The experts?

"I wouldn't mind getting my flashlight back," Ky admitted, but she wasn't really serious.

And so they have never followed up on the story. Ky always imagines she'll run into the Stranger one day in the nearby town. I hope I'm with her. Maybe I'll be up there for her birthday. Maybe it will be raining. Maybe we'll be coming out of a store and he'll be coming in wearing the big yellow poncho. He'll walk right by us, and Ky and I will turn just as he passes and whisper the magic words.

"Save the moon for Kerdy Dickus."

Then we'll hop in our saucer and slip off back to our own world.

1. RESPONDING TO THE STORY

a. Why do you think the Stranger appeared so alarmed and frightened by the Moris? How would you explain his behaviour?

b. In your opinion, who appears to have the more unusual characteristics in this story—the Stranger or the Moris? Explain your response in detail using examples from the selection.

c. Ky suggests to the Stranger that he should save some room for turkey dinner. What is relevant about this line?

d. How might the phrases "jumping to conclusions" and "more than meets the eye" apply to this story? Discuss with your class.

2. MEDIA ANALYSE NEWSPAPERS

The narrator mentions the *National Enquirer*, a tabloid newspaper. Unlike city or community newspapers, *tabloids* sensationalize and fabricate stories, and are sold to a national or international audience. Collect some tabloids and daily newspapers, and compare them. With three or four classmates, develop a comparison chart that includes such headings as "Layout," "Subject Matter," "Headlines," and "Photos."

Review your completed chart. What do you think makes tabloids popular? Do daily newspapers also appear to sensationalize stories? Explain. Write a two-paragraph summary stating your conclusions. Present your summary to the class.

3. LANGUAGE CONVENTIONS USE SIMPLE SENTENCES

In this story, Tim Wynne-Jones has used short, **simple sentences** to create his characters and describe the setting. Using short sentences helps make the selection easier to read because the writing is clear and concise. For example, recall how the father was introduced to us:

> A **simple sentence** is a group of words that expresses a complete thought. It has one subject and one verb. For example, *the cat plays in the yard.*

> **Tan Mori is Japanese. Here's how he looks.**
> **He wears clear rimmed glasses....**

Reread the story and pull out several sentences that you think are good examples of this technique. Try rewriting these sentences as one long sentence. What conclusions can you draw about using simple sentence structures in writing?

Alien
Song Lyrics by Kim Stockwood and Naoise Sheridan

There's people everywhere
New Year's Eve here in Times Square
Surrounded by all these souls
So why do I feel alone

Why don't I fit in
Am I not one of them
Am I an Alien
I swear to God I am

Dropped here from another planet
You know I don't belong
And I want to go home
Can anybody help me find my way
Will I ever find my home

Is there a handbook
I should've read
Instructions I didn't get
'Cause sometimes this place just makes no sense
Is it all some big experiment

GOALS AT A GLANCE

■ Respond critically and personally to the song.
■ Design a CD cover.

Why don't I fit in
Am I not one of them
Am I an Alien
I swear to God I am

Dropped here from another planet
You know I don't belong
And I want to go home
Can anybody help me find my way

Do you ever feel sometimes
Like a stranger in your own life
A million miles from what you see
An alien just like me
alien, alien, alien...

Do you ever feel sometimes
Like a stranger in your own life
A million miles from what you see
An alien just like me

----

1. RESPONDING TO THE SONG

a. Why does the songwriter refer to herself as an alien? Share your responses with a classmate.

b. Discuss the following with your class: Can you relate to the feelings expressed by the speaker? Are there times when you wish there was a "handbook" to help guide you through life, or would you rather keep things just as they are?

c. With a classmate, compare the characters, mood, and message of "Alien" and "Save the Moon for Kerdy Dickus."

2. MEDIA DESIGN A CD COVER

Examine some CD covers of musicians you like. What types of images are on the covers? What information is provided on them?

Reread this selection and think about how you would design a CD cover based on this song. You might use illustrations or photos from magazines, or create an image of your own. Incorporate some text from the song into the design. Display the CD cover for your class.

Discovering your special gift can make dreams come true.

The Life and Times of Diane Dupuy

PROFILE BY CATHERINE RONDINA

Diane Dupuy believes each of us has our own special gift and if we dig deep enough in our souls and discover that gift we can make our dreams come true. But discovering the gift isn't always easy.

Today Dupuy is the founding director of her own internationally successful theatre company, the Famous People Players, who celebrated their 25th anniversary in show business on June 1, 1999. This Toronto-based theatre group employs 54 people, most of whom are developmentally challenged performers who, like Dupuy, had to overcome many obstacles and prejudices to fulfil their dreams.

Famous People Players was founded in 1974. They've had two hit shows on Broadway, played

GOALS AT A GLANCE

■ Analyse and rewrite the introduction and conclusion.
■ Write a magazine article.

Radio City Music Hall, toured the world, opened their own dinner theatre in Toronto, and won the praise and financial support of celebrities like Paul Newman, Phil Collins, and Tom Cruise. But the road to success was a difficult one for Dupuy and her company, as they battled many non-believers.

Growing up in Hamilton, Ontario, Diane Thornton had little more than her dreams to hold on to. Her painful childhood was filled with disappointments and frustration. At school she was teased by bullies. "I couldn't concentrate in school. I was always bored and my mind wandered," recalls Dupuy, who failed three times before dropping out of school in Grade Nine. In today's world she probably would have been diagnosed as having a learning disability.

Dupuy's home life wasn't much better. Her father couldn't understand why his daughter couldn't learn and punished her by locking her in a dark basement. Alone, Dupuy played with her beloved puppets—a gift from her mother—and created her own little world where dreams *could* come true.

With her mother's encouragement she began to use the puppets to entertain her classmates at school, and it worked! Even the bullies were impressed with her talents. "My mother was very supportive," says Dupuy, whose parents eventually divorced.

After leaving school Dupuy tried a number of sales jobs that just didn't seem to work out. "I kept getting fired because I had trouble taking direction and my hair was always in my eyes and I didn't meet my bosses' standards," recalls Dupuy, who by this time was 20 years old and had abandoned her faithful puppets. When she rediscovered them, now too small for a grown woman to operate, her mother who owned a clothing design shop—offered to make new puppets for her to perform with. Before long Dupuy was hired to do her show for a department store and soon had a contract to do 16 shows at the Canadian National Exhibition in 1969. It was during these performances that she first started to use her "famous" people—celebrity look-alike puppets, with characters like Barbra Streisand and then-prime minister Pierre Trudeau. An audience member, who came backstage to congratulate her after a show, told her about "Black Light" theatre, in which the performers dress in black and are invisible to the audience. The admirer was comedian Bill Cosby.

Dupuy continued to do her one-woman show and accepted an invitation to perform for a group of adults who were developmentally challenged. She was so intrigued by the audience that she took a course in dealing with the developmentally challenged. She soon realized that her gift of entertaining could be used to fulfil not only her dreams, but the dreams of others.

So in 1974, at the age of 25, Dupuy obtained an $18 000 Opportunity for Youth Grant from the Canadian government, and Famous People Players was born. Her troupe of 11 developmentally challenged members was named after the famous puppets she planned to create. Remembering what Cosby had told her, Dupuy decided to "hide" the performers from their audience. This technique, which Dupuy refers to as "live animation," was first developed in Japan. By wearing black costumes the puppeteers are made "invisible" onstage as they manipulate brightly coloured, life-size puppets that are illuminated by ultraviolet black lights. Dupuy was determined that her performers would be known for their excellent work first, not because they were developmentally challenged.

From the very beginning Dupuy was a demanding boss. She expected hard work from her troupe members, many of whom were learning everyday life skills for the first time. "I wanted them to be self-sufficient and realize what they could do for themselves," explains Dupuy, who insisted that they learn to use the public transit system and get to rehearsals by themselves. "Training is still very difficult now," says Dupuy. "It can take a whole year for them to memorize a three-minute skit."

Their big break came just one year after the company was formed when showman Liberace saw their act and brought them to Las Vegas as part of his stage show. "Liberace came to see our show in Toronto," recalls Dupuy, who, ironically, had a "famous" puppet character of Liberace in her show. "When Liberace found out the cast was developmentally challenged he told us we better be good or he'd fire us like anyone else," recalls Dupuy. They were a smash hit and the professional relationship lasted ten years.

By the time they returned to Canada they had become an international success. Bookings were coming in from all over the world. In 1986 they opened on Broadway in *A Little Like Magic*. It was a proud moment for Dupuy and the cast, who would return a few years later in *A Little More Magic*.

Today, Famous People Players has grown into two full-time companies. One set of cast members appear at their Toronto dinner theatre, while the other members tour the world. And it's also a family affair for Dupuy, whose husband Bernard Dupuy is the company's general manager. Their two daughters, Jeanine and Joanne, are company members, and her mother, Mary Thornton, still designs and creates all the puppets and props for her daughter's company.

At 50, Diane Dupuy's childhood love of puppets has brought her fame and honour. A 1984 TV movie, *Special People*, was made about her life. She has received many awards, including the Order of Canada and honorary degrees from three universities. But what makes Dupuy the most proud is what her dreams have enabled others to do. "I found my special gift and I'm doing what I was born to do," says Dupuy, whose special gift seems to be helping others realize their dreams too.

Dupuy and her Famous People Players began performing a special production in 1999, paying tribute to their 25th anniversary. Written by Dupuy, *Leave the Porch Light On* chronicles the struggles of this unique theatre company.

----

1. RESPONDING TO THE PROFILE

a. Why did Diane Dupuy feel like an outsider in school and at home? How did she learn to cope with this feeling?

b. What was the turning point in Diane's life?

c. What is unique about the Famous People Players theatre group?

d. Why are people like Bill Cosby and Liberace so supportive of the performers and such fans of their stage performances?

e. What is the overall message of this selection?

2. EDITOR'S DESK INTRODUCTION AND CONCLUSION

Reread the article. Notice how the writer introduces and concludes the selection by repeating the same idea—finding your special gift in life. This is often referred to as a *wraparound technique* and is used to create unity in a selection. The writer may use a symbol, an event, or an idea. Has Catherine Rondina used this technique effectively? Explain.

Revise this selection by writing a new introduction and conclusion, and using this wraparound technique. Share your revision with a partner. Consider using this technique the next time you write an article.

SELF-ASSESSMENT: What sentence did you use in your introduction? Did you rephrase this to write your conclusion? How difficult or easy was it to revise the article?

STRATEGIES

3. MEDIA MAGAZINE ARTICLE

With a partner, examine some popular magazines for teens to see how the articles are written and designed. Discuss, using these questions as a guide:

- What types of articles do these magazines contain?
- What features do these articles have in common?
- Which types of people are most often profiled in the articles?

Write a two-page feature article for a teen magazine. The focus of your article could be the need to find one's special gift, or it could be a topic that connects to the theme of "Popular Culture." Remember that using a wraparound technique can create a more unified article.

Ask a classmate to read your first draft and give you feedback on the writing style, organization, and interest level. Use this feedback to revise your work. Discuss how you will design your piece to make it look like a magazine article.

Use a computer to develop a final draft in three columns. Add a catchy title and illustrations or photos.

Your article, and those of your classmates, could be placed in a class binder or posted on your school's Web site.

Have you ever thought about the power of advertising? Read on for Arthur Black's opinion on the…

Running Shoe Run-Around

Satirical Essay by Arthur Black

Jared Ogden, Catwalk Arête, Cirque of the Unclimbables, Northwest Territories, Canada
Photo: Gordon Wiltsie

Your troubles **cannot climb, walk or roam.**

Over the past 30 years, gear from The North Face has taken adventurers higher and farther than they ever thought possible. Today, we're introducing a line of trekking footwear as technical as the rest of our equipment. The X-2™ midsole design with dual-density polyurethane technology supports the midfoot while cushioning the heel and forefoot. Rugged, multi-dimensional lug design provides superior all-terrain traction and the Dri-lex™ lining keeps the foot dry. Trekking footwear from The North Face. Exploration gear for the feet.

GORE-TEX®

Gore-Tex is a registered trademark of W.L. Gore & Associates, Inc.

Palisade Crest Gore-Tex®   Cathedral Pass   Triple Divide

NEVER STOP EXPLORING™

It's interesting how tiny, trivial things can sometimes thread themselves through the whole tapestry of your life. Take running shoes. Running shoes are responsible for my first sense of being a Canadian. Must have been thirty-five years ago on a dock in Muskoka. I remember this loud blond brushcut teenager wearing a shiny new pair of strange-looking running shoes with little rubber disks on the ankles. He was bragging about his brand-new "sneakahs."

289

"Sneakers?" I thought, what is this guy—a cat burglar?

Naw. He was just an American. Americans called them sneakers; we called them running shoes. I kinda preferred the name sneakers, but I stubbornly continued to call them running shoes. Patriotism sometimes roots in pretty sandy soil.

Mind you, none of us had much running-shoe imagination back then. Not like today.

We just had the standard-issue, rubber-bottom, canvas-top $6.98 shoes that laced up to the ankle and lasted from first mud till the snow flew again. Today? Phew. I spent part of yesterday afternoon window-shopping in a downtown shoe store. An *athletic*...shoe store. They've got court shoes, tennis shoes, jogging shoes, and sprinting shoes. They've got aerobics shoes and warm-up shoes, track shoes, and cycling shoes.

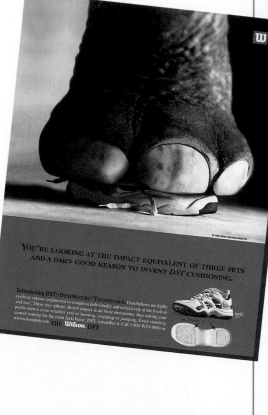

They've even got an entire line of walking shoes—which you would think would have to represent full circle for the athletic shoe business, but I doubt it. Don't sell these merchandising guys short. I expect any day to walk by that store window and see the all new Napping Shoe—revolutionary footwear that fights fallen arches and corrects pigeon toes while you doze in front of the TV.

Mind you, it's not all advertising hype. Modern running shoes are a far technological cry from my old $6.98 blacktops.

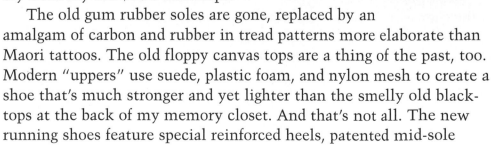

is the top of the hill.

All that waits atop the hill

Glory doesn't wait atop the hill.

Money doesn't wait atop the hill.

achieve new balance

The old gum rubber soles are gone, replaced by an amalgam of carbon and rubber in tread patterns more elaborate than Maori tattoos. The old floppy canvas tops are a thing of the past, too. Modern "uppers" use suede, plastic foam, and nylon mesh to create a shoe that's much stronger and yet lighter than the smelly old black-tops at the back of my memory closet. And that's not all. The new running shoes feature special reinforced heels, patented mid-sole

SAUCONY

Loyal to the sport

POWER IS

Power is pounding the road into submission with every step.

KNOWING THAT

Power is the beat of your heart.

NO RUN IS OVER

Fit is everything.

UNTIL YOU

Wear Saucony.

DECIDE IT IS.

Grid Stabil

©Saucony 1999

800·365·7282 • saucony.com • Canada 888·203·8118

shock absorbers, and all manner of gizmos to make runners run faster and more comfortably. Tiger Brand shoes feature a gel insert to absorb the thump of feet hitting the ground. I've got a pair of shoes here that have air capsules under the heel to do the same thing. All this is not, of course, included in the old $6.98 price. Actually, you can get a pretty brisk cardiovascular workout just reading the price tags on these new running shoes. Know what the irony is?

Know what all these flotation devices and miracle fibres and kinetic wedges are trying to recreate? Something that world-famous runners like Kipoge Keno, Zola Budd, and gold-medal marathon runner Abede Bikila discovered a long time ago. That when it comes to running, nothing beats the efficiency of...bare feet. Those runners all run in their bare feet.

Which of course come a lot cheaper. Cheaper even than $6.98.

1. RESPONDING TO THE ESSAY

a. How would you describe the tone of this essay?

b. What is the point or message of this essay? What literary device is Arthur Black using to get his point across?

c. Examine the images and layout of "Running Shoe Run-Around." With your class, discuss how the images and text work together. What messages do the ads send? How does this work with the message of the essay?

2. ESSAY CRAFT PERSONAL ESSAY

Arthur Black has used both humour and **situational irony** to make his point in this essay. Where in the essay do we find this? With your class, discuss how effectively this essay uses humour and situational irony.

> **Situational irony** occurs when a set of circumstances turns out differently from what the reader expects or anticipates.

Think about something you own—like an old sweater or favourite belonging—that might be considered out of style according to today's standards of what's "in." Write a short personal essay in which you express how you feel about this item. Remember to use humour and, if appropriate, include an ironic ending.

3. MEDIA ANALYSE MESSAGES

The comic strip on page 288 and the essay on page 289 approach the same subject in different ways. Which one expressed its main idea more clearly? Why do you think so?

Choose one of the following activities:

- Write a 200-word personal commentary for a TV news program. Describe how you think the media influence consumer spending on items like expensive running shoes. Include your own opinion. You can use information from Arthur Black's essay to help you.
- Develop a comic strip that examines why we purchase overpriced items like running shoes. Look at "For Better or For Worse" on page 288 for ideas on creating the art and frame(s), and writing the dialogue.

Share your work with a classmate.

PEER ASSESSMENT: Examine the language your partner has used. Is the wording clear and concise? Does your partner use a humorous or serious tone effectively? Explain.

4. MEDIA DEVELOP AN AD

With three or four classmates, examine the magazine ads on pages 289–292. Discuss their features, contents, and messages. Do you think these ads are effective? Why or why not? What would you change about them?

With your group, develop an ad for a running shoe. Who is your audience? Decide whether your ad is intended for magazines, newspapers, or TV. Where exactly would you place your ad? on the back cover of a teen fashion magazine? during a TV drama intended for kids? Design an ad with a clear message and a strong image. Share it with your classmates, explaining who your target market is and how the ad was developed.

Have you ever responded to an ad in the
back of a magazine or comic book?
What happened?

Fool Proof

MEMOIR BY MARY COOK

Father was sitting with his feet propped up on the oven door. He had his chair tilted back, and the door was simply a steadying device, so that he wouldn't tumble backwards and break his neck, which Mother predicted regularly was one day bound to happen. It was a blistering hot day, but Father still wore heavy grey knitted work socks, and his laced boots sat beside the straight-back kitchen chair like two obedient dogs waiting for the call of their master.

His glasses, which he had bought at the Five-to-a-Dollar store in Renfrew for seventy-five cents, were sitting on the end of his nose, and he was reading the *Family Herald and Weekly Star*, which he favoured over the *Ottawa Farm Journal* at noontime.

Then something struck his fancy, and he was out of the chair in one leap and over to the kitchen table where we were dawdling over the last crumbs of a big chocolate cake Mother had made that morning. He jabbed his pipe at a square advertisement that appeared in the upper corner of the paper. "Read that...right there. By gar, that's what we need on this here farm, and by the holy thunder I'm going to send for it!" His fist came down with such a bang that he rattled the dishes on the table.

GOALS AT A GLANCE

■ Present a dramatization of a scene.
■ Respond personally to ads through journal entries.

"In fact," he said, "I'm going to send for two of them." All of us rushed over to the end of the table—even Mother, who knew it had to be something special to get Father to spend a dime on anything other than the bare necessities of life.

The ad was about ten centimetres square. Guaranteed to kill your potato bugs, it said. Absolutely foolproof. Send one dollar for this amazing kit.

Well, if there was anything we all hated on the farm it was killing potato bugs. And because they seemed to come to our potato plants by the thousands, every last one of us was pressed into service. It was a laborious and backbreaking job. Father would fill honey pails or old baking powder tins half full of coal oil, and we went up and down the rows popping the bugs into the cans. And God have mercy on you if you missed a bug, because Father went up and down the rows after you to make sure the job was done to his satisfaction.

Mother agreed that anything would be better than picking off the potato bugs and popping them into tins of coal oil. Father went to the sideboard, took down the blue sugar bowl, and drew out two one-dollar bills. Audrey was ordered to address the envelope. Father personally put in the two bills with his name and address written on a piece of paper, and Emerson was dispatched to the mailbox at the end of the lane.

Father said that for the next few days *he* would look after fetching the mail. He was just beside himself with excitement, and said he couldn't wait to get his hands on this wonderful invention that was going to end forever one of the most hateful jobs on the farm.

In those days it didn't take a month to get a letter out west and a return answer. So in less than a week Father retrieved a small parcel from the mailbox, and headed right for the kitchen. We were as excited as he was.

Audrey fetched the scissors, and Everett offered to cut the string. Inside was a plain brown cardboard box. Father lifted the lid. He took out four pieces of board about fifteen centimetres square. Two pieces were tied together with more string and a sheet of instructions was anchored to the top.

Father turned the boards over in his hand. Then he asked Audrey to read the instructions. She read, "Untie the string. See small circle drawn on one of the boards. Place potato bug on circle. Bang other piece of board on top of bug in circle."

That's all there was to it. Father scrounged around in the box to see if anything was missing. No one said a word. Father took a match out of his pocket, scratched it on the leg of his overalls and lit his pipe. Then he lit another match, went over to the Findlay Oval, and touched the match to the paper and kindling that were always at the ready. He walked back to the table, picked up the box, paper, and the four pieces of wood, took them over to the stove, and fed them into the firebox.

He turned on his heel and headed for the door. Not a word was spoken. All of us rushed to the window. We saw him at the drive shed filling the small tin cans with coal oil. ◆

1. Responding to the Memoir

a. What parts of the memoir give the reader a sense of the past?

b. How does responding to the ad for the potato bug killer change the father and his family? What expectations do they have about the gadget before they actually receive it?

c. After the potato bug killer is opened, what actions does the father take? What words would you use to describe his mood? Explain.

d. With a partner, list the events of the memoir. How does this list reflect the five elements of plot—introduction, rising action, climax, falling action, and resolution?

2. Oral Communication   Present a Scene

In small groups, prepare a dramatization of one scene from this memoir. Reread the selection and choose the scene you'd like to recreate. What dialogue do you need to include? If possible, use props, sound effects, or lighting to enhance this scene for your audience. Perform it for the class.

Group Assessment: Did you pay attention to the dialogue and setting of the memoir when you created your improvisation? How did this add to your performance?

3. Language Conventions   Interjections

Many authors include **interjections** in dialogue to make speech seem more natural. Reread the memoir with a partner, and list the interjections. Have you ever heard these expressions before? What do they mean? What emotions do they express?

Look through the short stories in your writing folder. How could you use interjections to add colour to your stories? Remember that many interjections are considered to be slang, and should not be used in more formal writing.

> An **interjection** is an expression of surprise, sorrow, or delight, with no grammatical connection to what precedes or follows it. For example, *Wow! Look at that plane.*

4. Media   Personal Response

Have you or your friends ever purchased or been tempted to order an item through the mail? What were the results? Write a journal entry about the experience. Include how you felt when you first saw the ad and decided to purchase the product, and how you felt when you received it.

REFLECTING ON THE UNIT

SELF-ASSESSMENT: MEDIA

As you worked on the activities in this unit, what did you learn about
- magazine or newspaper editorials?
- TV commentaries?
- opinion pieces like tributes, essays, and memoirs?
- analysing media messages?
- designing CD covers?
- creating ads?
- constructing Web sites?

MEDIA MESSAGES

Look around your classroom and think about the various media and messages
you see. What types of media do you see as you travel home from school?
What types of media do you see at home? As a class, discuss how people
are constantly surrounded by a variety of media. What messages do these
different media send? How much are we influenced by these messages?
Are you attracted to one type of medium over another? Explain.

VISUAL COMMUNICATION REPRESENT A SUBJECT

Pick a subject of importance to you in this unit, such as what you like about
movies or what you dislike about ads. Design an image that effectively shows
your point of view. You could create an image that reflects the medium—
comic strip, CD cover, Web site, etc. Display your work on your class's
Media Messages bulletin board.

WRITING PARAGRAPHS EXPRESSING VIEWPOINTS

Think about how the media have changed since you first started school in
Grade One. Write two short paragraphs, explaining what the media are like
now, and how you think they will change in the next ten to fifteen years.
Include both factual information and personal opinion in your paragraphs.

To help you develop ideas, think about some of the media discussed in
this unit. Also consider using the Internet to find further ideas on future
changes in technology and media.

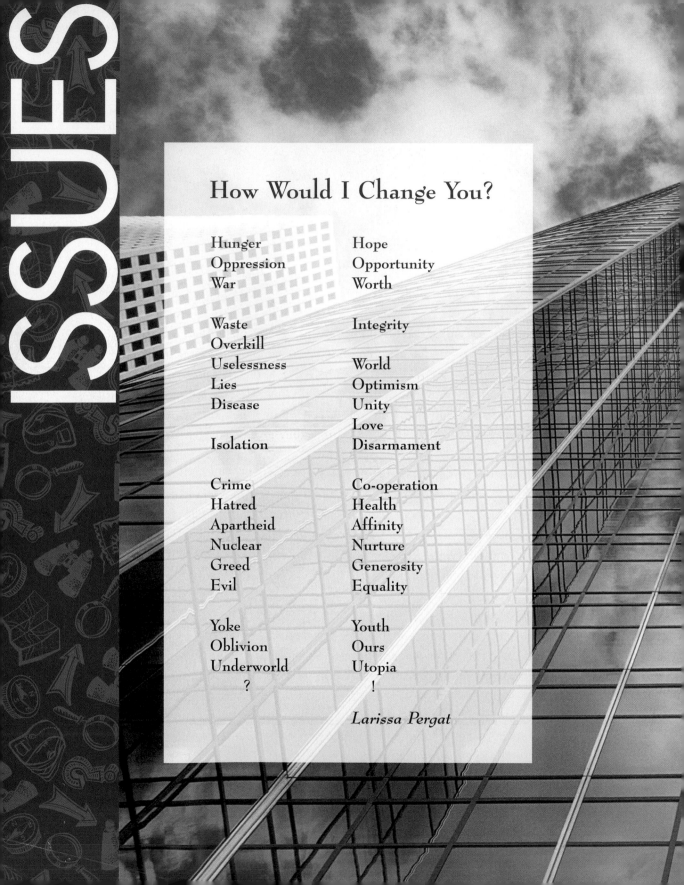

ISSUES

How Would I Change You?

Hunger	Hope
Oppression	Opportunity
War	Worth
Waste	Integrity
Overkill	
Uselessness	World
Lies	Optimism
Disease	Unity
	Love
Isolation	Disarmament
Crime	Co-operation
Hatred	Health
Apartheid	Affinity
Nuclear	Nurture
Greed	Generosity
Evil	Equality
Yoke	Youth
Oblivion	Ours
Underworld	Utopia
?	!

Larissa Pergat

VIEWPOINTS

UNIT AT A GLANCE

Sometimes one incident can dramatically alter
how we see the people in our lives.

Mrs. Buell

SHORT STORY BY JEAN LITTLE

For years and years, for what seems like forever, I've gone to BUELLS when I had a dime to spare. It's a run-down, not very clean, corner store. Kids go there mostly, for licorice and bubble gum and jawbreakers and popsicles and comic books and cones. She only has three flavours and the cones taste stale. Still, she'll sell you one scoop for fifteen cents. It's not a full scoop but it's cheaper than anywhere else. It's the only place I know where a kid can spend one penny.

Mrs. Buell is run-down too, and a grouch. She never smiles or asks you how you are. Little kids are scared to go in there alone. We laugh at them but really, we understand. We felt it too, when we were smaller and had to face her towering behind the counter.

She was always the same except that once. I tripped going in, and fell and scraped my knee. It hurt so much that I couldn't move for a second. I was winded too, and I had to gasp for breath. I managed not to cry out but I couldn't keep back the tears.

Mrs. Buell is big but she moved like lightning. She hauled a battered wooden chair out from behind the curtain that hung across the back. Then, without a word, she picked me up and sat me down on it. We were alone in the store but I wasn't afraid. Her hands, scooping me up, had been work-roughened; hard but kind.

■ Examine a story's purpose.
■ Develop oral storytelling skills.

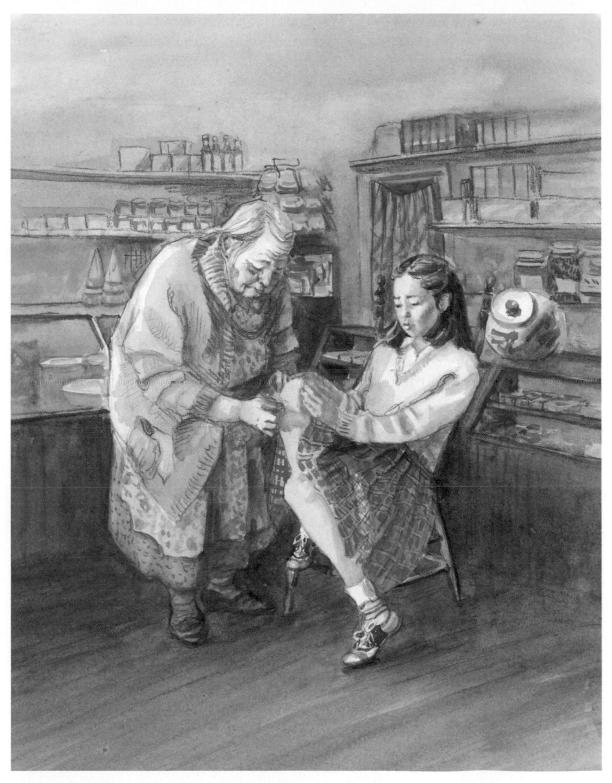

She still didn't speak. Instead, she took a bit of rag out of her sweater pocket, bent down, and wiped the smear of blood off my knee. The rag looked greyish but her hands were gentle. I think she liked doing it. Then she fetched a Band-Aid and stuck it on.

"Does it still sting?" she asked, speaking at last, in a voice I'd never heard her use before.

I shook my head. And she smiled. At least I think she did. It only lasted a fraction of a second. And I wasn't looking straight at her.

At that moment Johnny Tresano came in with one nickel clutched in his fist. He was so intent on the candies he hardly noticed me. He stood and stood, trying to decide.

"Make up your mind or take yourself off," she growled.

She had gone back behind the counter. I waited for her to look at me again so that I could thank her. But when he left she turned her back and began moving things around on the shelves. I had meant to buy some jujubes but I lost my nerve. After all, everybody knew she hated kids. She was probably sorry now that she'd fixed my knee. I slunk out without once opening my mouth.

Yet, whenever I looked down and saw the Band-Aid, I felt guilty. As soon as one corner came loose, I pulled it off and threw it away. I didn't go near the store for weeks.

She was terribly big. She got so hot in summer that her hair hung down in wet strings and her clothes looked limp. In winter she wore the same sweater every day, a man's grey one, too big, with the sleeves pushed up. They kept slipping down and she'd shove them back a million times a day. Yet she never rolled up the cuffs to make them shorter.

She never took days off. She was always there. We didn't like her or hate her. We sort of knew that selling stuff to kids for a trickle of small change wasn't a job anybody would choose— especially in that pokey little place with flies in summer and the door being opened all winter, letting in blasts of cold air. Even after that day when she fixed my knee, I didn't once wonder about her life.

Then I stopped at BUELLS one afternoon and she wasn't there. Instead, a man and woman I'd never laid eyes on were behind the counter sorting through stacks of stuff. They were getting some boxes down off a high shelf right then so they didn't hear me come in. I was so amazed I just stood there gawking.

"How Ma stood this cruddy hole I'll never know!" the woman said, backing away from a cloud of dust. "Didn't she ever clean?"

"Give the subject a rest, Glo," he answered. "She's dead. She won't bother you any longer."

"I tried, Harry. You know I tried. Over and over, I told her she could move in with us. God knows I could have used a bit of cash and her help looking after those kids."

I think I must have made a sound then. Anyway, she whirled around and saw me.

"This place is closed," she snapped. "Harry, I thought I told you to lock the door. What did you want?"

I didn't want anything from her. But I still could not believe Mrs. Buell wasn't there. I stared around.

"I said we're shut. If you don't want anything, beat it," she told me.

The minute I got home I phoned Emily. She said her mother had just read it in the paper.

"She had a daughter!" Emily said, her voice echoing my own sense of shock. "She died of a heart attack. Kate, her whole name was Katharine Ann Buell."

"Katharine," I said slowly. My name is really Katharine although only Dad calls me by it. "I can't believe it somehow."

"No," Emily said. "She was always just Mrs. Buell."

I told her about Glo and Harry. After we hung up though, I tried to imagine Mrs. Buell as a child. Instead, I saw her bending down putting that Band-Aid on my knee. Her hair had been thin on top, I remembered, and she'd had dandruff. She had tried not to hurt me. Glo's voice, talking about her, had been so cold. Had she had anyone who loved her? It seemed unlikely. Why hadn't I smiled back?

But, to be honest, something else bothered me even more. Her going had left a hole in my life. Because of it I knew, for the first time, that nothing was safe—not even the everyday, taken for granted, background of my being. Like Mrs. Buell, pushing up her sweater sleeves and giving me my change. ◆

1. RESPONDING TO THE STORY

a. Why do you think Mrs. Buell reacts so differently to Kate when she falls on the steps? What might this indicate about Mrs. Buell's true feelings for the children who come to her store?

b. What is significant about Kate finding out Mrs. Buell's first name? How does this affect her?

c. What kind of relationship did Mrs. Buell have with her daughter, Glo? How might this have affected how Mrs. Buell treated children?

d. Have you ever had an experience similar to the one Kate had? Share this story with a partner.

2. STORY CRAFT EXAMINE PURPOSE

What do you think was the author's purpose in writing this story? Discuss this in a small group. The *purpose* refers to the author's intention to either entertain or inform readers. What message is Jean Little conveying? Summarize your response in a short paragraph.

STRATEGIES

3. ORAL COMMUNICATION STORYTELLING

Storytelling involves remembering and sharing an experience from your past. Using both your memory and imagination, recreate the sights, sounds, and smells that you associate with a special place from your childhood. As these details come to mind, jot them down in your notebook. Then use these notes to "tell" your story. Be sure to follow these tips:

- Rehearse several times before you present.
- Speak clearly and confidently, varying your tone and volume.
- Use facial gestures and body movement.
- Keep the story moving by "ad libbing" or improvising when you forget something.

Share your story with a classmate.

PEER EVALUATION: Did your classmate tell a good story? Why or why not? Could you experience the story as though you were there? If so, how did your classmate achieve this?

Island Clay

Song Lyrics by Lennie Gallant

This old house once stood proud up on a hill
Of pine and cedar from the land
Cut by my father's hand
And hauled up from the mill
Now she stares, at her life spread on the lawn
At strangers picking through her bones
They take them for their own
And haul them far away

GOALS AT A GLANCE

- Create a web to organize ideas.
- Write diary entries.

The auctioneer he sings his songs and the people pay
Old voices echo from this house now dark and grey
And cold as Island clay

This old farm, 80 acres of a life
Sweat and iron reddened soil,
Paid little for my toil
But saw us through all right
Till the company came
And bought land up all around
Soon the market prices fell
I took another loan
And ploughed it underground

But tomorrow morning they will come and have their way
Though their hands touch not the soil and never will pay
The price of Island clay

These old hands turned the sod and tossed the seed,
These hands worked hard and they were strong
But they couldn't hold a printed paper deed

From the moment that they signed this land away
These old hands are getting colder every day
As cold as Island clay

----

1. RESPONDING TO THE SONG LYRICS

a. What does "Island clay" refer to in the song? Why is it cold? Are there any phrases in this song whose meaning you do not understand? Discuss these phrases with a partner.

b. Why do you think people who live and work on farms feel so close to the land? In what ways are they different from people who live and work in a city?

c. Lennie Gallant, singer and songwriter, tells this song partly from the viewpoint of a woman who must sell all of her possessions. What other viewpoint has he used?

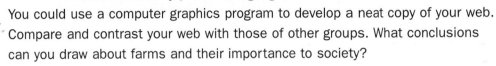
2. ORAL COMMUNICATION CREATE A WEB

With a small group, create a web on the topic "How Farms Contribute to the Well-Being of Society." Record this topic in the middle circle, and place your supporting ideas in circles that surround it and are attached. Follow these steps:

- Choose one person to record your ideas.
- Brainstorm with your group.
- Record all suggestions without editing or deleting ideas.
- Choose which key points to highlight.

You could use a computer graphics program to develop a neat copy of your web. Compare and contrast your web with those of other groups. What conclusions can you draw about farms and their importance to society?

3. WRITING DIARY ENTRIES

In the role of the woman in this song, write a series of diary entries about the last few months on your farm. Use phrases from the song, original drawings, magazine photos, or newspaper text to enhance your writing.

SELF-ASSESSMENT: Has writing the diary entries given you a better understanding of the feelings expressed by the narrator? If so, how? Record your response in your journal.

A confused young teen discovers the harsh reality of living on the streets.

The Runaway

SCRIPT BY ROBERT MAURO

CHARACTERS

MADGE, *a homeless woman;*

JENNY, *a runaway*

TIME:
Fall, just before winter

SETTING:
A park bench, trees behind bench,
city skyline in background, moonlight

AT RISE:
MADGE *enters. She pushes a shopping cart*
that contains shopping bags and all her possessions.

Madge: *(Talking to herself as she pushes her cart back and forth, back and forth across stage)* I don't know. I don't know. First they take away my room, then they tear down my little house— okay, okay, so what if it was a cardboard house? It was from good cardboard. A big box. But they tore it down, then they chase me out of the subway, out of the bus terminal, and out of the train station. Where do I go now? The Ritz? The Waldorf? Where do I sleep? They steal my money. They scare me away and say, "Get lost, you old goat!" Is that a nice way to treat an old woman? I ask you. Is it? That's for me to know and for you to find out. Whatever happened to respect for your elders? Take care of them. Treat them like human beings, like a person. I am a person, you know. *(Bangs her chest with her fist.)* I have feelings. Dignity! The doctors said I was sick. In the head. Me? Ha. I was never sick a day in my life. I was a mother! I had... *(Thinks, then)* three, four kids. Where are they now? *(Stops to think, then continues to pace.)* They all forgot about me. The children, the city, the people. They try to act like we're invisible. We have no homeless, no bag people, no bums. Well, I'm not a bum. I'm a person. I've got feelings. I'm not invisible. I'm right here. *(To skyline)* See? *(To audience)* See? I'm a real person. I'm alive. I wasn't homeless all my life. No. I had a home once. A nice home. *(Thinks, then)* It was somewhere. I was someone. Then I got sick. I told them I wasn't sick. "I am not sick," I told them. No, I was not sick. I was fine. Just let me alone, leave me be. Go away, I told them. *(She walks over to bench and sits, takes a few breaths; she's puffing.)* Just let me rest. I'll be fine in a moment. And so here I am. I guess they let me out. They finally realized I was fine. So here we are. *(Looks around.)* Where are we? Looks like the park again. I don't like the park. I can't sleep here. Keep one eye open at all times, Madge, old girl. They want to take everything else you have. And don't put up a fight. Don't struggle. Just give in to their demands. You're old. They are young. They are strong. You aren't. So let them have it all, everything. Or they might hurt you. And what will you have then? *(Thinks)* My dignity? *(Shrugs)* Or did I lose that long ago with my pride, my home, my family, my children? And here I am.

Still...I am my own boss. No one tells Madge what to do, where to go, where to sleep. I have my independence. I am an independent woman. Yes, yes. I have that. No one is going to take away my independence. *(Pulls cart closer, protecting it.)*

Or my bags. And don't tell me to go to those shelters. I prefer the park. It may not be as warm at night, but it's a lot safer here. That's what I say. Oh, they tell me different. But they lie. They all lie. You have to be careful. They're all liars today. Don't trust a soul. *(Just then* JENNY *runs onstage.* MADGE *sees* JENNY *and quickly grabs her cart, protecting it.* JENNY *looks around, trying to hide from someone.)*

JENNY: *(Afraid, puffing, she sits on bench beside* MADGE, *who moves away carefully.)* You see anyone after me?

MADGE: *(Scared)* No. I didn't see anyone.

JENNY: Good, because I ran away from home yesterday and I think the cops are after me.

MADGE: You ran away? From home?

JENNY: Yeah.

MADGE: Me too.

JENNY: When?

MADGE: *(Thinks, then)* Not yesterday. Long ago...I think. I forget just when. Why did you run away?

JENNY: I'm tired of everyone telling me what to do.

MADGE: I know what you mean.

JENNY: You do?

MADGE: Sure. You want to be your own boss. Be independent. Have no one telling you to do this, do that. Wear this, wear that.

JENNY: Right. How did you guess?

MADGE: You remind me of me.

JENNY: *(Not happy about that)* I do?

MADGE: You do. I hate people telling me where to go, what to do, when to get up, when to dress, what to wear. Now I do what I want when I want and wear what I want when I want. *(Shows her her clothes.)* See? I found this myself. But I'm not sure where. Like it?

JENNY: *(Appalled)* It's...okay, I guess.

MADGE: It's perfect. *(Looks down at her garment.)* Not one flea. *(Picks a flea off.)* Well, maybe one. But no ticks or lice. Nope. It's a good fabric. Did I tell you the best garbage was on Fifth Avenue? Or was it Fifty-seventh Street? Excellent garbage.

JENNY: Garbage?

MADGE: Yes. Excellent selection. Very fashionable, so long as you're thirty or forty years behind the times. Very few holes or fleas. *(Sees a big hole in coat.)* Well, maybe one.

JENNY: You got that coat out of the garbage?

MADGE: No, I bought it at Bloomingdale's. *(Points to blouse.)* And this at Macy's. *(Points at pants.)* And this at Gimbel's.

JENNY: Gimbel's went out of business years ago.

MADGE: Really?

JENNY: Yes. Really.

MADGE: Well, I think I got these pants there. *(Thinks)* Or maybe I got them at the Salvation Army. Maybe they were a gift? I don't know. I don't recall. So you been on the street long?

JENNY: Just this morning. I was at a friend's house last night.

MADGE: You have a friend?

JENNY: Yes. Don't you?

MADGE: *(Shakes her head no.)* No. You can't afford them on the street. "Trust no one" is my motto.

JENNY: Do you trust me?

MADGE: About as far as I can throw you.

JENNY: That's not very nice.

MADGE: Nice? Nice is for family and friends. Out here on the street, you have to be careful. So you settle for cold, aloof, distant.

JENNY: Can't we be friends?

MADGE: *(Backing away a bit)* Why?

JENNY: Everyone needs a friend.

MADGE: No, thank you. I had one once and he beat me up.

JENNY: You don't think I would beat you up, do you?

MADGE: *(Backing away a bit more)* You might. You look strong enough yet. You're new.

JENNY: New?

MADGE: On the street. You're still strong. But after you get pneumonia a few times, bit by a rat or two, mugged, or worse, you won't be so strong. Then you'll be smarter. You won't be so nosey.

JENNY: I just want to be your friend. That's all. I don't want to rip you off, beat you up. Really. Don't you believe me?

MADGE: Why should I? I don't know you. Who are you?

JENNY: My name is Jenny. *(Puts her hand out to shake.)*

MADGE: *(Moves away more.)* So?

JENNY: What's your name?

MADGE: That's for me to know and for you to find out.

JENNY: That's not very friendly. I just want to be your friend.

MADGE: Why?

JENNY: I told you. Everyone needs a friend.

MADGE: Well...I don't. I just want to be left alone. I like my freedom. I like my independence. *(Looks at* JENNY, *who smiles at* MADGE *and puts her hand out.)* I like being alone. *(Quickly shakes* JENNY's *hand.)* My name is Madge.

JENNY: Hi, Madge. Happy to meet you.

MADGE: Yeah? Why?

JENNY: *(Shrugs)* I guess because you're the first one I've talked to all day.

MADGE: Oh. Me too.

JENNY: I'm the first one you talked to all day?

MADGE: All month.

JENNY: Madge, aren't you lonely?

MADGE: *(Looks away from* JENNY.) Why should I be lonely?

JENNY: I don't know. I haven't talked to anyone for only a few hours and I'm lonely already.

MADGE: You'll get over that. Soon you'll forget all your old friends and they'll forget you. Your mother and father will forget you, you'll forget them. Do you have a boyfriend?

JENNY: I did.

MADGE: They're the first to forget. Men. Here today, gone tomorrow.

JENNY: Yeah. I hate my life.

MADGE: I hate my life. No. Wait. I hate your life. Yes. My life I like. It's you who hates my life.

Or do you like it? So, Jenny, do you like life on the street?

JENNY: It's certainly free.

MADGE: Yep. Just stay out of the way of the police, the muggers, the crazies, the bums, the wild dogs—

JENNY: Wild dogs?

MADGE: Yeah. And rats. Rabies. Don't feed them. Hit them with a stick! Hard. It's them or us.

JENNY: I guess.

MADGE: You guess? Girl, it's a fact. Facts of life on the street. Here, you're not careful, and you're suddenly living in Potter's Field, only you aren't living. So why you run away—besides the usual bad parents thing!

JENNY: That's it.

MADGE: Were they mean to you? Abusive?

JENNY: My parents?

MADGE: No, mine. Yes, your parents.

JENNY: No. They were just... parents.

MADGE: Did you have a colour TV?

JENNY: Yeah. So? Possessions aren't everything.

MADGE: True. But I was just wondering if Blase Lantana on that soap *The Edge of Death* is as cute as they say.

JENNY: He is.

MADGE: I knew it.

JENNY: Don't you ever see TV?

MADGE: Occasionally, in store windows. But lately they chase me away before I get a chance to see the soaps.

JENNY: Oh.

MADGE: You'll see. Now they'll all love you. You look like money to them. A "yuppie puppy" I think they call it. You say to them: here's someone who'll be buying a colour TV, a VCR, a CD player, a Walkman. Me? When they see me, they see an eyesore—strange, unattractive odours—no sale. I upset them. Unnerve them. Give it time. Soon they'll want to throw you out too. You like sleeping in the park?

JENNY: I don't know. Is it safe?

MADGE: No. There's the mosquitoes, the rats, the gangs, the police. I keep one eye open at all times.

JENNY: Don't you have a home?

MADGE: Oh, yes. A condo on Park Avenue and a winter place in Miami. No. (Points to bench.) This is my home.

JENNY: This bench?

MADGE: The whole thing— (Looking at JENNY sitting on bench) or part of it anyway. (JENNY gets up.)

JENNY: Sorry, I didn't realize it was yours.

MADGE: Sit. Sit! (JENNY sits.) My house is your house.

JENNY: Thanks, Madge.

MADGE: (Backs away a bit.) How'd you know my name?

JENNY: You told me.

MADGE: I did?

JENNY: You did.

MADGE: Funny. I don't usually do that.

JENNY: So you don't have a home and you don't have a family, Madge?

MADGE: I did once. Long time ago. (Goes to get photo album out of her cart.) My photo album. (It contains her life's history and family photos before she hit the street. MADGE looks for it.)

JENNY: You carry your family album with you?

MADGE: Sure. I carry all the essentials, all the important things. (Holds each item up.) My toothbrush, my insect spray, my galoshes, my toilet paper, a comb, my teacup, (Holds up a teddy bear) my baby's teddy. I think it was my baby's. It was someone's baby's. And my photo album. (Sits close to JENNY.) Want to see?

JENNY: Okay.

MADGE: It's old, but it's mine.

JENNY: Who's that? She's really pretty. Is she a model? Is that your daughter?

MADGE: That's me.

JENNY: It is?

MADGE: Yes. I told you it was a long time ago. *(Looks at picture, thinks, smiles.)* All the boys were crazy about me at school.

JENNY: *(Points to another picture.)* Who's this hunk? He's cute.

MADGE: *(Turning page very coldly)* My father. You wouldn't like him.

JENNY: Why not?

MADGE: That's for me to know and for you to find out. *(Turns page.)*

JENNY: *(Looking at picture)* Nice house. Yours?

MADGE: Yes. I loved that house. You were never cold in that house. There were no rats to bite you. No dirt or mess. Mama was very neat.

JENNY: Who's this woman with the baby?

MADGE: My mother. She died when I was two. That's me in her arms. *(Kisses picture and turns page.)* Look. See this guy?

JENNY: The chubby guy?

MADGE: *(Big smile)* Yeah. Uncle Sal. I wanted to go live with him and Aunt Jo.

JENNY: You didn't want to live with your father?

MADGE: That's for me to know and for you to find out.

JENNY: *(Looking at picture)* Is that you on your father's lap?

MADGE: *(Turning page quickly)* That's—

MADGE AND JENNY: *(Together)* For me to know and for you to find out.

JENNY: I don't think you liked your father very much. (MADGE *is silent.)* So you wanted to run away and live with your Uncle Sal.

MADGE: And Aunt Jo. They always loved me. They had such beautiful Christmas trees. Uncle Sal would play Santa. *(Points to photo.)* See? Didn't even need a pillow for his belly. He'd decorate the house with a million lights.

JENNY: And your father didn't?

MADGE: No. I said I'd decorate, but he said no. And no was no. He didn't like Uncle Sal or Aunt Jo, but he ate their food. And borrowed money for beer and cigarettes. But he hated them. I loved them.

JENNY: Where are they now?

MADGE: *(Closes album.)* Dead. Everyone's dead. *(Puts album away.)* It's just me and the rats now. You're a lucky kid.

Your family is still alive. And they don't hurt you. Lucky.

JENNY: Sure, sure. Give me a break. All day it's Jenny do this, Jenny do that; Jenny, don't go out with this boy; Jenny, don't go out with that boy. Pick up your clothes, clean your room, lower the stereo. They never stop!

MADGE: When they stop, then you should run away. My father never had two words for me. *(Mumbles)* He did other things...but never talked to me. He never really loved me. Your parents love you?

JENNY: *(Thinks, then shrugs.)* I guess. They just want me to do all the things I hate.

MADGE: Like clean your room?

JENNY: Yeah.

MADGE: Do they beat you?

JENNY: *(Shocked)* No. Never.

MADGE: You're lucky. Do they talk to you?

JENNY: All the time. They never stop.

MADGE: How's Christmas at your house?

JENNY: Daddy always brings home a big tree.

MADGE: Is he a good man?

JENNY: Both of my parents are okay. They just don't understand me. I don't understand me.

MADGE: They don't understand you? And you don't understand you. I don't understand you. They love you, you have a nice home, a big Christmas tree, a stereo, occasionally a *loud* stereo, and you want to live in the park on this bench with me?

JENNY: I don't know what I want.

MADGE: Ah, that's different. You're a normal teenager. What normal teenager knows what he or she wants?

JENNY: I'm so confused.

MADGE: It's your job to be confused. Accept it, kiddo. When you're old like me you can be unconfused. You can be smart. You can choose to abandon your life of opulence for the good life of meagre rations, hungry rats, and this bench. Hey, go home, kid. Have some milk and cookies. *(Taps seat of bench.)* I'll keep your place warm for you. It'll always be right here. In ten, fifteen years when Prince Charming does you wrong, or you don't become a woman on Wall Street Week, you can come back, live in the park, and we can go over *your* family album. Be sure to bring your family album. *(Mumbles to herself.)* Because someday it will be all that's left.

JENNY: I think I want to go home.

MADGE: Wait.

JENNY: Wait?

MADGE: Yes. Will you visit me?

JENNY: Here?

MADGE: Where else? The Waldorf? So will you? Visit me?

JENNY: Sure. (JENNY *gets up to go.*) Well...bye.

MADGE: Yeah. Right. Bye, kid.

JENNY: My name's Jenny, Madge.

MADGE: Sure. Right. Memory's a little fuzzy these days. It's all that ozone in the air if you ask me.

JENNY: I guess. (JENNY *is sorry to leave* MADGE.) Bye, Madge.

MADGE: Bye, already. Geez. Go.

JENNY: You're going to be okay?

MADGE: I have my Raid and my Mace. What more do I need?

JENNY: I'll be back. I'll bring you some food or something.

MADGE: Sure, kid.

JENNY: Jenny.

MADGE: Bye.

JENNY: Bye. You sure you're going to be all right?

MADGE: Yeah. Get home. (JENNY *waves and exits.*) I thought she'd never leave. (*She spreads out newspapers on bench, sprays some insect spray around and on her.*) Am I all right? (*A little laugh, she lies on bench.*) That's for me to know and for you to find out. (*She covers her head with newspaper and goes to sleep as curtain falls.*)

---

1. RESPONDING TO THE SCRIPT

a. Madge's motto is "Trust no one." With a partner, list examples from the script that indicate Madge's life on the street is difficult and dangerous.

b. Madge, who once had a house and a home, winds up living on a park bench. How can this happen? What does this say about life? our society?

c. Madge repeats that she is an independent woman who likes her freedom. What price did she pay for this? Is she truly free? Why or why not?

d. Jenny runs away from home in order to be free of parents who hassle her about picking up her clothes and turning down the stereo. Is this something you can relate to? Explain.

2. ORAL COMMUNICATION PRESENT A SCRIPT

In a small group, plan a presentation based on one important scene from this play. Begin by rewriting the script from the perspective of two teens. As you rewrite, change the dialogue to reflect the interests, concerns, and speech of teenagers. Finalize the script and rehearse it with your group. Use costumes, lighting, sound effects, or music in your presentation. Perform for another group.

GROUP ASSESSMENT: How easy or difficult was it to rewrite a scene for a play? What do you think worked well?

3. WRITING A FORMAL LETTER

Homelessness is an issue that concerns people in cities and towns across Canada. Gather some research on homelessness by visiting your library or using the Internet. You might also consider contacting local social service agencies for reference material.

Once you have gathered and analysed the information, compose a formal letter to the Prime Minister of Canada or your local provincial representative. Offer suggestions about how to provide food and shelter for the many people who currently live on the streets. With a partner, review the format of formal letters before you complete a final draft.

4. LANGUAGE CONVENTIONS SENTENCE FRAGMENTS

With a partner, find and discuss any **sentence fragments** within the script. Why do you think the author used them? Is the meaning of each sentence fragment clear? Should they have been corrected? What would be the effect if they were all changed into complete sentences?

Remember that sentence fragments are acceptable in informal writing, dialogue, and spoken English, but are not appropriate in formal writing.

> A **sentence fragment** is a group of words that is set off like a sentence, but lacks either a verb or a subject. For example, *My dignity*.

HOW TO

PRESENT A PLAY

Goals at a Glance

- Work co-operatively to present a stage play. • Analyse oral presentations.

Start with the Script

The script tells who the characters are, what they look like, and what they say to each other. Usually scripts include **stage directions** that describe where the action takes place, what the stage should look like, what special lighting and sound effects are required, and how the characters move and behave.

Some scripts contain very precise stage directions. Others, such as the script for "The Runaway," say very little about how the play should be brought to life.

If you are going to present a play, familiarize yourself with the script first to see how much detail it contains. Keep your audience in mind when you are making decisions about costumes, music, setting, and so on. For example, you might use one kind of back-ground music if you were performing for children, but a different kind for an audience of classmates.

Divide the Tasks

To present a play, you and your classmates will have to decide who will take responsibility for the different tasks that are required.

Director: contributes to all decisions, co-ordinates all personnel, helps to shape the way the actors move and speak

Actors: perform one or more roles, bring the characters to life

Stage Manager: in charge of set construction, oversees lighting, sound, props, etc.

Lighting Technician: installs and/or operates lighting

Sound Technician: creates sound effects

Prop Manager: obtains and keeps track of all props

Costume Person: obtains and keeps track of all costumes

Make-up Person: designs and applies the actors' make-up

Prompter: helps the actors remember their lines in rehearsals and performances

PROCESS

Helpers: assist with set construction, scene changes, and so on

Plan the Process

Even if you are presenting a short play in a very simple way, you should take time as a group to create a plan. It should show what tasks are to be done, who will do them, and when they will be completed. Read the script carefully as a group and discuss what will be needed to bring the play to life.

Make the key decisions at the beginning. Where will the presentation take place? Do sets have to be constructed or painted? What furniture and props are required? Will there be special costumes? Do you need lighting or sound effects or background music? Will actors wear make-up or masks?

The actors should begin to practise and learn their parts while the others get underway with the set and other technical details.

The actors should first read their lines while sitting, then read them in position, then recite them from memory while moving on stage.

Incorporate props, sound effects, music, and lighting into the rehearsals as they are ready. Everyone needs to practise, not just the actors!

Include a *dress rehearsal* in your plan. A dress rehearsal is a trial performance with all details in place.

Present Your Play

Actors should speak loudly so that everyone can hear.

Don't let a mistake stop the play. Ignore a flubbed line or a missed sound effect.

Members of the crew should remain quiet behind the scenes.

Self-Assessment

❑ Did each person have a clear role?
❑ Did I start by reading the script carefully and discussing it?
❑ Did I create a clear plan for my presentation?
❑ Did I include a dress rehearsal?
❑ Did we work as a team?

What were the strengths of the presentation? What were its weaknesses? List three ways the presentation could be improved.

PROCESS

NEW CANADIAN VOICES:

SELECTIONS FROM CANADIAN KIDS

GOALS AT A GLANCE

■ Respond critically to the selections.
■ Respond personally by writing journal entries.

A MULTICULTURAL NATION

MEMOIR BY WINSTON LOUI

What does it mean to be a Canadian? Does an official document make one "Canadian"? I have often wondered why people question their own identity and why I need to question my own.

Fifteen years ago, I arrived in Toronto with my family. It was a cool summer evening. I felt a chilling freshness in the air; it was different from the warmth of my tropical island home town in Trinidad. In the days that followed, I busily observed the wonders of the big city. But, everywhere I went, eyes stared at me, or so it seemed. Was it the colour of my skin or was it my accented English? I was intimidated by these thoughts. I did not want to brave the new any more. For some time, I only wanted to stand quietly and observe. Fortunately, I began to discover people's friendly natures. They showed interest in my background. They even offered their friendship.

In the meantime, I still had doubts about fitting into Canadian society. But I was determined to establish myself (prove my existence) in some way. I felt impelled to follow what "Canadians" did. Yet somehow, I was not comfortable doing that. It was then that I realized that the Canadian culture is a blend of the cultures and the traditions of the different people living in Canada.

To be Canadian, I simply have to be myself. If I cannot accept myself or appreciate others, how can I expect to live in this multicultural nation? To make my life in Canada worthwhile, I must share my unique heritage.

Today I do not question myself. Canada is my home. And, certainly, I do not have to label myself with a sign that says, "I am Canadian." Why should I? After all, I am one of those different people living in Canada—a Canadian.

TOO **OLD** TO **CHANGE**

DIALOGUE BY VICTOR CHANG

Son: Morning Dad! Where would you like to go today? I'd planned to take you out to see some of Toronto.

Father: I just want to go to Chinatown.

Son: How about going to Yonge Street and the Eaton Centre after we've had our morning tea in Chinatown? Wouldn't you like that?

Father: Morning tea in Chinatown is excellent, but Mom and I don't want to go to Yonge Street. Instead, we want to buy some fresh seafood in Chinatown. Then we'll come back and prepare our supper.

Son: You should try to go somewhere else besides Chinatown. You don't know anything else about the rest of Toronto.

Father: No, Yonge Street isn't suitable for us. We aren't interested in it. I'd rather stay home instead of going there.

Son: Don't stick to Chinatown only! Don't you feel bored always going to Chinatown?

Father: Of course we don't! We are Chinese, and it reminds us of home. Don't force us to change our ways. We feel more comfortable with our own language and our own people. We're too old to change.

Son: Won't you just try to experience something new for a change?

Father: Don't force us, son! We're quite satisfied with the life we lead. I hope you'll understand when you get older.

DO AS I SAY

DIALOGUE BY ASIF KHAN

Father: If you speak one more word of English to your sisters in front of me, I will be really annoyed with you. Is this clear?

Son: But this is the best way to learn English.

Father: You can practise English outside if you want, but not here. You know I don't understand English.

Son: But you should learn English if you want to live happily in Canada. You're being unreasonable. Can't we speak English at home? We feel as comfortable in English as we do in Urdu.

Father: I'm afraid you will forget your own language.

Son: No, I could never forget my mother tongue. After all, I've been speaking it for 18 years.

Father: Many Pakistanis who have been living in Canada all their lives forget Urdu, and when their children are born, they never learn to speak Urdu properly.

Son: No, I can't see any reason for not speaking English at home.

Father: Will you stop arguing and do as I say!

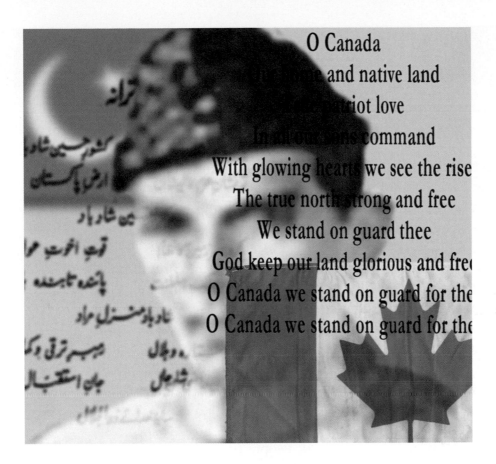

O Canada
and native land
...riot love
...command
With glowing hearts we see the rise
The true north strong and free
We stand on guard thee
God keep our land glorious and free
O Canada we stand on guard for the
O Canada we stand on guard for the

1. RESPONDING TO THE SELECTIONS

In small groups, compare the content, mood, message, and experiences presented in the three selections in "New Canadian Voices." How are these students' feelings and experiences similar? different?

2. WRITING PERSONAL JOURNAL ENTRIES

These three young writers are presenting real experiences they've had. Think about a time when you had a similar experience or felt the same way as one of these writers. Write about this in your journal. Include a description of the setting and the people, and relate details of the event in chronological order.

A Mother's Voice

Poem by Julia, Grade Eight,
James Lick Middle School, San Francisco

I never knew much about her, not as much as a daughter should
know. Sure, I knew those big chunks like how many languages
she knew and her education, but those things aren't important,
not to me.

What I want to know is the sound of her voice. I remember her
telling me to lay on my stomach when it hurt, but I don't
remember the voice that said it.

I want to know how it feels to have a mother hug me. I feel guilty
about not remembering, and there is nothing I can do about it.
I know how it felt ten years ago, but that is a long time ago,
especially if you are only thirteen years old.

I want to know how she acted. People try to tell me only the
good things, but I also want to know about the bad. They say
I act like her. I wouldn't know if I did.

I wish I could see what she looked like. I have a million
photographs of her, but those don't show every freckle, every
line, every eyelash.

Big chunks don't make a life. It's the little things that make a
person human and a human an individual. Remember people
when they are there and don't forget them when they are gone.

GOALS AT A GLANCE

■ Create a scrapbook.
■ Organize and present information effectively.

VISUAL COMMUNICATION CREATE A SCRAPBOOK

Julia tells us, "Remember people when they are there and don't forget them when they are gone." Think of a friend, relative, or pet that is important to you. In your notebook, list the special traits and characteristics of your subject. Use this list to help you create a scrapbook in which you pay tribute to this individual. Include pieces of music, drawings, photos, and any other objects that are important. How will you organize these items to highlight the person's accomplishments and character? Avoid putting too much on one page—if an item is particularly important you might want to leave a full page for it. Add captions if necessary. Share your scrapbook with others in your class.

SELF-ASSESSMENT: What did you learn from compiling this scrapbook?

Find out how one young man overcomes racism—
with the support of his friends.

A Mason-Dixon Memory

Memoir by Clifton Davis

Dondre Green glanced uneasily at the civic leaders and sports figures filling the hotel ballroom in Cleveland. They had come from across the nation to attend a fundraiser for the National Minority College Golf Scholarship Foundation. I was the banquet's featured entertainer. Dondre, an eighteen-year-old high-school senior from Monroe, Louisiana, was the evening's honoured guest.

"Nervous?" I asked the handsome young man in his starched white shirt and rented tuxedo.

"A little," he whispered, grinning.

One month earlier, Dondre had been just one more black student attending a predominantly white Southern school. Although most of his friends and classmates were white, Dondre's race had never been an issue. Then, on April 17, 1991, Dondre's black skin provoked an incident that made nationwide news.

"Ladies and gentlemen," the emcee said, "our special guest, Dondre Green."

As the audience stood applauding, Dondre walked to the micro-phone and began his story. "I love golf," he said quietly. "For the past two years, I've been a member of the St. Frederick High School golf team. And though I was the only black member, I've always felt at home playing at mostly white country clubs across Louisiana."

The audience leaned forward; even the waiters and busboys stopped to listen. As I listened, a memory buried in my heart since childhood began fighting its way to life.

"Our team had driven from Monroe," Dondre continued. "When

we arrived at the Caldwell Parish Country Club in Columbia, we walked to the putting green."

Dondre and his teammates were too absorbed to notice the conversation between a man and St. Frederick athletic director James Murphy. After disappearing into the clubhouse, Murphy returned to his players.

"I want to see the seniors," he said. "On the double!" His face seemed strained as he gathered the four students, including Dondre.

"I don't know how to tell you this," he said, "but the Caldwell Parish Country Club is reserved for whites only." Murphy paused and looked at Dondre. His teammates glanced at each other in disbelief. "I want you seniors to decide what our response should be," Murphy continued. "If we leave, we forfeit this tournament. If we stay, Dondre can't play."

As I listened, my own childhood memory from thirty-two years ago broke free.

In 1959, I was thirteen years old, a poor black kid living with my mother and stepfather in a small black ghetto on Long Island, New York. My mother worked nights in a hospital, and my stepfather drove a coal truck. Needless to say, our standard of living was somewhat short of the American dream.

Nevertheless, when my Grade Eight teacher announced a graduation trip to Washington, D.C., it never crossed my mind that I would be left behind. Besides a complete tour of the nation's capital, we would visit Glen Echo Amusement Park in Maryland. In my imagination, Glen Echo was Disneyland, Knott's Berry Farm, and Magic Mountain rolled into one.

My heart beating wildly, I raced home to deliver the mimeographed letter describing the journey. But when my mother saw how much the trip would cost, she just shook her head. We couldn't afford it.

After feeling sad for ten seconds, I decided to try to fund the trip myself. For the next eight weeks, I sold candy bars door-to-door, delivered newspapers, and mowed lawns. Three days before the deadline, I'd made just barely enough. I was going!

The day of the trip, trembling with excitement, I climbed onto the train. I was the only non-white in our section.

Our hotel was not far from the White House. My roommate was Frank Miller, the son of a businessman. Leaning together out of our window and dropping water balloons on tourists quickly cemented our new friendship.

Every morning, almost a hundred of us loaded noisily onto our bus for another adventure. We sang our school fight song dozens of times—en route to Arlington National Cemetery, and even on an afternoon cruise down the Potomac River.

We visited the Lincoln Memorial twice, once in daylight, the second time at dusk. My classmates and I fell silent as we walked in the shadows of those thirty-six marble columns, one for every state in the Union that Lincoln laboured to preserve. I stood next to Frank at the base of the almost fifty-metre seated statue. Spotlights made the white Georgian marble seem to glow. Together, we read those famous words from Lincoln's speech at Gettysburg remembering the most bloody battle in the War between the States: "...*we here highly resolve that these dead shall not have died in vain—that this nation, under God, shall have a new birth of freedom...*"

As Frank motioned me into place to take my picture, I took one last look at Lincoln's face. He seemed alive and so terribly sad.

The next morning I understood a little better why he wasn't smiling. "Clifton," a chaperone said, "could I see you for a moment?"

The other guys at my table, especially Frank, turned pale. We had been joking about the previous night's direct water balloon hit on a lady and her poodle. It was a stupid, dangerous act, but luckily nobody got hurt. We were celebrating our escape from punishment when the chaperone asked to see me.

"Clifton," she began, "do you know about the Mason-Dixon line?"

"No," I said, wondering what this had to do with drenching ladies.

"Before the Civil War," she explained, "the Mason-Dixon line was originally the boundary between Maryland and Pennsylvania—the dividing line between the slave and free states." Having escaped one disaster, I could feel another brewing. I noticed that her eyes were damp and her hands were shaking.

"Today," she continued, "the Mason-Dixon line is a kind of invisible border between the North and the South. When you cross that invisible line out of Washington, D.C., into Maryland, things change."

There was an ominous drift to this conversation, but I wasn't following it. Why did she look and sound so nervous?

"Glen Echo Amusement Park is in Maryland," she said at last, "and the management doesn't allow Negroes inside." She stared at me in silence.

I was still grinning and nodding when the meaning finally sank in.

"You mean I can't go to the park," I stuttered, "because I'm a Negro?"

She nodded slowly. "I'm sorry, Clifton," she said, taking my hand. "You'll have to stay in the hotel tonight. Why don't you and I watch a movie on television?"

I walked to the elevators feeling confusion, disbelief, anger and a deep sadness. "What happened, Clifton?" Frank said when I got back to the room. "Did the lady tell on us?"

Without saying a word, I walked over to my bed, lay down, and began to cry. Frank was stunned to silence. Junior-high boys didn't cry, at least not in front of each other.

It wasn't just missing the class adventure that made me feel so sad. For the first time in my life, I was learning what it felt like to be black.

Of course there was discrimination in the North, but the colour of my skin had never officially kept me out of a coffee shop, a church—or an amusement park.

"Clifton," Frank whispered, "what is the matter?"

"They won't let me go to Glen Echo Park tonight," I sobbed.

"Because of the water balloon?" he asked.

"No," I answered, "because I'm a Negro."

"Well, that's a relief!" Frank said, and then he laughed, obviously relieved to have escaped punishment for our caper with the balloons. "I thought it was serious."

Wiping away the tears with my sleeve, I stared at him. "It *is* serious. They don't let Negroes into the park. I can't go with you!" I shouted. "That's pretty serious to me."

I was about to wipe the silly grin off Frank's face with a blow to his jaw when I heard him say, "Then I won't go either."

For an instant we just froze. Then Frank grinned. I will never forget that moment. Frank was just a kid. He wanted to go to that amusement park as much as I did, but there was something even more important than the class night out. Still, he didn't explain or expand.

The next thing I knew, the room was filled with kids listening to Frank. "They don't allow Negroes in the park," he said, "so I'm staying with Clifton."

"Me too," a second boy said.

"Those jerks," a third muttered. "I'm with you, Clifton." My heart began to race. Suddenly, I was not alone. A pint-sized revolution had been born. The "water balloon brigade," eleven white boys from Long Island, had made its decision: "We won't go." And as I sat on my bed in the centre of it all, I felt grateful. But, above all, I was filled with pride.

Dondre Green's story brought that childhood memory back to life. His golfing teammates, like my childhood friends, had an important decision to make: standing by their friend when it would cost them dearly. But when it came time to decide, no one hesitated. "Let's get out of here," one of them whispered.

"They just turned and walked toward the van," Dondre told us. "They didn't debate it. And the younger players joined us without looking back."

Dondre was astounded by the response of his friends—and the people of Louisiana. The whole state was outraged and tried to make it right. The Louisiana House of Representatives proclaimed a Dondre Green Day and passed legislation permitting lawsuits for damages, attorneys' fees, and court costs against any private facility that invites a team, then bars any member because of race.

As Dondre concluded, his eyes glistened with tears. "I love my coach and my teammates for sticking by me," he said. "It goes to show that there are always good people who will not give in to bigotry. The kind of love they showed me that day will conquer hatred every time."

My friends, too, had shown that kind of love. As we sat in the hotel, a chaperone came in waving an envelope. "Boys!" he shouted. "I've just bought thirteen tickets to the Senators-Tigers game. Anybody want to go?"

The room erupted in cheers. Not one of us had ever been to a professional baseball game in a real baseball park.

On the way to the stadium, we grew silent as our driver paused before the Lincoln Memorial. For one long moment, I stared through the marble pillars at Mr. Lincoln, bathed in that warm, yellow light. There was still no smile and no sign of hope in his sad and tired eyes.

"...we here highly resolve...that this nation, under God, shall have a new birth of freedom..."

In his words and in his life, Lincoln had made it clear that freedom is not free. Every time the colour of a person's skin keeps that person out of an amusement park or off a country club fairway, the war for freedom begins again. Sometimes the battle is fought with fists and guns, but more often the most effective weapon is a simple act of love and courage.

Whenever I hear those words from Lincoln's speech at Gettysburg, I remember my eleven white friends, and I feel hope once again. I like to imagine that when we paused that night at the foot of his great monument, Mr. Lincoln smiled at last. As Dondre said, "The kind of love they showed me that day will conquer hatred every time."

1. Responding to the Memoir

a. With a partner, discuss how a **memoir** is different from or similar to other writing formats. Why do you think Davis wrote this piece as a memoir? If this were written in another format, would it have the same impact? Explain.

b. What are the similarities between Davis's experience as a young teen and Dondre's? What impact did these experiences have on them?

c. Why do you think both Clifton Davis and Dondre Green were surprised by the actions of their friends?

> A **memoir** is a record of a person's own experiences. Each experience is told like a story, and is written in *first person* (*I, me, we* and *us*).

2. Oral Communication   Class Debate

Clifton Davis states, "Sometimes the battle is fought with fists and guns, but more often the most effective weapon is a simple act of love and courage." Hold a class debate in which you agree or disagree with this statement. (See page 142 for tips on debating.) Decide who will be the chair, who will represent the opposing groups, and who will form the panel of judges.

Self-Assessment: How might you improve your debating skills?

3. Language Conventions   Use Dashes for Emphasis

Clifton Davis uses dashes (—) to add drama and impact to his memoir. The **dash** indicates a strong break or pause in a sentence so that an important point can be emphasized. Reread the memoir. With a partner, discuss where and why the author has used dashes. Were they necessary? If they weren't used, how would it have changed the selection? Explain.

Choose a few writing selections from your portfolio. Examine the use of dashes in your own writing. Are they used effectively? If you haven't used them before, what ways can you think of to incorporate them into your next piece of writing?

Find out how one woman took a stand against sexist behaviour.

What's Wrong with Playing "Like a Girl"?

Editorial by Dorothea Stillman

I started out watching my sons' games and practices just to cheer the boys on, but I quickly learned another important reason to be there. I found that, as often as not, while the coaches showed the kids how to shoot a basket, throw a strike, or head a soccer ball, they were also teaching them to regard girls as inferior to boys.

The co-ed basketball program was the worst offender. For three weeks I watched as the coaches belittled the girls and humiliated the boys by saying they were "playing like girls."

The 7-year-olds' division was about 30% girls. In the 10-year-olds' division there were no girls. Clearly, they were so discouraged by that age that they gave up.

One typical Saturday morning the gym rang with shouts as four groups of 7-year-olds excitedly waved their arms and urged their teammates to hurry. It was a relay dribbling race in my younger son's practice.

An all-girl team won against three other teams, all of which were made up

---

GOALS AT A GLANCE

■ Role-play a TV talk show interview.
■ Analyse the use of conjunctions.

exclusively or mostly of boys. As the last girl came to the finish, her teammates jumped up and exploded into cheers. A smirk came over the coach's face. He stood in the middle of the gym with a hand on one hip. "Are you going to let a bunch of girls beat you?" he roared at the boys.

The message was clear: if the girls won, it was because the boys hadn't been trying hard enough. The girls should feel no pride in their victory because it was a fluke. The natural order of things was that the boys should be superior to the girls—and be ashamed if they weren't.

The girls giggled uncertainly. The boys looked at each other sheepishly and shrugged. The fathers, helping out on the floor, smiled. The mothers, sitting on the sidelines, showed no reaction.

But I was riled, and I wasn't going to take it. For 3 weeks the director of the program had been asking for a volunteer to coach the 10-year-olds, and no one had come forward. When he made the appeal again at the end of practice, I said I'd do it. He looked shocked, but he could hardly say no. The alternative was to cut 10 kids from the program, and he knew it.

But it wasn't going to be that simple. No sooner had I picked up the assignment than men swooped in to take it away from me. A big man standing nearby pushed his way between me and the program director. "Ron can run the practices," he said. "He just can't be there for the games on Saturdays because he has to work." Ron joined in: "You could be there for the games, and some-times I'll be able to coach them, too, if I rearrange my lunch hour."

I went home and seethed. Ron would have been a fine coach if he had seen fit to volunteer on his own. But he hadn't. Ron never would have tried to use a man the way he was proposing to use me, and I was not willing to be used. I pulled myself together, called Ron, and told him thanks but no thanks. If I was going to be the coach, I wanted to run the practices myself.

Then I got busy. I knew next to nothing about basketball (neither did most of the fathers who were coaching), but I gave myself a crash course. I read books. I attended every game the local high-school team played. I watched the game on TV every day.

At first I could only recognize the obvious: the fast break, the slam-dunk. But before long I noticed the finer points— the fake, the curl, the pick-and-roll. At home my kids and I talked basketball day and night. I researched and watched and learned and developed drills and plays. I was so enthusiastic I even allowed my sons to dribble basketballs in the living room.

Before each of our games, the referees would ask the coaches for a roster of the players. My assistant was a man, and they approached him first every time.

"That's the coach over there," he would say, pointing to me. The refs would turn and scan the gym for another man. When they realized I was the one they were looking for, their eyebrows would shoot up. Or they'd break into a grin. Or their faces would freeze.

Out on the court the boys would be warming up. "Watch this, Coach," they'd call to me, eager to show off their fanciest moves, taking three-point shots, or dribbling between their legs. "You guys are looking good," I'd say, and they would beam with pride. To them I was no different from any other coach.

When I watched my younger son's practices, I chatted with the other mothers. My coaching had sent a ripple through them. One woman asked, "Is someone helping you? How can you do it?" She seemed to think women were incapable of understanding basketball. Another was more supportive: "It's about time we had a woman coach," she said. Best of all, a third woman joined the men out on the floor and helped run the last practice.

The season was ending, but something big was starting.

----

1. RESPONDING TO THE EDITORIAL

a. Why do you think Dorothea Stillman had such a strong reaction to the attitude of her son's coach? Would you have had the same reaction? Explain.

b. Several men volunteered to coach the basketball team after the author had shown some interest in the position. Why did they wait until after she volunteered? What might you assume about their actions?

c. With a partner, retell the events of this editorial from the perspective of another person—a different coach, a player on the team, or a parent.

2. MEDIA TV TALK SHOW

With four or five classmates, role-play a discussion between Dorothea Stillman and the director of the basketball program on a TV talk show. The theme of the show could be how children learn sexist behaviour and language in their homes and on playgrounds. One group member can assume the role of the talk show host, another Dorothea Stillman, and a third the director. The remaining group members can be the audience. Record your interview on either video- or audiotape. Present your tape to the class.

PEER ASSESSMENT: Evaluate the taped show for how well all three classmates expressed their key points. Write down two positive comments about the show and one specific suggestion as to how it could be improved.

3. LANGUAGE CONVENTIONS USE CONJUNCTIONS

Conjunctions link related words, phrases, clauses, or sentences together. Some common conjunctions are *and*, *but*, *or*, *if*, *when*, and *although*. Here's an example from the article.

> **Ron would have been a fine coach if**
> **he had seen fit to volunteer on his own.**

Reread this article and note how and when the author used conjunctions. How does using a variety of them make the editorial easier to read? How do they add impact to the writing? Compare your response with another classmate's. What conclusions can you draw?

images

Poem by Duncan Mercredi

i don't want to change you
you are what you are
i just want you to walk where i walk
see what i see
feel the stings of roses
disguised as beauty
till you hold them
then the prick of thorns cut you
and you curse at the lie
at the promise of a better life
it is still a mirage
i don't want to change you
why are you trying to make me into your image

----

1. RESPONDING TO THE POEM

a. How would you describe the mood of this poem? What words or phrases help to create this mood?

b. What is significant about the rose in this poem? Explain.

c. How would you interpret the last two lines of the poem? Do you feel these are the most or least important lines in the poem? Why?

2. POET'S CRAFT COMPARE AND ANALYSE POEMS

Turn back to the unit opener on page 300 and read the poem "How Would I Change You?" by Larissa Pergat. Now reread "images" by Duncan Mercredi. How would you compare the style, content, and structure of these two poems? Do they have similar messages? With a partner, jot down your observations about each poem. Write a paragraph in which you compare and analyse both poems.

GOALS AT A GLANCE

■ Respond critically to poetry.
■ Compare and analyse poems.

REFLECTING ON THE UNIT

SELF-ASSESSMENT: ORAL COMMUNICATION

As you worked on the activities in this unit, what did you learn about
- debating?
- storytelling?
- making a speech?
- defending or challenging opinions?
- role-playing?
- presenting a play?

Write your responses to each as a one- or two-line entry in your journal.

WRITING ORGANIZE AND SUMMARIZE INFORMATION

Working with a partner, make a T-chart. At the top of the column on the left, write the heading "Selections." Underneath this, list the titles of all the selections you've studied in this unit. At the top of the column on the right, write the heading "Issues."

Scan each selection quickly and decide what you think is the central issue. Summarize it in one or two sentences. Place a summary of each selection in the "Issues" column, opposite its title. After you have filled in both columns, discuss with your partner how each selection connects with the theme of this unit, "Viewpoints."

VISUAL COMMUNICATION REPRESENT CHARACTER OR ISSUE

Choose a favourite character or issue from one of the selections and create an image that you think best depicts it. Consider developing a character sketch, drawing, or photo for a favourite character. A poster, collage, or brochure may be a better way of representing an issue. Display your work for the class.

ORAL COMMUNICATION IMPROVISE

Choose two characters from two different selections in the unit. With a partner, improvise the dialogue that the characters might have if they met for the first time at a fund-raising party. What experiences might they share? What did they do in their lifetimes that had a lasting impact on themselves and others?

GLOSSARY

Adjective An adjective is the word that describes a noun or pronoun: *He felt a sharp pain. Her icy green eyes stared at the stars. He looked cold.* Adjectives, as well as describing, can also limit a noun: *I saw two movies on the weekend.*

Alliteration Alliteration involves the repetition of the same first sounds in a group of words or line of poetry: *The sun sank slowly.*

Anecdote An anecdote is a brief story that retells an incident or event. Like a story, it could be sad, funny, or adventurous, and often has a plot, characters, and setting.

Antagonist An antagonist is the person or thing in a story fighting against the main character or protagonist.

Biography A biography is the story of a person's life. It can be recorded in many formats: in writing, through pictures or artwork, or on film.

Clause A clause is a group of words that has a subject (a noun) and a predicate (a verb and sometimes adjectives, adverbs, and phrases).

An **independent** or **main clause** is complete thought and stands alone as a sentence: *I shut the door. The cat ran into the street.*

A **dependent** or **subordinate clause** is not a complete sentence and doesn't stand alone as a sentence: *Although she missed the bus. Whenever Jack got the chance.*

Comic Strip A comic strip is a series of drawings, especially cartoons, that tell a funny story, an adventure or a series of incidents. Comic strips involve recurring characters.

Conflict Conflict is a problem or struggle in a story that the main character has to solve or face. Conflict is created in four classic ways: human against self, human against human, human against nature, human against society. Writers may choose to use more than one conflict in a story, which can create an exciting plot.

Conjunction A conjunction is a word that connects other words, phrases, clauses, or sentences. There are three types of conjunctions.
- co-ordinating conjunctions *(and, or, nor, for, but, so, yet): Carla and I are best friends.*
- subordinating conjunctions: *(whenever, after, if, since, because, before, unless): I break out in a sweat whenever I get on an elevator.*
- correlative conjunctions *(but...and, either...or, neither...nor, not only...but also): My watch is neither on my wrist nor by my bed.*

Dialogue Dialogue is a conversation between characters. In narrative, every time a new character speaks a new paragraph is used. Quotation marks are used to indicate that dialogue is beginning and ending.

Ellipsis Points [...] Ellipsis points are a series of dots used to show that something has been left out. Use ellipsis points as follows.
- to show that one or more words have been left out of a quotation.
- to indicate that a sentence or thought has been left unfinished.

Fable A fable is a story that was created to teach a lesson. It is not necessarily a true story.

Five W's The five W's of journalism are the five questions that every newspaper or magazine article should answer: *who,* *what, where, when, why* (and sometimes *how*). By the end of the article, the reader should know who was involved in the story or event, what happened, where it happened, when it happened, why it happened, and how it happened.

Flashback A flashback is an event or scene that took place at an earlier point in a story. Writers use flashback to explain something that is presently occurring in the story. Flashbacks can also explain a character's motivation and help to clear up any unanswered questions in the plot.

Folk tale A folk tale is a story or legend that originated long ago and has been handed down from generation to generation.

Foreshadowing Foreshadowing is a writing device used to give a hint about what is to come in a story. The hint, however, should not be too obvious to the reader because it will give the plot away and affect the suspense. Foreshadowing is used mainly in mysteries and suspense stories, but can be used in other genres as well.

Homophones Homophones are two words that are pronounced alike but are spelled differently, such as *to, two,* and *too*. Homophones can easily be confused in speech and in writing.

Imagery Imagery is a technique poets and writers use to describe and appeal to the senses. There are many types of imagery including simile, metaphor, alliteration, and personification.

Interjection An interjection is an expression of surprise, sorrow, or delight, with no grammatical connection to what precedes or follows it. For example, *Wow! Look at that UFO!*

Irony Irony is a kind of humour that involves intentionally stating the opposite of what you mean in order to show what you truly mean. For example, calling a small bungalow a mansion is irony. Two common types of irony are dramatic and situational. **Dramatic irony** occurs when the audience knows something that a character does not. **Situational irony** takes place when circumstances turn out differently from what the reader expects or anticipates.

Lead A lead is the opening paragraph of a newspaper or magazine article. The lead should contain as many of the answers as possible to the five W's of journalism: *who, what, when, where,* and *why*.

Memoir A memoir is the recording of a person's own experiences, and involves the retelling of memorable experiences from that person's life. Each experience is told like a story, and is written from the first person point of view (*I, me, we, us*).

Metaphor A metaphor is a writing device in which a word or phrase that ordinarily means one thing is used to describe something else, suggesting that some common quality is shared by the two: *a heart of stone, copper sky*. As well as painting vivid pictures for the reader, metaphors help to make abstract ideas more concrete, add emotion, and show the writer's feelings.

Mood The mood or atmosphere is the feeling that pervades a piece of writing or work of art. *The mood of Frankenstein is sombre and dark*. Mood is created through description and through the plot and the setting.

Narration Narration is the telling of an event or series of events. Narration is used in all types of writing, including narrative, plays, and poetry.

Narrator The narrator is the person or character telling a story. See point of view.

Noun A noun is a word that refers to people, places, qualities, things, actions, or ideas. *When <u>Joe</u> was at the <u>library</u> in <u>Guelph</u>, <u>curiosity</u> caused him to read an <u>article</u> that claimed <u>fear</u> could be cured by <u>meditation</u>.*

Paragraph A paragraph is a group of sentences that develop one aspect of a topic, or one phase of a narrative. The sentences in a paragraph should be clearly related to each other. Sometimes, especially in essays, the aspect or point being developed is expressed in a topic sentence, and the other sentences in the paragraph expand on this statement.

Paraphrase To paraphrase a piece of writing, you restate the author's ideas in your own words. A good paraphrase will also reflect your own writing style.

Parody A parody is a humorous imitation of a serious writing format. It follows the form of the original, but changes its sense to nonsense. "The Transformations of Cindy R." by Anne Mazer is a parody of the story *Cinderella.*

Personification Personification is a literary device that gives human traits to non-humans: *The stream gurgled.*
Personification is used most often in poetry and narrative writing but can be used as a technique in print ads.

Phrase A phrase is a group of words, used together in a sentence, that does not have a subject and a verb:
Marcella spoke *for the first time.*
    (prepositional phrase)
Thinking fast, I covered my ears.
    (participial phrase)
Catrina wants *to be a scientist.*
    (infinitive phrase)

Plot The plot is the events in a story that make up the action. The plot in a story usually has five elements: the exposition (set-up), rising action, climax, falling action, and resolution.
- The **exposition** sets up the story by introducing the main characters, the setting, and the problem to be solved.
- The **rising action** is the main part of the story where the full problem develops. A number of events is involved that will lead to the climax.

- The **climax** is the highest point of the story where the most exciting events occur.
- The **falling action** follows the climax. It contains the events that bring the story to the conclusion.
- The **resolution** is the end of the story when all the problems are solved.

Point of View Point of view refers to the position from which the events of a story are presented to us. There are two main points of view: first-person and third-person narrative.
- **First-person** means the story is told through one character's eyes and the events are coloured through that character's experience.
- The **third-person** point of view means the story is told by an onlooker or narrator. There are two third-person points of view: **Omniscient** and **limited.** In the omniscient point of view, the narrator knows everything about all the characters and the events, and can shift from character to character. In the limited point of view, the author may choose to tell the story through one character or a group of characters' eyes.
- Many modern authors also use a "multiple point of view" in which we are shown the events from the position of two or more different characters.

Profile A profile is a concise description of a person's abilities, character, or career. It outlines the facts about someone.

Protagonist The protagonist is the main character in a story. The story is usually told from this person's point of view.

Rhyme Rhyme is the repetition of sound in different words, especially at the ends of words. For example, *see* rhymes with *bee.* Rhyme is one of the main techniques used in poetry.

Rhyme Scheme A rhyme scheme is the pattern of end rhymes used in a poem. The rhyme scheme is usually indicated by letters, for example, *abba abba cde cde* and *abab cdcd efef gg* are both rhyme schemes for a type of poetry called a sonnet.

Rhythm Rhythm is the arrangement of beats in a line of poetry. The beat is created by the accented and unaccented syllables in the words used in the line.

Run-on Sentence A run-on sentence is formed when two sentences run into one another. To fix a run-on sentence, add the proper punctuation, or change the wording to make it a single sentence.
Run-on: *The sky is clear it is spring at last.*
Better: *The sky is clear; it is spring at last.*
OR
The sky is clear, and it is spring at last.
OR
The sky is clear because it is spring at last.
You call two sentences separated by a comma a comma splice. Fix the comma splice the same way you would fix a run-on sentence.

Satire A satire is a type of writing that uses humour and irony to point out what is wrong with an organization, person, or society. Jonathan Swift's *Gulliver's Travels* is a satire.

Script A script is a story written to be performed as a play or developed into a movie or television show. The script tells a story with setting, plot, and characters. The story is told through dialogue between characters and through narration as well. Characters are usually listed on the left side of a script and their "lines" are included beside the character name. Scripts also contain stage directions that give instructions for setting up the stage and for the actors.

Semicolon [;] Use a semicolon to separate two related sentences: *I love watching television after school; it relaxes me.*
• A semicolon may also be used along with a co-ordinating conjunction (*and, or, nor, for, but, so, yet*) to join main clauses, if one or more of the clauses already contains a comma: *I threw on my coat, picked up my wallet, and raced to the bus stop; but the bus had already left.*
• Semicolons are also used to separate items in a list, when one or more of the items contains a comma: *Walter has lived in Tokyo, Japan; London, England; and Estavan, Saskatchewan.*

Sentence A sentence is a group of words that expresses a complete thought. Every sentence needs a subject and an action.

A **simple sentence** has one subject and one verb: *Yukio's house has five bedrooms.*

A **compound sentence** has two or more main clauses (that is smaller sentences that can stand alone). The sentences are usually joined together by a semicolon, or by a comma or semicolon followed by *and, or, nor, for, but, so,* or *yet: Yukio's house has five bedrooms, and the yard is huge.*

A **complex sentence** has a main clause that can stand alone as a sentence, and one or more subordinate clauses that cannot stand on their own as sentences. In the following example of a complex sentence, the main clause is underlined, and the subordinate clause is in italics:
<u>Yukio's house</u>, *which he built himself,* <u>has five bedrooms</u>.

Sentence Fragment A sentence fragment is a group of words that is set off like a sentence, but lacks either a verb or a subject. Sentence fragments are acceptable in informal writing, dialogue, and spoken English, but are not appropriate in formal writing:
Fragment: *We went to the game. Josh and I.* (lacks a verb)
Revised: *Josh and I went to the game.*

Setting The setting is the place and time where a story takes place. Setting plays an important role in many types of stories: science fiction, historical fiction, fantasy, and adventure stories.

Simile A simile is a comparison of two different things using the words *like* or *as:*

My ears buzzed like a mosquito. Similes are used in both prose and poetry.

Stereotype A stereotype is an oversimplified picture, usually of a group of people, giving them all a set of characteristics, without consideration for individual differences. Avoid stereotypes in your writing. Try to create fresh, real characters.

Suspense Suspense is a feeling of tension, anxiety, or excitement resulting from uncertainty. An author creates suspense to keep the reader interested.

Symbol/Symbolism A symbol is a person, place, thing or event that is used to represent something else. For example, a rainbow is often used as a symbol of hope.

Tone Tone is the atmosphere or mood of a piece. It can also refer to the author's attitude or feeling about the reader (formal, casual, intimate) and his subject (light, ironic, solemn, sarcastic, sentimental).

Tribute A tribute is an acknowledgment of someone's accomplishments.

Verb A verb is a word that expresses an action or a state of being. Verbs that express a state of being are sometimes called linking verbs, because they link the subject to another word that describes the subject.
Action verb: *Sunil <u>ran</u> to school.*
Linking verb: *Mariko <u>seemed</u> tired.*
The verb *be* is the most common linking verb, but verbs like *seem, appear, feel, smell,* and *look* can act as linking verbs.

INDEX OF ACTIVITIES

ACKNOWLEDGMENTS

Every reasonable effort has been made to trace ownership of copyrighted material. Information that would enable the publisher to correct any reference or credit in future editions would be appreciated.

10-25 "The Transformations of Cindy R." by Anne Mazer. © 1998 by Anne Mazer from *Stay True: Short Stories for Strong Girls* edited by Marilyn Singer, by permission of Scholastic Inc./ **28-29** "You Should Wear Khakis with That" from *Zits* by Jerry Scott and Jim Borgman./ **30-34** "Feeling Good, Looking Great" by Mary Walters Riskin from *Zoot Capri* (Summer 1992). Reprinted by permission of the Alberta Alcohol and Drug Abuse Commission./ **34-35** "At Face Value" by Lorna Renooy from *AboutFace* Newsletter, Spring, 1999 Vol. 13, No. 1./ **38-50** "Joy-riding" by Jim Naughton from *Ultimate Sports*./ **56** "How Feel I Do?" by Jim Wong-Chu. Reprinted by permission of the author./ **57** "I Lost My Talk" by Rita Joe from *Song of Eskasoni: More Poems by Rita Joe*, Ragweed Press./ **59-64** "A Hero's Welcome" by Barbara Haworth-Attard. Used by permission of the author./ **66** "Conversations with Myself" from *It Doesn't Always Have to Rhyme* by Eve Merriam. © 1964, 1992 by Eve Merriam. Reprinted by permission of Marian Reiner./ **70-84** "No Matter What" by Joan Lowery Nixon from *From One Experience to Another*./ **90-96** "The Water of Life" by Kay Stone from *At the Edge: A Book of Risky Stories*. Reprinted by permission of Ragweed Press./ **98** "Da Trang" by Tony Montague Reprinted by permission of Ragweed Press./ **107-114** "Iron Trails to Adventure" by Catherine George from *The Toronto Star*./ **116-120** From *Harlem* by Walter Dean Myers, illustrated by Christopher Myers. Published by Scholastic Press, a division of Scholastic Inc. Text © 1997 by Walter Dean Myers, illustrations © 1997 by Christopher Myers. Reprinted by permission of Scholastic Inc./ **121-133** "On the Road" by Joanne Findon from *Takes: Stories for Young Adults* (Thistledown Press, 1996). This version is an abridgement of the original./ **135-136** "Empty Fears" by Brian Lee from *Six of the Best: A Puffin Sextet of Poets*. Reprinted by permission of the author./ **138-141** "Out of This World" (originally entitled "Above and Beyond") by Andrew Philips from *Maclean's* magazine, May 17, 1999, and by Sarah Green, The Toronto Sun, May 29, 1999./ **144** "Greatness" from *The Mysterious Naked Man* by Alden Nowlan, © 1969 by Alden Nowlan. Reprinted by permission of Stoddart Publishing Co., Ltd./ **146-147** "Rainlight" from *West Coast Rhymes* by Jenny Nelson. Reprinted by permission of the author./ **148** "Haida Gwaii" by Jaalen Edenshaw from *West Coast Rhymes* by Jenny Nelson. Reprinted by permission of the author./ **149-150** "Hear Every Word" by Robertson Davies from *The Merry Heart*. Used by permission, McClelland & Stewart, Inc. *The Canadian Publishers*./ **152** "Formula" by Langston Hughes from *Collected Poems* by Langston Hughes. © 1994 by the Estate of Langston Hughes. Reprinted by permission of Alfred A. Knopf, Inc., a Division of Random House, Inc./ **153** "Helen Keller" by Langston Hughes from *Collected Poems* by Langston Hughes. © 1994 by the Estate of Langston Hughes. Reprinted by permission of Alfred A. Knopf, Inc., a Division of Random House, Inc./ **155** "Unconscious Came a Beauty" by May Swenson. Reprinted with the permission of Simon & Schuster Books for Young Readers, an imprint of Simon & Schuster Children's Publishing Division from *The Complete Poems to Solve* by May Swenson. Text © 1993 The Literary Estate of May Swenson./ **156-157** "Dreams of the Animals" from *Selected Poems 1966-1984* by Margaret Atwood. © 1990. Reprinted by permission of Oxford University Press Canada./ **159** "'Haiku' by Joso" from *One Hundred Poems From the Japanese* by Kenneth Rexroth. © All Rights Reserved by New Directions Publishing Corp. Reprinted by permission of New Directions Publishing Corp./ **159** "'Haiku' by Boncho" from *One Hundred Poems From the Japanese* by Kenneth Rexroth. © All Rights Reserved by New Directions Publishing Corp. Reprinted by permission of New Directions Publishing Corp./ **159** "'Haiku' by Basho."/ **159** "'Haiku' by Yayu."/ **160-161** "Poems in Your Pockets" by Karen Lewis. Reprinted, with permission, from *New Moon: The Magazine For Girls and Their Dreams* © New Moon Publishing, Duluth, MN. Subscriptions $29.00/6 issues. 1-800-381-4743 or, www.newmoon.org./ **163-166** "Smokeroom on the Kyle" from *The Chronicles of Uncle Moses* by Ted Russell. © Ted Russell Estate. Reprinted by permission of Breakwater Books./ **168-169** "Song of the Land" by Barry Brown. Reprinted by permission of Barry Brown Music Publishing Inc. and Southern Days Music./ **171** "#254" (originally entitled "Hope is the thing with feathers") by Emily Dickenson. Reprinted by permission of the publishers and the Trustees of Amherst College from *The Poems of Emily Dickinson*, Thomas H. Johnson, ed., Cambridge, Mass.; The Belknap Press of Harvard University Press © 1951, 1955, 1979, 1983 by the President and Fellows of Harvard College./ **172-176** "Called Back" (originally entitled "Emily Dickinson, American Poet") by Christina Ashton from *Cobblestone's* March 1995 issue, © 1995, Cobblestone Publishing Company, 30 Grove Street, Suite C, Peterborough, NH 03458. Reprinted by permission of the publisher./ **180-181** "The Base Stealer" by Robert Francis from *Orb Weaver* © 1960 by Robert Francis, Wesleyan University Press by permission of University Press of New England./ **183** "School Buses" by Russell Hoban from *Six of the Best: A Puffin Sextet of Poets*, Anne Harvey, ed./

185-188 "When Hallmark Just Won't Do" by Elizabeth Schaal. Reprinted by permission of the *National Post*./ 192-195 "A Desk for My Daughter" by Gardner McFall from *The Quiet Centre*. Reprinted by permission of HarperCollins Publishers./ 197-198 "Learn with BOOK" by R.J. Heathorn. © 1962 by Punch/Rothco. Reprinted by permission of Rothco Cartoons./ 200-203 "Instant Messaging" by Linda Matchan from *The Boston Globe*. © Globe Newspaper Co. (MA)./ 204 "Navigating Your Way Through Cyberspace" by Janice Turner. Reprinted by permission of The Toronto Star Syndicate./ 206-207 "The Path of Our Sorrow" from *Out of the Dust* by Karen Hesse. Published by Scholastic Press, a division of Scholastic Inc. © 1997 by Karen Hesse. Reprinted by permission of Scholastic Inc./ 208-209 "Ride Forever" by Paul Gross and David Keeley.Reprinted by permission of Lenz Entertainment/ 214-217 "A Mysterious Contraption" by Amelie Welden from *Girls who Rocked the World: Heroines from Sacagawea to Sheryl Swoopes*. © 1998 Amelie Weldon. Reprinted by permission of Beyond Words Publishing./ 219-230 "A Close Match" by Helen Dunmore. © 1998 by the author./ 244-247 "The Elders Are Watching" by David Bouchard. Text © 1997 by David Bouchard./ 252-254 "No Boring Parts Allowed" from *The D- Poems of Jeremy Bloom* by Gordon Korman and Bernice Korman. © 1992 by Gordon Korman and Bernice Korman. Reprinted by permission of Scholastic Inc./ 258-260 "Here's to You, Joe DiMaggio" by Paul Simon. Reprinted by permission of the author./ 262-263 "The Radio as Time Machine" by Lorna Crozier. Reprinted by permission of the author./ 265-278 "Save the Moon for Kerdy Dickus" from *Some of the Kinder Planets* by Tim Wynne-Jones. © 1993 by Tim Wynne-Jones./ 280 "Alien" lyrics by Kim Stockwood and Naoise Sheridan from the CD *12 years old*. Reprinted by permission of EMI Music Canada./ 288 "For Better or For Worse" by Lynn Johnston. © Lynn Johnston Productions Inc./Dist. by United Features Syndicate, Inc./ 289-292 "Running Shoe Run-Around" from *Arthur! Arthur!* © 1991 by Arthur Black. Reprinted by permission of Stoddart Publishing Co. Limited./ 295-297 "Fool Proof" from *Liar, Liar, Pants on Fire!* by Mary Cook, Creative bound Inc., ISBN 0-921165-40-4, 1995./ 300 "How Would I Change You?" by Larissa Pergat./ 302-305 "Mrs. Buell" from *Hey World, Here I Am!* by Jean Little./ 307-308 "Island Clay" by Lennie Gallant from CD *Breakwater*./ 310-320 "The Runaway" from *On stage! Short Plays for Acting Students* by Robert Mauro. © MCMXC Meriwether Publishing Ltd. Colorado Springs, CO. A royalty of $15.00 must be paid to Contemporary Drama Service PO Box 7710, Colorado Springs CO 80933 for any performance of this play whether or not admission is charged./ 325 "A Multicultural Nation" by Winston Loui from *New Canadian Voices*, edited by Jessie Porter, published by Wall & Emerson, Inc., Toronto, 1991./ 326-327 "Too Old to Change" by Victor Chang from *New Canadian Voices*, edited by Jessie Porter, published by Wall & Emerson, Inc., Toronto, 1991./ 328 "Do As I Say" by Asif Khan from *New Canadian Voices*, edited by Jessie Porter, published by Wall & Emerson, Inc., Toronto, 1991./ 330 "A Mother's Voice" by Julia from KidNews./ 332-338 "A Mason-Dixon Memory" by Clifton Davis from *Chicken Soup for the Teenage Soul: 101 Stories of Life, Love and Learning*, edited by Jack Canfield, Mark Victor Hansen, and Kimberly Kirberger./ 340-341 "What's Wrong with Playing 'Like a Girl'?" by Dorothea Stillman from *Newsweek*, March 22, 1999. All rights reserved. Reprinted by permission./ 344 "images" by Duncan Mercredi from *Wolf and Shadows*. Reprinted by permission of Pemmican Publications Inc.

Photo Credits
30-34, 198-203, 211 Ian Crysler; 35 Ani Aubin; 68-69 Kay Chernush/The Image Bank; 86 National Archives C-2772; 108 left Yukon Archives/Oral History Collection; 108 right Yukon Archives/MacBride Museum Collection, Vol. 2; 113 top Yukon Archives /Yukon Public Affairs Bureau; 113 bottom Yukon Archives/Vancouver Public Library Collection; 139, 141 NASA; 145 Toshihiko Chinami/The Image Bank; 152-153 Anselm Spring/The Image Bank; 154 Gordon Parks/Corbis; 183 Clair Morse/First Light; 185 Jeff Vinnick/National Post; 190-191 Harold Sund/The Image Bank; 214, 215 Corbis-Bettmann; 233, 234, 240 Urban and Northern Affairs Canada; 250-251 Weinberg-Clark/The Image Bank; 252 top The Kobal Collection; 252 bottom Warner Bros/Universal/The Kobal Collection; 253 The Kobal Collection; 254 top from Lethal Weapon/Warner Brothers/The Kobal Collection; 254 bottom Aquarius Library; 258-259 Corbis-Bettmann; 280 Visuals Unlimited; 285 Maclean's/CP Archive; 289 The North Face; 290 left Mizuno; 290 right Wilson; 291 New Balance North Shore; 292 Saucony, Inc.; 300-301 Peter Pearson/Tony Stone Images.

Illustrations
front cover, 8-9, 56, 66 Cathy Chatteron; 12, 15, 19, 23-24, 219, 221, 223, 226, 228 Linda Hendry; 36, 88, 178, 180-181, 238, 256, 322-323 Clarence Porter; 39, 43, 48 Stephen Taylor; 54 Bernadette Lau; 59, 63 Robert James Potvin; 71, 75, 78, 83, 340-341 Steve Schulman; 91, 95 Martin Springett; 99, 103 Emmanuel Lopez; 109 Deborah Crowle; 116-120 Christopher Myers; 150, 156-157, 173 Charles Weiss; 159 Masumi Suzuki; 163, 165 Norman Eyolfson; 193 Don Kilby; 206-209 Stephen Hutchings; 262-263 Farida Zaman; 268, 273, 277 Peter Lacalamita/3 in a Box; 296, 307 Joe Sampson; 303 Janet Wilson; 313, 316 Dennis Stilwell Martin; 324, 326-327, 329, 331 Richelle Forsey; 333, 335, 337 Patrick Fitzgerald.